MATT AND TO...

ULTIM
FOOTBALL...

KANE
VAN DIJK
MBAPPE

FROM THE PLAYGROUND
TO THE PITCH

DINO

First published in the UK in 2021 by Dino Books,
an imprint of Bonnier Books UK,
The Plaza, 535 King's Road, London SW10 0SZ
Owned by Bonnier Books,
Sveavägen 56, Stockholm, Sweden

🐦 @dinobooks
🐦 @footieheroesbks
www.heroesfootball.com
www.bonnierbooks.co.uk

Design by www.envydesign.co.uk

Paperback ISBN: 9781789465235

British Library Cataloguing-in-Publication Data:
A catalogue record for this book is available from the British Library.

Printed and bound in Great Britain by Clays Ltd, Elcograf S.p.A.

1 3 5 7 9 10 8 6 4 2

MIX
Paper from
responsible sources
FSC® C018072

For Dylan – a current and future superstar

ULTIMATE
FOOTBALL HEROES

Matt Oldfield is an accomplished writer and the editor-in-chief of football review site Of Pitch and Page. Tom Oldfield is a freelance sports writer and the author of biographies on Cristiano Ronaldo, Arsène Wenger and Rafael Nadal.

Cover illustration by Dan Leydon
To learn more about Dan visit danleydon.com
To purchase his artwork visit etsy.com/shop/footynews

KANE

TABLE OF CONTENTS

CHAPTER 1

ENGLAND HERO

Thursday, 5 October 2017

In the Wembley tunnel, Harry closed his eyes and soaked up the amazing atmosphere. He was back at the home of football, the stadium where he had first achieved his childhood dream of playing for England. 19 March 2015, England vs Lithuania – he remembered that game like it was yesterday. He had scored that day and now, with England facing Slovenia, he needed to do it again. As England's captain and Number 9, it was his job to shoot them to the 2018 World Cup.

'Come on, lads!' Harry called out to his teammates behind him: friends like Joe Hart, Kyle Walker and

Eric Dier. It was a real honour to be their leader. With a victory over Slovenia, they would all be on their way to the biggest tournament of their lives in Russia.

Harry looked down at the young mascot by his side and smiled at him. 'Right, let's do this!'

As the two of them led the England team out onto the pitch, the fans clapped and cheered. Harry didn't look up at the thousands of faces and flags; instead, he looked down at the grass in front of him. He was totally focused on his task: scoring goals and beating Slovenia.

'If you get a chance, test the keeper,' Harry said to his partners in attack, Raheem Sterling and Marcus Rashford, before kick-off. 'I'll be there for the rebound!'

Harry's new Premiership season with Tottenham Hotspur had not begun well in August, but by September he was back to his lethal best. That month alone, he scored an incredible thirteen goals, including two goals for England against Malta. He could score every type of goal – tap-ins, headers, one-on-ones, long-range shots, penalties, even free kicks. That's what made him such a dangerous striker.

With Slovenia defending well, Harry didn't get many chances in the first half. He got in good positions but the final ball never arrived.

'There's no need to panic yet,' Harry told his teammates in the dressing room. He really didn't want a repeat of England's terrible performance against Iceland at Euro 2016. That match still haunted him. 'We're good enough to win this by playing our natural game. Be patient!'

As Ryan Bertrand dribbled down the left wing, Harry sprinted towards the six-yard box. Ryan's cross didn't reach him but the ball fell to Raheem instead. His shot was going in until a defender deflected it wide.

'Unlucky!' Harry shouted, putting his hands on his head. 'Keep going, we're going to score!'

Without this kind of strong self-belief, Harry would never have made it to the top of European football. There had been lots of setbacks along the way: rejections, disappointments and bad form. But every time, Harry bounced back with crucial goals at crucial moments. That's what made him such a superstar.

A matter of seconds later, a rebound fell to him on the edge of the penalty area. Surely, this was his moment. He pulled back his left foot and curled a powerful shot towards the bottom corner. The fans were already up on their feet, ready to celebrate. Harry never missed… but this time he did. The ball flew just wide of the post. Harry couldn't believe it. He looked up at the sky and sighed.

On the sideline, England manager Gareth Southgate cheered his team on. 'That's much better – the goal is coming, lads!'

But after ninety minutes, the goal still hadn't come. The fourth official raised his board: eight minutes of injury time.

'It's not over yet, boys!' Harry shouted, to inspire his teammates.

The Slovenian goalkeeper tried to throw the ball out to his left-back but Kyle got there first. Straight away, Harry was on the move from the back post to the front post. After playing together for years at Tottenham, they knew how to score great goals.

As Kyle crossed it in, Harry used his burst of speed to get in front of the centre-back. Again, the England supporters stood and waited anxiously. The ball was perfect and Harry stretched out his long right leg to meet it. The keeper got a touch on his shot but he couldn't keep it out.

Goooooooooooooaaaaaaaaaaaaaaaaaaaallllllllllllllllllllll llllll!!!!!!!!!!!!!!!!!!!!!!!

He had done it! Joy, relief, pride – Harry felt every emotion as he ran towards the fans. This time, he hadn't let them down. He held up the Three Lions on his shirt and screamed until his throat got sore.

'Captain to the rescue!' Kyle laughed as they hugged by the corner flag.

'No, it was all thanks to you!' Harry replied.

At the final whistle, he threw his arms up in the air. It was a phenomenal feeling to qualify for the 2018 World Cup. He couldn't wait to lead England to glory.

'We are off to Russia!' a voice shouted over the loudspeakers and the whole stadium cheered.

It was yet another moment that Harry would

never forget. Against the odds, he was making his childhood dreams come true. He was the star striker for Tottenham, the club that he had supported all his life. And now, like his hero David Beckham, he was the captain of England.

Harry had never given up, even when it looked like he wouldn't make it as a professional footballer. With the support of his family and his coaches, and lots of hard work and dedication, he had proved everyone wrong to become a world-class goal machine.

It had been an incredible journey from Walthamstow to Wembley, and Harry was only just getting started.

CHAPTER 2

ALWAYS KICKING

'Mum!' Charlie shouted, stamping his feet.

Kim sighed and put her magazine down. 'What's happened now?'

'I spent ages building a Lego tower and Harry just kicked it over,' her older son answered. 'That was *my* tower!'

'I'm sorry, darling, but I'm sure Harry didn't mean it. Your brother doesn't know what he's doing with his little feet yet.'

Harry was nearly two years old and he was always on the move around their house in Walthamstow, North London. He had a few bumps on his head but it was his legs that caused the most trouble. Everywhere he went, they never stopped kicking. Kim wasn't surprised, though.

'Do you remember before your brother was born when he was still in my tummy?' she asked Charlie as she lifted Harry up onto the sofa. Charlie didn't reply; he was busy building a new tower. 'He was always kicking, even back then, wasn't he? I didn't get a good night's sleep for months!'

Kim held Harry up in the air to give his legs room to swing. 'No, you don't like letting me sleep, do you?' He smiled and wiggled his hands and feet. 'I knew you'd be a boy; there was no doubt about that. I told your Daddy that you were going to be sporty and do you know what he said? He said, "Great, he'll play for TOTTENHAM!"'

Harry's smile grew wider when he heard the name of their local football club. It was a word that his dad, Pat, said so often that it had become his favourite word. The Kane family lived only five miles away from Tottenham's stadium, White Hart Lane.

'Wow, you really love that idea, don't you!' Kim laughed. 'Well, your Grandad Eric was a good footballer in his day. Maybe you'll get his talent, rather than your Dad's. Bless him, he always says that bad injuries ruined his career but I think it was his bad first touch!'

It was a bright, sunny afternoon and so Kim took her two sons out to the local park. Hopefully, after a few hours of open space and fresh air, Charlie and Harry would sleep well that night, and so would their mum. Once they found a shady spot on the grass, Kim lay down the picnic rug and lifted Harry out of the pushchair.

'Charlie, you've got to stay where I can see you!' she called out as he chased after a squirrel.

After doing a few laps of the rug, Harry sat down and looked around him. He saw leaves and twigs and insects. He saw huge trees above him and patches of blue sky in between. Then his eyes fixed on the exciting scene in front of him. A group of kids were playing football with jumpers for goalposts. That looked like fun. He stood up and went over to explore.

'Harry, stop!' Kim shouted. She chased after her son and scooped him up just before he reached the other kids' football game. In her arms, Harry kept watching and his legs kept moving. He was desperate to kick the ball.

'Not today, darling,' his mum said, giving him a kiss on the cheek. 'But soon, I promise!'

*

'So, how was your day?' Pat asked, as they all ate dinner together. After a long day's work at the garage, he loved to come home to his happy family.

Charlie could now feed himself like a grown-up but Harry still needed a high chair and some help. Even with Pat holding the spoon, Harry got strawberry yoghurt all over his hands and face.

'I built an awesome tower but Harry broke it with his silly little feet,' Charlie told his dad. He was looking for sympathy, but Pat had other ideas.

'Good, your brother's getting ready for his big Tottenham career! Football runs in the family, you know. Just ask your Grandad – I was one of Ireland's best young players but sadly...'

Kim rolled her eyes. Not again! She decided not to mention Harry's kicking in the park. It would only get her husband's hopes up even more.

CHAPTER 3

HEROES AT WHITE HART LANE

'Have you been good boys today?' Pat asked his sons one evening as they all ate dinner together.

Charlie and Harry knew the right answer. 'Yes!'

Their dad smiled and reached into his trouser pocket. He took out three rectangles of white card and placed them down on the table. Then he watched and waited for his sons' reactions.

Harry thought he knew what they were but he didn't want to get his hopes up until he was sure. His dad had promised him that he could go to his first Tottenham game once he turned four. For his birthday, he got a Spurs shirt and a Spurs football, but no Spurs ticket. Charlie had been to White Hart Lane a few times and Harry was desperate to join them. Was his dream finally going to come true? There in the top left corner was the important word, written in navy blue – 'Tottenham'. He was right; they *were* match tickets! Harry jumped for joy.

'Wow, thanks!' he said, running over to give his dad a big hug. 'This is the best gift ever!'

Suddenly, Harry and Charlie weren't interested in eating anymore. Instead, they ran around the living room, waving the tickets in the air and chanting, 'We're going to White Hart Lane! We're going to White Hart Lane!'

Kim laughed. 'You'll need to keep a close eye on them,' she warned her husband. 'This is just the start!'

'Yes, I think I'll look after these,' Pat said, taking the tickets back from his over-excited sons.

It was a three o'clock kick-off on Saturday but Harry and Charlie were sitting in their Tottenham shirts at breakfast. They spent the morning playing football in the garden, pretending to be their heroes.

'David Ginola gets the ball on the left,' Charlie began the commentary, 'he dribbles past one defender and then another. Look at that skill! He's just outside the penalty area now, he looks up and...'

Harry didn't like playing in goal against his brother. He hardly ever made a save because Charlie's shots were too powerful.

...Gooooooooooooooooooaaaaaaaaaallllllllllllllllllllllll llllllllll!!!!!!!!!!!!!!!!!!!!

Charlie ran towards the corner of the garden and celebrated by pulling his Spurs shirt over his head.

'Right, my turn!' Harry said, picking up the ball.

His number one hero, Teddy Sheringham, had just left Tottenham to sign for Manchester United. But Harry already had his new favourite – German Jürgen Klinsmann. It was a hard name for a four-year-old to say but Harry did his best.

'Kiman runs towards the penalty area...'

He needed to strike the ball perfectly if he wanted to score past his older brother. Harry looked up at the goal and kicked it as hard as he could. The ball bounced and skipped towards the bottom corner...

...Goooooooooooooooooooaaaaaaaaaaaaaalllllllllllllll llllllllllll!!!!!!!!!!!!!!!!!!!!

Normally, Harry celebrated with the Klinsmann dive

but his Spurs shirt was white and he couldn't make
his White Hart Lane debut wearing a muddy shirt! So
instead, he jumped up and pumped
his fist. He could tell that it was going to be a very
good day.

After lunch, it was finally time for them to leave.

'Have you got your hats?' Kim asked at the front
door.

Harry nodded.

'Gloves?'

Harry nodded.

'Good, stay close to your dad and have a great
time!'

They were off! Harry couldn't wait to get to White
Hart Lane. On the bus, he imagined the people,
the noise, the goals. As they crossed through the
Walthamstow reservoirs, Charlie had a thought.

'Dad, have you got the tickets?'

There was panic on Pat's face as he checked all
of his pockets, once and then twice. 'Oh dear,' he
muttered.

Harry's face dropped with disappointment. How

had his dad forgotten the tickets? Why hadn't he checked before they left?

Suddenly, a smile spread across Pat's face, and he held up the tickets. 'Just kidding!' he cheered.

'Dad, don't scare us like that!' Harry shouted. He didn't find the joke funny at all.

When they got off the bus, the stadium was right there in front of them. Harry stood there looking up, his mouth wide open. It was even bigger than he'd expected.

'Come on, let's go in and find our seats!' his dad said. 'Don't let go of my hand, okay? If you get lost, Mum won't ever let us come back.'

Harry held on tightly as they moved through the crowds towards the turnstile, on their way to their seats. There were so many people everywhere and so much to see and hear.

'Get today's match programme here!' the sellers shouted.

Some Tottenham fans talked about their players in between bites of burgers and hot dogs. Other Tottenham fans were already singing songs even before they entered the stadium. It was all so exciting.

Once they were through the turnstile, Harry could see a square of green in the distance. His eyes lit up – the pitch! As they got closer, he couldn't believe the size of it. How did the players keep running from box to box for ninety minutes? It looked impossible.

'Look, there's Ginola!' Charlie shouted, pointing down at the players warming up. 'And there's Klinsmann!'

Harry stood up on his seat to get a better view. He was in the same stadium as his heroes; it didn't get any better than that.

Tottenham, Tottenham!

As the players ran out of the tunnel for the start of the game, the noise grew even louder. Spurs needed a win to stay out of the relegation zone. After a few minutes, Ginola got the ball on the left wing.

'Come on!' the Tottenham fans cheered, rising to their feet.

Ginola curled a brilliant cross into the penalty area. Harry held his breath as Klinsmann stretched to reach it…

Goooooooooooooooooooooooaaaaaaaaaaaaaaaaaallllll
llllllllllllllllll!!!!!!!!!!!!!!!!!!!!

What a start! Harry and Charlie jumped up and down together, cheering for their heroes.

The rest of the match was very tense but Tottenham held on for the victory. By the final whistle, Harry was exhausted but very happy. He was already looking forward to his next trip to White Hart Lane.

'So, who was man of the match?' Pat asked his sons on the bus home.

'Ginola!' Charlie replied.

'Klinsmann!' Harry replied.

Their dad shook his head. 'If we ever keep a clean sheet, it's always the goalkeeper!'

CHAPTER 4

RIDGEWAY ROVERS

'Why do we have to leave?' Charlie cried out. 'It's not fair. This is our home!'

Their parents had just given them some terrible news; the family was moving from Walthamstow to Chingford. They had never even heard of Chingford.

'We'll have more space there,' Kim replied. 'You'll have bigger bedrooms and a bigger football pitch in the garden too.'

'Look, we're not talking about Australia!' Pat said. 'Chingford is only a few miles away.'

'But all our friends are *here*,' Charlie argued.

As the conversation carried on, Harry had an important question to ask: 'How far is it from White Hart Lane?'

'It's only five miles away, the same distance as now.'

Kim and Pat finally won the family argument with a killer fact: David Beckham had grown up in Chingford.

'Really?' Harry asked excitedly. After the 1998 World Cup, Beckham was England's most famous footballer. Despite his red card versus Argentina, every kid in the country wanted to look and play like Becks.

His dad nodded. 'He played for a local team called Ridgeway Rovers.'

'Cool, can I play for Ridgeway Rovers too?'

'It's a deal!' Kim said, looking relieved.

Harry was determined to become a star striker for Tottenham and England, especially after visiting White Hart Lane. He practised all the time, with whatever he could find. In the garden and the park, he played with his own real football. It was his pride and joy, and he looked after it carefully. In the street, he played with any can or bottle that he could find. In the house, he swapped his football for rolled-up socks.

'STOP KICKING THINGS!' Charlie shouted angrily

from through his bedroom door.

'Sorry!' Harry replied quickly, running downstairs to help with dinner. He had been using his brother's door as a shooting target again. He knew that it wasn't allowed but he just couldn't help himself.

'Can I join Ridgeway Rovers now?' Harry asked his parents as they sat down to eat. He was desperate to test his talent against real opponents on a real pitch.

Pat knew that his son wasn't going to give up until it was sorted. Fifteen minutes later, he returned to the living room with good news. 'The Ridgeway Rovers trials are coming up in a couple of weeks. I'll take you along.'

'Thanks!' Harry cheered. He couldn't wait to follow in Becks' footsteps. But first, he had lots more practice to do.

'It's great to see so many of you down here,' Dave Bricknell, the Ridgeway Rovers coach, told the eager young faces at Loughton Rugby Club. 'Welcome! Today, we're looking for brilliant new players to join our club, but most importantly, we're going to have some fun, yes?'

'YES!' Harry cheered with the other boys.

As they all practised passing in pairs, Dave walked around the pitch. He was looking for a nice touch, as well as accuracy and power in the pass.

'Very good!' he called out to Harry.

Next up was dribbling. It wasn't Harry's favourite skill but he managed to keep the ball under control as he weaved in and out of the cones. He was relieved when it was over and he had only knocked one over.

'Right, it's the moment you've all been waiting for,' Dave said to the group. 'Shooting! Do we have a goalkeeper here?'

Everyone looked around but no-one stepped forward.

The coach looked surprised. 'Really? Not a single keeper?'

Harry was really looking forward to scoring some goals but he also didn't mind playing in goal, especially if it wasn't Charlie who was shooting at him. Slowly, he raised his arm.

'Great! What's your name?' Dave asked.

'Harry.'

'Thanks, Harry! You'll get a chance to shoot later on, I promise.'

He put on a pair of gloves, walked over to the goal and waited. As the first shot came towards him, he didn't even have to move. He caught the ball and rolled it to the side. The next shot was better and he had to throw himself across the goal to tip it round the post.

'What a save, Harry!' Dave clapped. 'I think we've found our new keeper!'

Harry enjoyed diving around but he didn't want to be Ian Walker or David Seaman. He wanted to be Teddy Sheringham or Jürgen Klinsmann.

'Coach,' he called out after the first round of shots, 'I don't really play in goal. I normally play outfield as a striker.'

'Not again!' Dave thought to himself. Young keepers always got bored and asked to move to attack for the glory. Even so, he made a promise to the boy:

'No problem, I'll put you up front for the match at the end. You're a natural in goal, though!'

Harry waited patiently for his chance to shine. It

29

took a little while, even once the match had started. But finally, his teammate kicked a long pass down the pitch and he was off, sprinting as fast as his little legs could go. He wasn't the fastest but he had a head start because of his clever run.

Harry beat the defender to the ball, took one touch to control it and calmly placed his shot in the bottom corner.

Goooooooooooooooooooaaaaaaaaaaaaaaaalllllllllllllllllllllllllllll!!!!!!!!!!!!!!!!!!!

Ten minutes later, Harry had a hat-trick and a place in the Ridgeway Rovers team.

'You're a natural keeper *and* a natural striker,' Dave laughed. 'I guess you're just a natural footballer!'

Harry couldn't wait for the real matches to begin. As he stepped out onto the field for the first time in the blue and white Ridgeway Rovers shirt, he felt unstoppable. This was it. He was ready for the big time, but was the big time ready for him?

When the ball came to him in the penalty area, Harry took a shot and it deflected off a defender and out for a corner.

'I'll take it!' Harry shouted, chasing over to the flag.

It was a long way from the corner to the penalty area, so he kicked it as hard as he could. The ball flew over the heads of everyone, including the goalkeeper. It landed in the back of the net.

Goooooooooooooooaaaaaaaaaaaaaaaaaalllllllllllllllllllllllllll lllllll!!!!!!!!!!!!!!!!!!!!!

Harry punched the air with joy – he was off the mark on his debut! It was a lucky strike but that didn't matter. Would he ever get tired of scoring goals? He really didn't think so.

CHAPTER 5

FOOTBALL, FOOTBALL, FOOTBALL

'That's it! Keep your head steady and lean over the ball as you kick it.'

At the weekends, Harry's dad often helped him with extra training in the back garden. There was so much that he wanted to improve, especially his shooting. He couldn't relax if he wanted to keep his place as Ridgeway Rovers' number one striker.

'Right, I think that's enough,' Pat said after an hour. 'You've got a game later today and you'll be too tired to score.'

'Okay, just three more shots,' Harry begged.

If his dad was busy, he went to the park with Charlie. When Harry was younger, his older brother used to make him stand between two trees and try to save his powerful shots for hours. That wasn't much fun but now that he was eight, Charlie let him join in properly. If there were other kids around, they'd play a big match but if it was just the two of them, they had long, competitive one-on-one battles. Harry was a skilful footballer but his older brother had one weapon that could defeat him: strength.

'Come on, that's not fair!' Harry shouted as he picked himself up off the grass. 'You can't just push me off the ball like that.'

Charlie shrugged. 'That was a shoulder-to-shoulder challenge. It's not my fault that I'm bigger than you.'

It was no use complaining; Harry just had to find other ways to beat his brother. Luckily, he was very determined. A few times he stormed off angrily but most of the time, Harry tried and tried until he succeeded.

'You're definitely getting better, bro!' Charlie told him as they walked back home together for lunch.

Harry smiled proudly; that was his aim. He didn't want to just be an average player; he wanted to become a great player like his Tottenham heroes. He didn't care how much time and effort that would take. Harry played football before school, at break-time, at lunchtime, and then after school too.

'See you later, Mum!' he called out as he gulped down a glass of water and threw his bag down.

Kim didn't need to ask where her son was going. She knew exactly where he would be and what he'd be doing. 'Just be careful and make sure you're back for dinner,' was all she said.

In the summer, Harry and his friends played in the park all day. But in the winter, it was too dark so they swapped grass for tarmac. Under the streetlights, their games could go on much longer, although there were more obstacles to deal with.

'Stop!' Harry called out. 'Car coming!'

All shots had to be low and soft. A few broken flowers were fine but broken windows meant game over.

'Kev, don't blast it!'

'Mrs Curtis is watching at the curtain!'

Harry loved their street games because they really

helped him to improve his technique. In the tight space between the pavements, his control had to be excellent and he had to look up quickly to find the pass. His movement had to be good too if he wanted to escape from the defenders and score.

'Yes!' he would scream as he made a sudden run towards goal. If he got it right, his marker wouldn't have time to turn and catch him.

Harry's hero, Teddy Sheringham, was back as Tottenham's Number 10. He watched him carefully in every match and tried to copy his movement. Teddy wasn't the quickest striker in the Premier League but he was always alert and clever around the penalty area.

'Stay tight on Harry,' his opponents would say. 'Don't switch off or he'll score!'

Normally, their street games were friendly and fun, but not always. If the result came down to next goal wins, everyone took it very seriously.

'No way! That went straight over the jumper – that's not a goal.'

'What are you talking about? That was post and in!'

'Stop cheating!'

'You're the one who's cheating!'

Of course, there was no referee, so Harry often had to be the peacemaker. He wanted to win just as much as the other boys, if not more, but he always stayed calm. Getting angry didn't help anyone. If Harry ended up on the losing team one day, he just worked even harder the next day.

Harry's days started and ended with football. It was all he thought about. In bed, he lay there imagining his Tottenham debut:

It was 0–0 with ten minutes to go and he came on to replace Les Ferdinand up front. Darren Anderton got the ball in midfield and played a brilliant through-ball. Harry ran towards goal, and he was one-on-one with the goalkeeper. Could he stay calm and find the net?

Unfortunately, he fell asleep before he found out the answer.

CHAPTER 6

ARSENAL

Harry was used to seeing Premier League scouts at Ridgeway Rovers matches. There was lots of young talent in north east London and no club wanted to miss out on the next David Beckham. If he kept scoring, Harry believed that it could be him.

'Well played, today,' said Ian Marshall, the Chairman of Ridgeway Rovers, as he ruffled the boy's short hair. 'How many is that for the season now?'

Harry pretended to count but he knew the answer. 'Eighteen in fifteen games.'

'You're our little Alan Shearer!'

Harry shook his head. 'I prefer Sheringham.'

Ian laughed. 'Of course, Teddy it is then! Do you mind if I have a quick chat with your dad please?'

While Harry practised his keepie-uppies nearby, the adults chatted.

'We had an Arsenal scout here today,' Ian said. 'He wants your boy to go for a trial there.'

Pat wasn't surprised; he already knew that his son was a very good player. But he wanted to do what was best for him.

'What do you think?' he asked Ian. 'He's still only eight – is he too young to join an academy? I want Harry to keep enjoying his football.'

The Ridgeway Rovers coach nodded. 'I understand. Look, I don't think there's any harm in him trying it out. If he doesn't like it, he can just come back here. We'll always have a place for him.'

Pat thanked Ian. 'Harry loves everything about football but I just don't want to get his hopes up. It can be a very cruel business for youngsters.'

As soon as they were in the car, Harry wanted to know everything. 'What were you and Ian talking about?'

'Wait until we get home. I need to talk to your mum first.'

'Okay, but was it a Tottenham scout?'

'Harry!'

'A West Ham scout?'

'HARRY!'

After a whispered chat with Kim in the kitchen, Pat shared the good news with his son. 'Arsenal want to offer you a trial. What do you think?'

Harry's first thoughts were a mix of pride and disappointment. It was amazing news that a Premier League club wanted him, but why did it have to be Arsenal, Tottenham's biggest rivals?

'But we hate Arsenal, Dad!'

Pat laughed. 'We don't really hate them, son. It's just a football rivalry. They're a great club and they're doing very well at the moment.'

His dad was right; Arsenal were the second-best team in England, just behind Manchester United. They had exciting superstars like Dennis Bergkamp, Patrick Vieira and Thierry Henry. Tottenham, meanwhile, were down in mid-table.

That was enough to make Harry change his mind. 'Okay, so when can I start?'

For the big day, Harry decided not to wear his Tottenham shirt. He was already going to be the new kid at Arsenal and he didn't want to make things even harder.

'How are you feeling?' his mum asked on the journey to London Colney, Arsenal's training ground location.

'Fine,' Harry replied but really, he was getting more and more nervous in the backseat of the car. It was going to be a massive challenge for him, and what if he failed? What if he wasn't good enough and made a fool of himself? This wasn't Ridgeway Rovers anymore.

'You'll be brilliant,' Kim told him, giving his hand a squeeze. 'But maybe don't tell your new coaches that you're a Spurs fan straight away!'

Harry smiled and felt a bit more relaxed. As long as he tried his best, what more could he do?

As they drove into the Arsenal Training Centre, Harry couldn't believe his eyes. Compared to Ridgeway's Peter May Sports Centre, it looked like a whole city. There were ten perfect, full-size pitches, as well as lots of indoor facilities.

'Not bad, is it?' his dad joked.

Once the session began, Harry's nerves turned into adrenaline. 'I can do this!' he told himself. Everything felt better with a football at his feet.

In the drills, he showed off his best touch and passing. Some of the other boys had incredible technique already, but Harry didn't let that get him down. He was waiting for his moment to shine – shooting. When that moment arrived, the Arsenal goalkeepers didn't have a chance. Bottom left, top right, straight down the middle; Harry scored every time.

'Great work!' the coach clapped.

That trial session soon turned into a whole season at Arsenal. At first, it felt strange to play for Tottenham's enemies but Harry soon forgot about that. He was having so much fun. He wasn't as skilful as some of his teammates, but that wasn't really his role – he was the one who scored the goals. He didn't play every minute of every match but he tried to make the most of every opportunity.

At the end of the season, the Arsenal academy had to choose which youngsters to keep and which youngsters to let go. Harry crossed his fingers tightly for weeks but unfortunately, it was bad news. The coaches decided that he was too small for his age.

'I'm so sorry,' his dad said, giving him a hug. 'Be proud and keep going. Once you've had your growth spurt, Arsenal are going to regret it!'

For the next few days, Harry was so angry and upset that he wanted to give up. But luckily, that feeling didn't last long. He realised that he loved football too much to stop. If Arsenal didn't want him, he knew another team that hopefully still did.

'Dad, can I go and play for Ridgeway Rovers again?'

The Peter May Sports Centre would always feel like home.

'Welcome back, kid!' Ian said with a wink. 'What we're looking for is a goalscorer, a fox in the box – do you know of anyone like that?'

Harry grinned. 'Yes – me!'

CHAPTER 7

CHINGFORD FOUNDATION SCHOOL

After playing for Ridgeway Rovers, Harry was soon
following in David Beckham's footsteps for a second
time when he started at Chingford Foundation School.
Becks' signed shirt hung proudly in the entrance lobby
at Chingford. Harry looked at it every morning as
he arrived at school, hoping that it would bring him
luck, but especially on the day of the trial for the Year
7 football team. Chingford had one of the best track
records in Greater London and Harry was ready to be
their next star.

'I'm the striker that they need and I'll show them
at the trial,' he told his brother, Charlie, on the way

to school. He wasn't quite as confident as he sounded but he was as determined as ever.

Harry loved scoring goals. It was an amazing feeling when a shot hit the back of the net. But he could do a lot more than just that. During his year at Arsenal, he had improved his all-round game. He was good in possession, and creative too. Setting up chances for his teammates was almost as much fun as scoring.

'Just don't be too selfish,' Charlie warned. 'Mr Leadon hates a show-off!'

Harry didn't forget his brother's advice. After changing into his white Tottenham shirt, he made his way out onto the pitch with the other boys.

'Good luck!' Harry told his mates. They were all competing for places now.

After a warm-up and some passing exercises, Mark Leadon, Chingford's football coach, split the boys up and gave half of them orange bibs.

'I'm looking for team players today,' he told them. 'If you just want to show off how many tricks you can do, go do that in the playground. I want to see how you can work together and help each other to win.

Right, let's play!'

Most of Harry's schoolmates knew that he was a good footballer because they had seen him play in the lunchtime games. They knew that he had played for Arsenal, but he was still quite small and he didn't have the flashy skills and speed to dribble past everyone. There were other boys who looked more talented but Harry hadn't played at his best. Yet.

'If we pass the ball around, they'll get tired and the chances will come,' he told his teammates. He had made himself the leader.

Harry was ready to be patient but he didn't need to be. The opposition defenders couldn't cope with his clever runs into space. As the cross came in, he made a late run to beat his marker to the ball.

Goooooooooooooooaaaaaaaaaaaaaaaaaaalllllllllllllllllllllllllll!!!!!!!!!!!!!!!!!!!!!

Harry didn't run off and celebrate on his own; he ran straight to thank the teammate who had set him up. Together, they ran back for the restart. They had more goals to score.

'I like this kid,' Mark thought to himself on

the sidelines. 'For an eleven-year-old, he really understands football. He knows where to go and he knows where his teammates are going to go too.'

Harry didn't stop running until Mark blew the whistle to end the game. By then, it had turned into a thrashing. When he found room to shoot, Harry shot and scored. When he could see another player in space, he passed for them to score instead. He was involved in every part of his team's victory.

They walked off the pitch together, with their arms around each other's shoulders. Their man of the match was right at the centre of the gang.

'Well played,' Mark said to them but he was looking straight at Harry.

'Thanks, sir,' he replied politely, but inside, he was buzzing with pride.

Mark was very impressed. Every year, he had excellent young footballers in his school team but this boy seemed special. He had technique, vision, movement *and* work-rate. Mark could tell that it was going to be a good season.

'So, how did it go?' Charlie asked when his brother

got home from school that evening.

Harry smiled and shrugged modestly. 'It went okay, I think.'

Harry became the first name on a very successful teamsheet. His goals led Chingford to school cup glory.

'If you keep working hard, your shirt could be hanging up there with Becks one day!' Mark Leadon told him.

CHAPTER 8

HEROES AND DREAMS

'Welcome!' David Beckham announced to a group
of sixteen boys and girls. The England superstar was
in East London to launch his brand-new football
academy. With his white Adidas tracksuit and trendy
haircut, he looked so cool. 'Today, we're going to
practise some of my favourite skills.'

Harry wasn't really listening; he was too busy
staring at his hero. He was one of the Chingford
Foundation School footballers who had been selected
to go to the academy launch. So now, Becks was right
next to him, giving him football tips! Surely, it was too
good to be true? But no, it was really happening.

Like Becks, Harry wore an Adidas tracksuit, but

their hairstyles didn't match. Harry's head was shaved short, like Becks way back in 2000, but Becks had tried five different looks since then! Harry felt very nervous. Not only was Becks watching him but there were also cameras everywhere. Still, he was desperate to impress. Harry dribbled the ball carefully from end to end, and kept his keepie-uppies simple.

'That's it, great work everyone!' Becks called out.

At the end of the day, he shook each of them by the hand and chatted with them. When it was Harry's turn, he was too nervous and shy to speak. Luckily, Becks went first.

'Well done today. Are you one of the lads from Chingford?' he asked.

Harry nodded. 'A-and I play for Ridgeway Rovers too.'

Becks smiled. 'Great club, so what's next? What's your dream?'

Harry didn't need to think about that one. 'I want to play for England at Wembley!'

'Good choice, it's the best feeling in the world. If

you keep working hard, you can do it. Good luck!'

As Harry travelled home with his mum, he could still hear his hero's inspirational words in his head – 'you can do it'.

*

'Play the pass now!' Harry shouted, as he sprinted towards goal. It was only one of their street games, but that didn't matter. Every football match was important. The pass never arrived, however.

'Car!' one of his mates shouted, picking up the ball.

As he moved over towards the pavement, Harry noticed two strange things about this particular car. Firstly, it wasn't the typical old banger that usually drove through the area. It was a huge black Range Rover and it looked brand-new. Secondly, the car didn't speed off once they were out of the way. Instead, it stopped and the driver's door opened.

'Hey guys, do you fancy a game?' the man said with a big smile on his face.

Harry's jaw dropped. Was he dreaming? Was Jermain Defoe, Spurs' star striker, really standing there asking to play with them?

'Yes, Jermain's on our team!'

'Hey, that's not fair!'

After a few minutes of arguing, the decision was made: Harry and Jermain would play on opposite teams.

'Let's see what you've got!' Jermain told him with a wink.

Harry loved a challenge but this one was impossible. He knew that he couldn't compete with a top Premier League striker yet but he did his best. He chased every pass and got on the ball as often as possible. He wanted to show off all his skills.

When he wasn't racing around the pitch, Harry tried to watch his superstar opponent in action. Jermain scored lots of goals but Harry was more interested in the rest of his play. With a powerful burst of speed, he could escape from any tackle. Jermain was always thinking one step ahead, playing quick passes to get his teammates into really dangerous areas. If there was a loose ball, or a goalmouth scramble, he was always the first to react.

First Becks and now Jermain; Harry was learning from the very best.

After half an hour, Jermain had to leave. 'Thanks for the game, lads!'

The boys all stood and watched as the black Range Rover drove away. Then they looked at each other, their faces full of wonder. It was a night that none of them would ever forget.

'They're not going to believe us at school, are they?' Harry said.

His mates shook their heads. 'Not in a million years.'

CHAPTER 9

TOTTENHAM AT LAST

'I can't believe you're leaving us again,' Ian Marshall said with a wink and a handshake. 'I hope it goes well for you, lad, but if not, just come back home!'

Harry would miss playing for Ridgeway Rovers but Watford had offered him a trial. They weren't as big as Arsenal or Tottenham, but they were a good Championship team. It was the sort of new challenge that he needed.

'Good luck!' Pat called from the car window as he dropped Harry off at the Watford training centre. His son hadn't said much during the journey and he hoped that he wasn't brooding on his experience at

Arsenal. Harry was at a different club now and there was nothing to worry about.

But Harry wasn't worried; he was just focused on doing his best. He might only have a few weeks to impress his new coaches, so he had to get things right. If Harry missed one shot, he had to score the next one.

'How did it go?' Pat asked when he returned to pick him up.

'It was good,' was all Harry said. This time, he was taking it one step at a time. He didn't want to get carried away. It was just nice to be training with a professional team again.

But it turned out that Watford weren't the only ones chasing him. Another club was also interested, the only club in Harry's heart – Tottenham.

Tottenham's youth scout Mark O'Toole had been watching Harry's Ridgeway Rovers performances for nearly a year. Harry was easily the best player in his team. He was a natural finisher and he had good technique. So, what was Mark waiting for?

'He knows exactly where the goal is but most

strikers are either big or quick,' he discussed with the other scouts. 'Harry's neither!'

Mark liked to be 100 per cent certain before he told the Tottenham youth coaches to offer a youngster a trial. But when he heard that Harry was at Watford, he decided to take a risk, and advised the coaches:

'I want you to take a look at a kid who plays for Ridgeway Rovers. He scores lots of goals but he's not a classic striker. I guess he's more like Teddy Sheringham than Alan Shearer.'

'Interesting! What's his name?'

'Harry Kane.'

'Well, tell him to come down for a trial.'

When his dad told him the news, Harry thought his family were playing a prank on him. How could they be so mean? Surely, they knew how much he wanted to play for his local club.

'No, I'm serious!' Pat told him. He tried to look serious but he couldn't stop smiling. 'I got a call from a Tottenham youth scout. They want you to go down to the training centre next week.'

After checking a few times, Harry celebrated with a

lap of the living room.

'I'm going to play for Tottenham! I'm going to play for Tottenham!'

He had only been training with Watford for about a month, but there was no way that he could say no to Spurs. His dream team was calling him.

Harry waited and worried but finally the big day arrived.

'How are you feeling?' Pat asked as they drove to Spurs Lodge in Epping Forest.

Harry nodded. His heart was beating so fast that he thought it might jump out of his mouth if he tried to speak.

'Just remember to enjoy it, son,' his dad told him. 'It's a big opportunity but you've got to have fun, okay?'

Harry nodded again. Nothing was as fun as scoring goals.

As they parked their car, Harry could see the other boys warming up on the pitch. In their matching club tracksuits, they seemed to be having a great time together. This was the Under-13s but they all looked at least fifteen. Harry was still waiting for his growth spurt. What if they didn't want a little kid to join their group? What if he made a fool of himself? No, he couldn't think like that. He had to keep believing in himself.

Mark O'Toole was there at the entrance to greet them. 'Welcome to Tottenham! Are you ready for this, kid?'

This time, Harry had to speak. 'Yes, thanks.'

After a deep breath, he walked out onto the pitch in his lucky Tottenham shirt. He had nothing to lose.

Two hours later, Harry was on his way back home, sweaty and buzzing.

'They scored first but I knew we would win it. We had all the best players. George is really good in midfield and Danny can dribble past anyone. I reckon he can kick it even harder than Charlie! The other team didn't stand a chance, really. We had to work hard but–'

'Whoa, slow down, kiddo!' his dad laughed. 'So, you had a good time out there?'

'It was so much fun! I scored the winning goal!'

'I know – it was a great strike too.'

Harry frowned. 'How do you know that?'

His dad laughed. 'I watched from the car! I didn't want to put extra pressure on you by standing there on the sidelines but I wasn't going to miss your first session. Well done, you played really well tonight.'

After six weeks on trial, Harry became a proper Spurs youth team player. It was the proudest moment of his life but he had lots of hard work ahead of him. He had been the best player at Ridgeway Rovers, but he was now just average at Tottenham. It was like starting school all over again.

Luckily, Harry was a quick and willing learner. If it meant he got to play for Spurs, he would do anything the coaches asked him to do.

'Excellent effort, Harry!' John Moncur, the head of youth development, shouted.

Harry was enjoying himself but as summer approached, he began to worry. Soon, it would be time for the end-of-season letters again. Would Spurs decide to keep him for another year? After his experience at Arsenal, he couldn't bear another rejection. The day the post arrived, Harry's hands were shaking.

'Open it!' his brother Charlie demanded impatiently.

When he tore open the envelope, Harry read the dreaded word and his heart sank: '*Unfortunately…*'. It was the release letter. He tried to hold back the tears but he couldn't. 'I don't understand – I had a good season!'

The phone rang and Pat went to answer it. Within seconds, the sadness was gone from his voice. Instead, he sounded relieved. 'Don't worry, these things happen…Yes, I'll tell him right now.'

'Panic over!' Pat called out as he returned to the living room. Harry looked up and saw a big smile on his dad's face. What was going on? 'They sent you the wrong letter by mistake. Spurs want you to stay!'

CHAPTER 10

ONE MORE YEAR

Alex Inglethorpe was Tottenham's Under-18s coach but once a week, he helped out with the Under-14s training. He liked to keep an eye on the younger age groups because the most talented boys would soon move up into his team. Ryan Mason and Andros Townsend were already making the step-up. Who would be next?

During the session, Alex offered lots of advice, especially to the team's best players. There were a couple of speedy full-backs, plus a tall centre-back and a classy playmaker in central midfield. And then there was Harry.

Harry didn't really stand out as an amazing young

footballer, but Alex loved the boy's attitude. He played
with so much desire and all he wanted to do was
score goals for his team. Harry understood that he
wasn't as strong or quick as the other strikers, but he
didn't let that stop him. He loved a challenge, and
competing with Tottenham's best young players was
certainly a challenge. With the pressure on, he never
panicked. He just made the most of his technique and
worked hard on his weaknesses.

'That's it, Harry! Shield the ball from the defender
and wait until the pass is on. Lovely!'

Harry was the perfect student. After most sessions,
he would stay behind for extra shooting practice. For a
youth coach, that desire was a very good sign.

'Let's wait and see what happens when he grows
a bit,' Alex kept telling everyone at the Tottenham
academy. But they couldn't wait forever. Next year,
Harry would be moving up to the Under-16s. Before
then, they had to make a big decision about his future.

'Thanks for coming,' the Under-14s coach said,
shaking hands with Harry's parents. 'I wanted to
talk to you about your son's progress. As you know,

everyone loves Harry here at Spurs. He works so hard and he's a pleasure to work with.'

Pat and Kim could tell that there was a 'But' coming.

'But we're worried. He's still small for his age and he's not a speedy little striker like Jermain Defoe. Don't get me wrong, Harry's got a very good understanding of the game but he needs more than just that if he wants to play up front for Spurs.'

'Okay, so how long does he have to get better?' Pat asked. Once they knew the timeframe, they could make a plan.

The Under-14s coach frowned. 'Every age group is a big new challenge and unless we see real improvement, we don't think that Harry will make it in the Under-16s next year.'

So, one more year. When they got home, Pat sat Harry down in the living room and told him the news. He could see the tears building in his son's eyes. First Arsenal and now Tottenham…

'Don't worry, this isn't over,' Pat said, putting an arm around Harry's shoulder. 'We just have to work even harder to prove them wrong. We believe in you. Do you want to give up?'

Harry shook his head firmly. 'No.'

His dad smiled. 'Good, that's my boy! We'll make a plan tomorrow.'

For the next twelve months, Harry trained with Tottenham as normal, but he also did extra sessions away from the club.

'I want to help but me and you kicking a ball around in the garden won't cut it anymore,' his dad joked. 'It's time to get serious!'

At first, 'serious' just meant lots of boring running and not much actual football. Harry did short sprints until he could barely lift his legs. 'What's the point of this?' he thought to himself as he stood there panting in the rain. This wasn't the beautiful game that he loved.

'Let's have a chat,' his coach said. He could tell that Harry was hating every second of it. 'Look kid, you're never going to be a 100-metre champion but a short burst of pace can make a huge difference for a striker.'

Harry thought back to Jermain Defoe during that street game a few years earlier. He was really good at making space for the shot and his reaction speed was amazing. That was what Harry needed. If the ball dropped in the penalty area, he had to get there first. If a goalkeeper made a save, he had to win the race to the rebound.

'Brilliant, Harry!' his coach cried out a few minutes later. 'That's your best time yet!'

Soon, they moved on to ball work. Harry practised his hold-up play, his heading and, of course, his shooting. He could feel the improvement and so could Tottenham. After a few months, Harry was looking fitter and much more confident on the pitch. Most importantly, he was a better striker and he was scoring more goals.

'Congratulations, kid!' Alex told him after another brilliant performance. 'I knew you'd prove them wrong. And you're getting taller every time I see you.'

Yes, Harry was finally growing! Everything was falling into place at just the right time. Thanks to lots of extra effort, Spurs wanted him to stay. Now, Harry just needed to grow into his tall new body.

CHAPTER 11

MEXICO AND SWITZERLAND

By the time he turned fifteen, Harry had become one of Tottenham's hottest prospects. He still played a lot of games for the Under-16s but he was also getting experience at higher levels. No matter who he played against, Harry kept scoring goals.

'That kid is one of the best natural finishers I've ever seen,' Spurs coach Tim Sherwood told Alex Inglethorpe. 'Why have I never heard of him until now?'

The Under-18s coach laughed. 'He's a late developer!'

'Okay, well look after him carefully – he could be our next goal machine.'

At the start of the 2008–09 season, Jonathan Obika had been Alex's number one striker in the Spurs academy side but the team played lots of matches and it was good to have competition for places.

'Welcome to the squad!' Alex said as he gave Harry the good news. 'At first, you'll be on the bench but if you keep making the most of your opportunities, you'll force your way into the starting line-up. You deserve this.'

Harry was delighted. Not only was he moving up but he was joining a very good side. There was Steven Caulker at the back, Ryan Mason in the middle and Andros Townsend on the wing. With teammates like that, he was going to get plenty of chances to score. Harry couldn't wait.

'If I grab a few goals, I could be playing for the first team soon!' he told Charlie excitedly.

It was his older brother's job to keep his feet on the ground. 'And if you miss a few sitters, you could be playing for the Under-16s again!' Charlie teased.

Luckily, that didn't happen. Harry kept on scoring and soon he was off on an exciting international adventure.

'I'm going to Mexico!' he told his family in December. 'I made the Spurs team for the Copa Chivas.'

'Never heard of it!' Charlie replied with a smile. He was very proud of his younger brother, but it wasn't very cool to show it.

Kim was more concerned about Christmas. 'When do you leave?' she asked.

Harry shrugged; he wasn't bothered about the details. He was playing football for Tottenham; that was all he needed to know. 'In January, I think.'

It was going to be the trip of a lifetime. He couldn't wait to have lots of fun with Ryan, Steven and Andros and win the tournament. What an experience it would be!

'Just you behave yourself,' his mum told him at the airport. 'Don't let the older boys get you into trouble!'

After a long flight, the squad arrived in Guadalajara and found the familiar Tottenham cockerel on the side of a big coach.

'We're famous!' Ryan joked as they all got on board.

In the Copa Chivas, Tottenham faced teams from Spain, Costa Rica, Brazil, Paraguay, Norway and, of course, Mexico.

'Come on boys, we're representing England here!' Harry said, looking down at their white Spurs shirts.

It was hard work in the heat but Tottenham did well. In eight matches, Harry managed to score three goals.

'Only Ryan got more than me!' he told his parents proudly when he returned to Chingford. It had been the best trip ever, but he was glad to get back to his own bedroom and home cooking.

A few months later, Harry was off again. Tottenham were playing in the *Torneo Bellinzona* in Switzerland against big clubs like Sporting Lisbon and Barcelona.

'Barca who?' Steven joked. They weren't scared of anyone.

Harry started two of their five matches and, although he didn't score, he played a big role in helping his team to win the tournament.

'I like setting up goals too, you know!' he reminded Ryan after their final win. It was a great feeling but nothing beat scoring goals.

Harry had really enjoyed his travels and he had learnt a lot from playing against teams from other countries. But back in England, it was time to think about his Spurs future. With his sixteenth birthday coming up, would Tottenham offer him a scholarship contract? He felt like he was improving all the time but he didn't want to get his hopes up. As time went by, his fears grew.

'Harry, have you got any plans for Tuesday?' John McDermott, the head of the academy, asked him casually.

He quickly worked out the date in his head. 'That's my birthday! Why?'

John smiled. 'Do you think you'll have time to come in and sign your contract?

Harry had never felt so relieved. He couldn't wait to tell his family and friends. After all his hard work, he was finally getting his reward. Signing with Spurs would be the best birthday present ever.

CHAPTER 12

GETTING CLOSER

Ahead of the 2009–10 season, the Tottenham Under-18s lined up for their squad photo. Harry had grown so much that the cameraman placed him on the back row next to the goalkeepers. He wasn't yet important enough to sit in the front row, but that was where he aimed to be next year.

Once everyone was in position, the cameraman counted down. '3, 2, 1... Click!'

Most of his teammates looked very serious in the photos but Harry couldn't help smiling. Why shouldn't he be happy? He was playing football for his favourite club in the world!

Harry's season started in Belgium at Eurofoot. Ryan, Andros and Steven had all gone out on loan, so he was suddenly a senior member of the youth squad.

'A lot of excellent players have played in this tournament,' coach Alex Inglethorpe told them. 'This is going to be a great experience for all of you. We will be playing a lot of games while we're out here, so get ready to test your fitness!'

After his successful trips to Mexico and Switzerland, Harry couldn't wait for his next international adventure. He was a year older now and a much better striker. The tournament schedule was really tiring but Harry scored three goals in his first four games.

'You're on fire!' his strike partner Kudus Oyenuga cheered as they celebrated their win over Dutch team Willem II.

In the end, Tottenham didn't reach the semi-finals but Harry had his shooting boots on, ready for the Premier Academy League to begin. Or so he thought, anyway. But after four matches, he still hadn't scored.

'Just be patient,' Kudus kept telling him.

It was easy for Kudus to say; he had already found the net three times. 'But scoring goals is what I do best!' Harry argued.

'I think you're just trying too hard,' Tom Carroll, their tiny midfield playmaker, suggested. 'Just relax and I bet the goals will come.'

Harry was grateful for his teammates' support and advice. He scored in his next match against Fulham and once he started, he didn't stop. After two free-kick strikes against Watford, first-team coach Harry Redknapp picked him as a sub for the League Cup match against Everton.

'No way! This is too good to be true,' Harry said when he saw the squad list. His name was there next to top professionals like Jermaine Jenas and Vedran Ćorluka.

Alex laughed. 'No, it's for real! Just don't get your hopes up; you probably won't get off the bench.'

Harry didn't come on, but he got to train with his heroes and share a dressing room with them. The experience inspired him to keep working hard. He could feel himself getting closer and closer to his Tottenham dream.

By Christmas, Harry was the Under-18s top scorer

with nine goals, and the new academy captain.

'Alex always had a good feeling about you,' John McDermott said as he congratulated Harry. 'You're certainly proving him right these days! If you keep it up, the future is yours.'

Harry celebrated by scoring his first hat-trick of the season against Coventry City. And the great news just kept coming. In January 2010, he was called up to the England Under-17s for the Algarve Tournament in Portugal.

'Welcome!' the coach John Peacock said at his first squad meeting. 'I guess you must know a lot of these guys from the Premier Academy League?'

'Yes,' Harry replied, trying to hide his nerves. He had played against Benik Afobe, Ross Barkley and Nathaniel Chalobah before but they probably didn't even remember him. He was the new kid and he suddenly felt very shy. Luckily, his new teammates were very friendly.

'Nice to meet you, we needed a new striker,' Nathaniel grinned. 'Benik already thinks he's Thierry Henry!'

Harry soon felt like one of the gang. Off the pitch, they had lots of fun together but on the pitch, they were a focused team. The Under-17 European Championships were only a few months away, and so the Algarve Tournament was a chance for players to secure their places.

As he walked onto the pitch wearing the Three Lions on his shirt for the first time, Harry had to pinch himself to check that he wasn't dreaming. A few years earlier, Spurs had been close to letting him go – but now look at him! It was hard to believe. Harry didn't score against France or Ukraine but he would never forget those matches. He was an England youth international now.

Harry knew that if he played well until May, he had a chance of going to the Euros in Liechtenstein. That's what he wanted more than anything. He kept scoring goals for the Tottenham Under-18s and the Reserves, and crossed his fingers. He finished with eighteen goals in only twenty-two Premier Academy League games. Surely that would be enough to make the England squad?

In the end, Harry never found out because he was too ill to go to the tournament. Instead of representing his country at the Euros, he had to sit at home and watch Nathaniel, Ross and Benik winning without him. When England beat Spain in the final, Harry was both delighted and devastated.

'Congratulations, guys!' he texted his teammates but inside, he was very jealous. He should have been there with them, lifting the trophy.

'You'll get more chances,' his mum told him as he lay on the sofa feeling sorry for himself.

It didn't seem that way at the time, but Harry always bounced back from disappointments. There was a new season to prepare for, and a first professional Tottenham contract to sign. That was more than enough to lift him out of his bad mood. It was the best feeling in the world as he signed his name on the papers.

'Thanks for always believing in me,' Harry told Alex as they chatted afterwards. 'I couldn't have done this without you.'

His Under-18s coach shook his head. 'You did it all

yourself but you haven't achieved anything yet, kid. The next step is the hardest but you've got what it takes.'

Harry smiled. It was true; he wouldn't give up until he made it into the Spurs first team.

CHAPTER 13

EXPERIENCE NEEDED

At seventeen, Harry was on his way to becoming
a Spurs superstar but he still had a lot to learn.
Luckily, there were plenty of teachers around him at
Tottenham. In the Reserves, he often played alongside
first team stars who were recovering from injuries, like
David Bentley and Robbie Keane. Harry loved those
matches. He was always watching and listening for
new tips.

'If you need to, take a touch but if you hit it early,
you might catch the keeper out.'

'Don't just assume that he's going to catch it. Get
there in case he drops it!'

By 2010, Harry was also training regularly with

Harry Redknapp's squad. It was hard to believe that he was sharing a pitch with world-class players like Gareth Bale, Luka Modrić and Rafael van der Vaart. But best of all, Harry was working with his hero, Jermain Defoe. Eventually, he plucked up the courage to talk about that street game.

'Oh yeah, I remember that!' Jermain laughed. 'That was you? Wow, I feel *really* old now!'

Jermain became Harry's mentor and invited him to his extra shooting sessions.

'You're a natural goalscorer, H, but it takes more than instinct to become a top striker. You need to practise, practise, practise! What are you aiming for when you shoot?'

It seemed like a really stupid question. 'The goal,' he replied.

'Okay, but what part of the goal? Top corner, bottom corner?'

'Err, I don't know, I guess I–'

Jermain interrupted Harry. 'No, no, no! You've got to know exactly what you're aiming at, H. Before you hit this one, I want you to picture the goal in your head and then aim for the top right corner.'

Harry took his time and placed the ball carefully into the top right corner.

'Good, but you won't get that long to think in a real match.'

Jermain called a young defender over: 'As soon as I play the pass to Harry, close him down.'

Under pressure, Harry hit the target again but his shot went straight down the middle of the goal. 'No, the keeper would have saved that,' Jermain said. So Harry tried again and again until he hit that top right corner.

'Nice! Now let's work on making that space to shoot. Let's hope you're quicker than you look!' Jermain teased.

He was very impressed by Harry's attitude. Not only did he love scoring goals but he also loved improving his game. That was a winning combination. Jermain kept telling the Spurs coaches, 'If you give him a chance, I promise you he'll score!'

But for now, Redknapp already had Jermain, Roman Pavlyuchenko and Peter Crouch in his squad. Harry would have to wait for his chance. He was doing well for the Reserves but was that the best place for him to develop? Spurs' youth coaches didn't think so.

'He's a great kid and a talented player but what's his best position?' Les Ferdinand asked Tim Sherwood.

That was a difficult question. Harry was a natural finisher but he was also good on the ball. He could read the game well as a second striker, linking the midfield and attack.

Sherwood's silence proved Ferdinand's point. 'That's the big issue. He's a goalscorer but he's not strong enough to battle against big centre-backs.'

'Not yet, no.'

'Plus, he's not quick enough to get in behind the defence.'

This time, Sherwood disagreed. 'He's quicker than he looks and he's lethal in the box.'

After a long discussion, the Spurs coaches agreed on an action plan – Harry would go out on loan in January 2011 to a lower league club.

'We've spoken to Leyton Orient and they want to take you for the rest of the season,' Sherwood told him in a meeting.

At first, Harry was surprised and upset. He didn't want to leave Tottenham, even if it was only for a few months.

'Look, kid, a spell in League One will be good for you,' Sherwood explained. 'You need first-team experience and you're not going to get that here at the moment, I'm afraid. We also need to toughen you up a bit, put some muscle on that skinny frame. Don't worry – we're not going to forget about you!'

Harry spoke to his parents and he spoke to his teammates. They all agreed that it was a good idea.

'Everyone goes out on loan at some point,' Ryan told him. 'It's better than being stuck in the Reserves, trust me!'

'I was at Orient last season,' Andros told him. 'It's a good club and they'll look after you. At least, Spurs aren't asking you to go miles from home. Leyton is just up the road!'

They were right, of course. If a loan move to Leyton Orient would help him to improve and get into the Tottenham first team, Harry would go. It really helped that he wouldn't be going alone.

'Let's do this!' Tom cheered as they travelled to their first training session together.

CHAPTER 14

LEYTON ORIENT

Rochdale's pitch looked bad even before the match kicked off. Where had all the grass gone? As the Leyton Orient squad warmed up, they kept away from the boggy penalty areas and corners. They didn't want to make things worse. When Harry tried a short sprint, his boots sank into the squelch and it was difficult to lift them out. How was he supposed to make runs into the box?

Orient's striker Scott McGleish watched and laughed. 'Welcome to League One, kid!'

The Spotland Stadium was certainly no White Hart Lane. After seventy minutes of football and heavy rain, it looked more like a mud bath than a pitch. On the bench, Harry sat with his hood up, shaking his legs to keep warm. The score was 1–1, perfect for a super sub...

'Harry, you're coming on!' the assistant manager Kevin Nugent turned and shouted.

This was it – his Leyton Orient debut. Harry jumped to his feet and took off his tracksuit. As he waited on the touchline, he didn't even notice the rain falling. He was so focused on making a good first impression for his new club.

'It's fun out there today!' Scott joked, high-fiving Harry as he left the field.

Harry grinned and ran on. He was desperate to make a difference, either by scoring or creating the winning goal. He chased after every ball but before he knew it, the final whistle went.

'Well done, lad,' his manager Russell Slade said, slapping his wet, muddy back.

Harry had enjoyed his first short battle against the big League One centre-backs. They wanted to teach the Premier League youngster about 'real football', and he wanted to show them that this Premier League youngster could cope with 'real football'. Scott was right; it *was* fun!

'So, how did you find it?' Kevin asked back in the dressing room. Alex Inglethorpe had left him in charge of Harry and Tom during their loan spell at the club.

'It's different, that's for sure!' Harry replied after a nice hot shower. 'I need to get stronger but I'm ready for the challenge.'

Orient's assistant manager was impressed. The kid had a great attitude and that was very important in professional football. He could see the hunger in his eyes.

Harry was picked to start the next home game against Sheffield Wednesday. It was a big responsibility for a seventeen-year-old. He fought hard up front but it wasn't easy against really experienced defenders. At half-time, it was still 0–0.

'You're causing them lots of problems,' Kevin reassured him. 'Keep doing what you're doing and be patient.'

Harry felt more confident as he ran out for the second half. He had fifteen, or maybe twenty, minutes to grab a goal before the manager took him off. 'I can do this,' he told himself.

When Orient took the lead, the whole team breathed a sigh of relief. They started passing the ball around nicely and creating more chances. Harry only needed one. When it arrived, he steadied himself and placed his shot carefully.

Goooooooooooooooaaaaaaaaaaaaaaaaaaalllllllllllllllllllllll llll!!!!!!!!!!!!!!!!!!!!!!

He had scored on his full debut! Harry ran towards the Orient fans to celebrate. It felt like the start of big things.

'You're one of us now!' Scott cheered as they high-fived on the touchline.

*

'So, how is Harry getting on?' Alex asked Kevin when they met up a few months later.

The Orient assistant manager chuckled. 'That boy's a real fighter, isn't he? His legs are no bigger than matchsticks but he's fearless. He's good in front of goal, too.'

'What about that red card against Huddersfield?'

Kevin shook his head. 'The second yellow was very harsh,' he explained. 'I'm not sure he even touched the guy! You know that's not Harry's way. He's one of the good guys.'

Tottenham's youth coach nodded. He knew all about Harry's character. Some youngsters really struggled to adapt to new environments, but clearly not him. Alex never had any doubt that Harry would make the most of his first-team experience.

With Orient chasing a playoff spot, Harry was back on the bench for the last few matches of the season. It wasn't where he wanted to be but he was pretty pleased with his record of five goals in eighteen games. It was a decent start to his professional career.

'Welcome back, stranger!' Ryan joked when Harry returned to Tottenham in May.

Despite going out on loan, he had never really left his beloved club. After training with Orient, Harry often went back to do extra sessions with the Spurs Under-21s. They couldn't get rid of him that easily.

Over the summer of 2011, Redknapp sold Peter Crouch and Robbie Keane, and replaced them with

Emmanuel Adebayor. Harry was feeling positive about his sums.

'Two strikers left and only one came in,' he thought to himself. 'That means one spare spot for me!'

It looked that way at the start of the 2011–12 season. In August, Harry made his Tottenham debut at White Hart Lane, against Hearts in the UEFA Europa League. They were already 5–0 up from the first leg, so Redknapp threw him straight into the starting line-up, with Andros and Tom. Harry had never been so excited.

'I'm keeping Jermain out of the team!' he joked with his brother.

'What shirt number did they give you?' Charlie asked.

'37.'

'And what number is Jermain?'

'18.'

'Well, you're not the star striker yet then, bro!'

But Harry wasn't giving up until he *was* Tottenham's star striker. In the twenty-eighth minute, he chased after Tom's brilliant through-ball. It was a move that they had practised so many times in the Spurs youth teams. Harry got there first, just ahead of the Hearts keeper, who tripped him. Penalty!

Harry picked himself up and walked over to get the ball. This was *his* penalty, a great opportunity to score on his Spurs debut. He placed it down on the spot and took a few steps back. He tried to ignore the goalkeeper bouncing on his line. He pictured the goal in his head, just like Jermain had taught him.

After a deep breath, he ran towards the ball but suddenly, doubts crept into his head. Was it a bad idea to shoot bottom left like he usually did? He paused just before he kicked it and that gave the keeper time to make the save. Harry ran in for the rebound but it was no use; he had missed the penalty.

Harry was devastated but he didn't stand there with his head in his hands. The nightmares could wait until after the match. For now, he kept hunting for his next chance to become a Tottenham hero...

CHAPTER 15

MILLWALL

'Go out there and score!' Jermain shouted as Harry ran on to replace him.

Tottenham were already 3–0 up against Shamrock Rovers. There was still time for him to grab a fourth.

Danny Rose's cross flew over Harry's head but Andros was there at the back post. As he knocked it down, Harry reacted first and shot past the defender on the line.

Goooooooooooooooooaaaaaaaaaaaaaaaaalllllllllllllllllll llllll!!!!!!!!!!!!!!!!!!!!!!

Harry turned away to celebrate with Andros. What a feeling! He roared up at the sky. He was a Tottenham goalscorer now, and he could put that awful penalty miss behind him.

Unfortunately, however, that was the end of Tottenham's Europa League campaign. It was a real blow for their young players because the tournament was their big chance to shine. What would happen now? There wasn't space for them in Spurs' Premier League squad, so they would either have to go back to the Reserves or out on loan again.

'Right now, I just want to play week in week out,' Harry told his dad. 'I don't care where!'

Pat smiled. 'Be careful what you wish for. You wouldn't like the cold winters in Russia!'

In the end, Harry and Ryan were sent on loan to Millwall in January 2012. The Lions were fighting to stay in the Championship and they needed goals.

'We only scored one goal in the whole of December,' Harry's new manager Kenny Jackett moaned. 'We played five matches, that's over 450 minutes of football!'

Harry's job was clear and he couldn't wait to help his new team. In his Millwall debut against Bristol City, he had a few chances to score but he couldn't get past former England goalkeeper David James.

When City won the match with a last-minute goal, Harry couldn't believe it. He trudged off the pitch with tears in his eyes.

'Hard luck, kid,' Jackett said, putting an arm around his shoulder. 'You played well. The goals will come.'

His new strike partner, Andy Keogh, gave him similar advice. 'Just forget about the misses. If you keep thinking about them, you'll never score!'

The Millwall players and coaches liked Harry and they wanted him to do well. Despite his talent, he wasn't an arrogant wonderkid who thought he was way too good for them. He was a friendly guy, who worked hard for the team and always wanted to improve.

But six weeks later, Harry was still waiting for his first league goal for Millwall. It was the longest drought of his whole life. What was going wrong? Why couldn't he just put the ball in the net? Eventually, he did it away at Burnley.

He made the perfect run and James Henry played the perfect pass. Harry was through on goal. Surely, he couldn't miss this one! The goalkeeper rushed out to stop him but he stayed calm and used his side foot to guide the ball into the bottom corner.

*Goooooooooooooooooaaaaaaaaaaaaaaaaalllllllllllllllllllll
lllllllllll!!!!!!!!!!!!!!!!!!!!!!*

Harry pumped his fists and jumped into the air. It was finally over! James threw himself into Harry's arms.

'Thanks mate!' Millwall's new goalscorer shouted above the noise of the fans. 'There's no stopping me now!'

With his confidence back, Harry became a goal machine once more. The Championship defenders just couldn't handle his movement. He was deadly in the penalty area, hitting the target with every shot and header. But he was also brilliant when he played behind the striker. In a deeper role, he had the technique and vision to set up goals.

'Cheers!' Andy shouted after scoring from his perfect pass.

Harry also loved to hit a long-range rocket. Against Peterborough, he spun away from his marker and chased after the ball. It was bouncing high and he was on his weaker left foot, but Harry was feeling bold. Why not? Jermain and Robbie had taught him a very important lesson at Tottenham – if you shoot early, the keeper won't be ready. Harry struck his shot powerfully and accurately into the far corner.

Gooooooooooooooooooooooaaaaaaaaaaaaaaaaaallllllll llllllllllllllllll!!!!!!!!!!!!!!

Harry ran towards the fans and slid across the grass on his knees.

'You're on fire!' Andy cheered as they celebrated together.

With his nine goals, Harry won Millwall's Young Player of the Season award. It was a proud moment for him and a nice way to say goodbye to the club.

'We're going to miss you!' Jackett told him after his last training session. 'It's been a pleasure working with you. Good luck back at Spurs – you're going to be great.'

Harry was sad to leave Millwall but he was also excited about returning to Tottenham. He had learnt a lot from his loan experience. He was now a stronger player, both physically and mentally. It was much harder to push him off the ball, and much harder to stop him scoring.

'2012–13 is going to be my season!' Harry told his family confidently.

But first, he was off to play for England at the UEFA European Under-19 Championships in Estonia. Nathaniel, Benik and Ross were in the squad too, along with some exciting new players: Eric Dier was a tough defender and Nathan Redmond was a tricky winger.

'There's no reason why we can't win this!' their manager Noel Blake told them.

Although he wore the Number 10 shirt, Harry played in midfield behind Benik and Nathan. He enjoyed his playmaker role but it made it harder for him to do his favourite thing – scoring goals. After a draw against Croatia and a win over Serbia, England needed to beat France to reach the semi-finals.

As the corner came in, most of the England attackers charged towards the goal. But not Harry. He waited around the penalty spot because he had noticed that the French goalkeeper wasn't very good at catching crosses. When he fumbled the ball, it fell straight to Harry, who was totally unmarked. He calmly volleyed it into the net.

Goooooooooooooooooooooaaaaaaaaaaaaaaaalllllllllllllll lllllllllllll!!!!!!!!!!!!!!!!!!!!!!!!

2–1 to England! Harry pumped his fists and pointed up at the sky. He was delighted to score such an important goal for his country.

'You're a genius!' Eric cheered as the whole team celebrated.

Unfortunately, Harry wasn't there to be England's hero in the semi-final against Greece. He had to watch from the bench as his teammates lost in extra-time. It was such a horrible way to crash out of the tournament.

'At least we've got the Under-20 World Cup next summer!' Harry said, trying to make everyone feel a little bit better.

He focused once again on his top target – breaking into the Tottenham first team.

CHAPTER 16

TOUGH TIMES

On the opening day of the 2013–14 season, Harry
travelled up to Newcastle with the Tottenham squad.
New manager André Villas-Boas wanted to give his
young players a chance. Jake Livermore started the
match, and Harry and Andros waited impatiently on
the subs bench. Would this be the day when they
made their Premier League debuts?

'Is it bad to hope that someone gets injured?'
Andros joked.

With ten minutes to go, Newcastle scored a penalty
to make it 2–1. Harry's heart was racing; surely, this
was going to be his moment. Tottenham needed to
score again and he was the only striker on the bench.

'Harry, you're coming on!'

He quickly took off his yellow bib, and then his grey tracksuit. He pulled up his socks and re-laced his boots. He tucked his navy-blue Spurs shirt into his white shorts. '37 KANE' was ready for action.

'Good luck!' Andros said as Harry walked down to the touchline.

'Get a goal!' Villas-Boas said as Harry waited to come on.

'Let's do this!' Jermain cheered as Harry ran on to join him up front.

Harry had less than ten minutes to score and become an instant Spurs hero. Anything was possible but Newcastle were in control of the game. Harry's Premier League debut was over before he'd really touched the ball.

'Don't worry, that was just a first taste of the action,' Jermain promised him.

Harry hoped that his mentor was right. He shook hands with his opponents and the match officials. Then he walked over to clap the Tottenham fans in the away stand. He had done his best to save the day for his club.

He couldn't wait for his next chance to play but he wasn't even a substitute for their next match against West Brom. With Emmanuel Adebayor back in the team, he was back in the Reserves. Harry was disappointed but he didn't give up.

'I'm still only nineteen,' he told himself. 'I've got plenty of time to shine.'

A few days later, he joined Norwich City on loan for the rest of the season. The Canaries were in the Premier League, so this was a great opportunity to show Spurs that he was good enough to play at the top level.

'Bring it on!' he told his new manager Chris Hughton.

Against West Ham, Harry came on with twenty minutes to go. That gave him plenty of time to score. He dribbled forward, cut inside and curled the ball just wide of the post.

'So close!' Harry groaned, putting his hands on his head.

Minutes later, he beat the West Ham right-back and

pulled the ball back to Robert Snodgrass… but his shot was blocked on the line! Somehow, the match finished 0–0 but Harry was happy with his debut.

Afterwards, Hughton told the media, 'I think Kane will be a super player'.

Harry was delighted with the praise. His first start for Norwich soon arrived against Doncaster in the League Cup. He couldn't wait.

'I'm definitely going to score!' he told his teammates.

Sadly, Harry didn't score and he only lasted fifty minutes. He tried to carry on but he couldn't; his foot was way too painful. He winced and limped off the pitch.

'What happened?' his brother asked as he rested on the sofa back at home.

'I've fractured a metatarsal,' Harry explained.

'Isn't that what Becks did before the 2002 World Cup?' Charlie joked, trying to cheer his brother up. 'You've got to stop copying him!'

Harry smiled, but he was dreading the surgery and then the months without football. It would drive him crazy.

'You're a strong character,' Alex Inglethorpe told him when he returned to Tottenham, 'and you're going to come back even stronger!'

Harry's new girlfriend helped to take his mind off his injury. He and Katie had gone to the same primary and secondary schools but it was only later that they started dating. They got on really well and made each other laugh, even during the tough times.

Harry spent October and November in the gym, slowly getting his foot ready to play football again. It was long, boring work but he had to do it if he wanted to be playing again before the new year.

That was his big aim. In December, Harry started training with the first team again, and starring for the Reserves.

'I'm feeling good!' Harry told his manager Chris Hughton with a big smile on his face. It was great to be playing football again. He had missed it so much.

On 29 December 2012, he was a sub for the Manchester City match. By half-time, Norwich were losing 2–1.

'They're down to ten men, so let's get forward and

attack,' Hughton told his players in the dressing room. 'We can win this! Harry, you're coming on to replace Steve.'

Harry's eyes lit up. He had been hoping for ten, maybe fifteen, minutes at the end but instead he was going to play the whole second half.

This was his biggest challenge yet. Harry was up against City's captain Vincent Kompany, one of the best centre-backs in the world. These were the big battles that he dreamed about. Harry held the ball up well and made clever runs into space. He didn't score but he was back in business.

'Boss, that was just the start!' he promised Hughton.

Before long, however, Harry was told that he had to return to Tottenham. Villas-Boas wanted a third striker as back-up for Jermain and Emmanuel. Harry was happy to help his club but he wanted to play regular football. What was the point of him being there if he wasn't even getting on the bench? A few weeks later, Villas-Boas sent him back out on loan to Leicester City.

'This is all so confusing!' Harry moaned to Katie. It

had turned into a very topsy-turvy season. 'Do Spurs want me or not?'

It was a question that no-one could answer. Harry tried his best to adapt to another new club but soon after scoring on his home debut against Blackburn, he was dropped from the Leicester starting line-up. It was a massive disappointment. It felt like his career was going backwards.

'If I'm only a sub in the Championship, how am I ever going to make it at Spurs?' he complained to his dad on the phone. Leicester felt like a very long way away from Chingford.

Pat had seen his son looking this sad before. 'Remember when you were fourteen and Tottenham told you that you weren't good enough?' he reminded him. 'You didn't give up back then and you're not going to give up now!'

Harry nodded. He *was* good enough! All he needed was a run of games and a chance to get back into goalscoring form. He just had to believe that the breakthrough would come.

CHAPTER 17

BREAKTHROUGH

'I'm not going anywhere this season,' Harry told Tottenham firmly. After four loan spells, he was determined to stay at the club. 'I'm going to prove that I should be playing here week in, week out!'

Harry wasn't a raw, skinny teenager anymore. He was now twenty years old and he looked like a fit, powerful striker at last. That was thanks to his Football League experience and lots of hard work in the gym to build up his strength. He now had even more power in his shot.

'Looking good, H!' Jermain said in pre-season training. His encouragement was working. Harry was getting better and better.

The 2013 U-20 World Cup in Turkey had been a

very disappointing tournament for England, but not
for Harry. He set up their first goal against Iraq with
a brilliant header, and a few days later scored a great
equaliser against Chile from outside the penalty area.
He hit the ball perfectly into the bottom corner, just
like he did again and again on the training ground.

'What a strike!' England teammate Ross Barkley
said to Harry as they high-fived.

When he returned to England in July, Harry felt
ready to become a Premier League star but again,
Spurs had signed a new striker. Roberto Soldado cost
£26 million after scoring lots of goals for Valencia in
La Liga. Watching his rival in action, Harry didn't
give up. He believed in himself more than ever.

For now, cup matches were Harry's chance to
shine. In the fourth round of the League Cup, Spurs
were heading for a disastrous defeat as opponents
Hull took the lead in extra-time. Could Harry save
the day?

When Jermain passed the ball to him, he had his
back to goal, and needed to turn as quickly as possible.
Harry used his strength and speed to spin cleverly past

his marker. With a second touch, he dribbled towards the penalty area. He was in shooting range now. There were defenders right in front of him, blocking the goal, but he knew exactly where the bottom corner was. Harry could picture it in his head.

Goooooooooooooooooooooooaaaaaaaaaaaaaaaaalllllllllllll llllllllllllll!!!!!!!!!!!!!!!!

Yes! Harry pumped his fists and ran towards the fans. The job wasn't done yet but his strike had put Spurs back in the game. When the tie went to penalties, he was one of the first to volunteer.

'I've got this,' he told Spurs manager André Villas-Boas. It was time to make up for that miss in the Europa League.

Harry was Spurs' fifth penalty taker. The pressure was on – he had to score, otherwise they were out of the competition. This time, he felt confident. He had a plan and he was going to stick to it, no matter what. As the goalkeeper dived to the right, Harry slammed his shot straight down the middle. The net bulged – what a relief!

'Well done, you showed a lot of guts there,' Tim

Sherwood told him afterwards, giving him a hug. 'Your time is coming!'

In December 2013, Sherwood took over as Tottenham manager for the rest of the season, after the sacking of Villas-Boas. Harry didn't want to get his hopes up but he knew that his former Under-21 coach believed in his talent. Hopefully, Sherwood would give him more opportunities now. By February, he was coming off the bench more regularly but only because Jermain had signed for Toronto FC in Canada.

'I can't believe you're leaving!' Harry told him as they said goodbye. It was one of his saddest days at White Hart Lane. 'It won't be the same around here without you.'

Jermain smiled. 'It's time for me to move on and it's time for you to step up. I want you to wear this next season.'

It was Jermain's Number 18 shirt. Harry couldn't believe it.

'Wow, are you sure?' he asked. It would be such an honour to follow in his hero's footsteps. 'I promise to do you proud!'

Harry did just that when he finally got his
first Premier League start for Tottenham against
Sunderland in April. After years of waiting, Harry's
time had come. He had never been so nervous in
his life.

'Relax, just do what you do best,' Sherwood told
him before kick-off. He was showing lots of faith in his
young striker. 'Score!'

In the second half, Christian Eriksen curled a
beautiful cross into the six-yard box. As the ball
bounced, Harry made a late run and snuck in ahead
of the centre-back to steer the ball into the bottom
corner.

*Goooooooooooooooooooooaaaaaaaaaaaaaalllllllllllllllllll
lllllllllll!!!!!!!!!!!!!!!!!!!!!!*

Harry was buzzing. With his arms out wide like
an aeroplane, he ran towards the Spurs fans near
the corner flag. He had scored his first Premier League
goal for Tottenham. It was time to celebrate in style.

Aaron Lennon chased after him and jumped up on
his back. 'Yes, mate, what a goal!' he cheered.

Harry was soon in the middle of a big player

hug. He was part of the team now and that was the greatest feeling ever.

There were six more league matches in the season and Harry started all of them. He was full of confidence and full of goals. Against West Bromwich, Aaron dribbled down the right wing and crossed into the six-yard box. Harry jumped highest and headed the ball past the defender on the line.

Goooooooooooooooooooaaaaaaaaaaaaaaaaallllllllllllll llllllllllllllll!!!!!!!!!!!!!!!!!!!!

A week later, they did it again. Aaron crossed the ball and Harry flicked it in. 2–1 to Tottenham!

'You've scored in three games in a row,' Emmanuel Adebayor shouted over the White Hart Lane noise. 'You're a goal machine!'

Harry had also already become a favourite with the fans. They loved nothing more than cheering for their local hero.

> *He's one of our own,*
> *He's one of our own,*
> *Harry Kane – he's one of our own!*

Even an own goal against West Ham didn't stop
Harry's rise. In only six weeks, he had gone from sub
to England's hottest new striker.

'What an end to the season!' Tim Sherwood said as
they walked off the pitch together. 'You'll be playing
for a different manager next season, but don't worry.
If you keep banging in the goals, you're going to be a
Tottenham hero, no matter what!'

CHAPTER 18

EXCITING TIMES AT TOTTENHAM

'Do you think he'll bring in a big new striker?' Harry asked Andros during preseason.

His friend and teammate just shrugged. They would have to wait and see what the new Tottenham manager, Mauricio Pochettino, would do.

As the 2014–15 season kicked off, Spurs had signed a new goalkeeper, some new defenders and a new midfielder. But no new striker! That left only Emmanuel, Roberto and Harry. Harry was feeling really good about his chances. He worked extra hard to impress Pochettino.

'Great work, you've certainly got the desire that I'm looking for in my players,' his manager told him. 'This could be a huge season for you!'

Emmanuel started up front against West Ham in the Premier League but it was Harry, not Roberto, who came on for the last ten minutes. That was a good sign. If he kept scoring goals in other competitions, surely Pochettino would have no choice but to let him play. Harry got five goals in the Europa League and three in the League Cup.

'Kane needs to start in the Premier League!' the fans shouted in the stands.

Harry was making a name for himself with the England Under-21s too. He loved representing his country, especially in the big games. Against France, he positioned himself between the two centre-backs and waited like a predator. When Tom Ince played the through-ball, Harry was already on the move, chasing after it. He was too smart for the French defenders and he chipped his shot over the diving goalkeeper.

Goooooooooooooooooooaaaaaaaaaaaaaaaaaaaallllllllllll llllllllllllll!!!!!!!!!!!!!!!

Two minutes later, Tom crossed from the right and Harry was there in the six-yard box to tap the ball into the net.

'That's a proper striker's goal!' his teammate told him as they celebrated together.

Tom was right. Harry was a real goalscorer now, always in the right place at the right time. 'That's thirteen goals in twelve games!' he replied proudly.

By November 2014, there was lots of pressure on Pochettino to give Harry more game-time in the Premier League. Away at Aston Villa, he came on for Emmanuel with half an hour to go.

'Come on, we can still win this match!' his old friend Ryan Mason told him. Soon, Andros was on the pitch too. They were all living their Spurs dreams together.

In injury time, Tottenham won a free kick just outside the penalty area. It was Harry's last chance to save the day for Spurs. Érik Lamela wanted to take it but Harry wasn't letting his big opportunity go. He took a long, deep breath to calm his beating heart. He looked down at the ball and then up at the goal. 'This is going in!' he told himself.

He pumped his legs hard as he ran towards the

ball. He needed as much power as possible. But rather than kicking it with the top of his boot, he kicked it with the side. As the ball swerved through the air, it deflected off the head of a Villa defender and past their scrambling keeper.

Goooooooooooooooooaaaaaaaaaaaaaaaaaalllllllllllllllllll lllllllll!!!!!!!!!!!!!!!!!!!!!!

It was the biggest goal that Harry had ever scored. He ran screaming towards the corner flag with all of his teammates behind him. In all the excitement, Harry threw himself down onto the grass for his favourite childhood celebration – the Klinsmann dive. Soon, he was at the bottom of a pile of happy players.

'What a beauty!' Danny Rose cheered in his face.

After scoring the match-winner, Harry was the talk of Tottenham. The fans had a new local hero and they wanted him to play every minute of every game. Against Hull City, Christian Eriksen's free kick hit the post but who was there to score the rebound? Harry!

Even when he didn't score for a few matches, Pochettino stuck with Harry. As a young player, he was still learning about playing at the top level.

'I believe in you,' his manager told him. 'You've got lots of potential and you've got the hunger to improve.'

With Pochettino's support, Harry bounced back against Swansea City. As Christian whipped in the corner kick, Harry made a late run into the box. He leapt high above his marker and powered his header down into the bottom corner.

Goooooooooooooooooooooaaaaaaaaaaaaaalllllllllllllllllll llllllll!!!!!!!!!!!!!!!!!

Once he started scoring, Harry couldn't stop. He was such a natural finisher. On Boxing Day, Harry even scored against one of his old teams. Only eighteen months earlier, he had been sitting on the Leicester City bench. Now, he was causing them all kinds of problems as Tottenham's star striker. With hard work and great support, he was proving everyone wrong yet again.

Pochettino was delighted with his young striker's form but he didn't want him to burn out. 'Get some rest because we've got big games coming up.'

Harry was so excited about the 2015 fixture list ahead – Chelsea on New Year's Day and then a few weeks later, the biggest game of them all: The North London Derby – Tottenham vs Arsenal.

'Don't worry, boss,' he said with a big smile. 'I'll be ready to score some more!'

CHAPTER 19

GOALS, GOALS AND MORE GOALS

As the Tottenham team walked out of the tunnel at White Hart Lane, Harry was second in line, right behind their goalkeeper and captain, Hugo Lloris. He had come so far in the last eighteen months – it was still hard to believe. There were thousands of fans in the stadium, cheering loudly for their team, and cheering loudly for him.

> *He's one of our own,*
> *He's one of our own,*
> *Harry Kane – he's one of our own!*

Harry looked down at the young mascot who was

holding his hand. Ten years before, that had been one of his biggest dreams – to walk out on to the pitch with his Spurs heroes. Now, he was the Spurs hero, so what was his new dream? Goals, goals and more goals, starting against their London rivals Chelsea.

'Come on, we can't let them beat us again!' Harry shouted to Ryan and Andros. They were all fired up and ready to win.

Chelsea took the lead, but Harry didn't let his head drop. It just made him even more determined to score. He got the ball on the left wing and dribbled infield. He beat one player and then shrugged off another. He only had one thing on his mind – goals. When he was just outside the penalty area, he looked up.

He was still a long way out and there were lots of Chelsea players in his way, but Harry could shoot from anywhere. The Premier League would soon know just how lethal he was. For now, however, the defenders gave him just enough space. His low, powerful strike skidded across the wet grass, past the keeper and right into the bottom corner.

Goooooooooooooooaaaaaaaaaaaaaaaaaallllllllllllllllllllll llllll!!!!!!!!!!!!!!!!!!!!!!!

Game on! Harry ran towards the Tottenham fans and jumped into the air. He was used to scoring goals now, but this was one of his best and most important.

'You could outshoot a cowboy!' Kyle Walker joked as he climbed up on Harry's back.

At half-time, Spurs were winning 3–1 but Harry wanted more. 'We're not safe yet,' he warned his teammates. 'We've got to keep going!'

As the pass came towards him, Harry was just inside the Chelsea box with his back to goal. It didn't look dangerous at first but one lovely touch and spin later, it was very dangerous indeed. Harry stayed calm and placed his shot past the goalkeeper. It was like he'd been scoring top goals for years.

'Kane, that's gorgeous!' the TV commentator shouted. 'How good is *he*?'

The answer was: unstoppable. Even one of the best defences in the world couldn't handle him. The match finished 5–3. It was a famous victory for Tottenham and Harry was their hero. After shaking hands with the Chelsea players, he walked around the pitch, clapping the supporters. Harry loved making them happy.

'If we play like that against Arsenal, we'll win that too!' he told Andros.

Harry got ready for the big North London Derby by scoring goals, goals and more goals. The timing was perfect; he was in the best form of his life just as Arsenal were coming to White Hart Lane. Revenge would be so sweet for Harry. Arsenal would soon realise their big mistake in letting him go.

After five minutes, Harry cut in from the left and curled a brilliant shot towards goal. He got ready to celebrate because the ball was heading for the bottom corner yet again. But the Arsenal keeper made a great save to tip it just round the post. So close! Harry put his hands to his head for a second but then kept going. If at first you don't score, shoot, shoot again.

At half-time, Tottenham were losing 1–0. 'We're still in this game,' Pochettino told his players in the dressing room. 'If we keep creating chances, we'll score!'

When Érik took the corner, Harry stood lurking near the back post. He was waiting for the rebound. The keeper saved Mousa Dembélé's header but the ball bounced down in the box. Before the Arsenal defenders could react, Harry pounced to sweep it into the net.

Gooooooooooooooooooaaaaaaaaaaaaaaaallllllllllllllll llllllll!!!!!!!!!!!!!!!!!!!

Harry roared and pumped his fists. Scoring for Spurs against Arsenal meant the world to him. He had dreamed about it ever since his first trip to White Hart Lane.

'Right, let's go and win this now!' Harry told his teammates.

With five minutes to go, it looked like it was going to be a draw. As Nabil Benteleb's cross drifted into the box, Harry's eyes never left the ball. He took a couple of steps backwards and then leapt high above Laurent Koscielny. It was a very difficult chance. To score, his header would have to be really powerful and really accurate.

As soon as the ball left his head, Harry knew that he had got the angle right. It was looping towards the corner but would the keeper have time to stop it? No, Harry's perfect technique gave David Ospina no chance.

Goooooooooooooooooaaaaaaaaaaaaaaaallllllllllllllllllll llll!!!!!!!!!!!!!!!!!!!!!

As the ball landed in the net, Harry turned away to celebrate. What a moment! With the adrenaline flooding through his veins, he slid across the grass, screaming. As he looked up, he could see the Spurs fans going crazy in the crowd. All that joy was because of him!

The final minutes felt like hours but eventually, the referee blew the final whistle. Tottenham 2, Arsenal 1! The party went on and on, both down on the pitch and up in the stands.

'I might as well retire now!' Harry joked with Ryan. 'Nothing will ever beat scoring the winner in the North London Derby.'

'Not even playing for England?' his teammate asked him. 'Mate, Roy Hodgson would be a fool not to call you up to the squad!'

Harry was desperate to play for his country. Like his hero Becks, he wanted to be the national captain one day. After doing well for the Under-21s, he was now ready to step up into the senior team. He had won both the January and February Premier League Player of the Month awards. Then, in March, Harry got the call he had been waiting for.

'I'm in!' he told his partner Katie excitedly. He wanted to tell the whole world.

'In what?' she asked. 'What are you talking about?'

'The England squad!'

The amazing news spread throughout his family. Everyone wanted a ticket to watch his international debut.

'I might not even play!' Harry warned them, but they didn't care.

He was glad to see that lots of his Tottenham teammates were in the England team too. Training with superstars like Wayne Rooney and Gary Cahill would be a lot less scary with Kyle, Andros and Danny by his side. A week later, Ryan also joined the Spurs gang.

'Thank goodness Fabian Delph got injured!' he laughed. 'I was gutted to be the only one left behind.'

They were all named as substitutes for the Euro 2016 qualifier against Lithuania at Wembley. But would any of them get to come on and play? They all sat there on the England bench, crossing their fingers and shaking with nerves.

With seventy minutes gone, England were winning 3–0. It was time for Roy Hodgson to give his young players a chance. Harry's England youth teammate Ross Barkley was the first substitute and Harry himself was the second. He was replacing Wayne Rooney.

'Good luck!' Ryan and Andros said, patting him on the back.

Harry tried to forget that he was making his England debut at Wembley. That was something he could enjoy later when the match was over. For now, he just wanted to score.

As Raheem Sterling dribbled down the left wing, Harry took up his favourite striking position near the back post. Raheem's cross came straight towards him;

he couldn't miss. Harry had all the time in the world to place his header past the keeper.

*Gooooooooooooooooooaaaaaaaaaaaaaaaallllllllllllllllllll
llllllllll!!!!!!!!!!!!!!!*

In his excitement, Harry bumped straight into the assistant referee. 'Sorry!' he called over his shoulder as he ran towards the corner flag.

'Was that your first touch?' Danny Welbeck asked as they celebrated.

'No, it was my third or fourth,' Harry replied with a cheeky grin. 'But I've only been on the field for about a minute!'

There had been so many highlights for Harry during the 2014–15 season already, but this was the best of all. He had scored for England on his debut. All of his dedication had paid off and he felt so proud of his achievements. Harry's childhood dream had come true.

CHAPTER 20

HARRY AND DELE

'So, do you think you can score as many this season?'
Charlie asked his brother.

Lots of people thought Harry's twenty-one Premier
League goals were a one-off, a fluke. They argued that
the PFA Young Player of the Year wouldn't be as good
in 2015–16 because defenders would know all about
him now. They would mark him out of
the game.

But Harry knew that wasn't true. 'Of course I can.
In fact, I'm aiming for even more this time!'

Charlie smiled. 'Good, because when you scored
those goals against Arsenal, the guys in the pub

bought me drinks all night. Sometimes, it's fun being your brother!'

Harry was still getting used to his fame. It was crazy! Every time he took his Labradors Brady and Wilson out for a walk, there were cameras waiting for him. They even took photos of Katie when she went out shopping.

'Our normal life is over!' she complained as she flicked through the newspapers.

After a very disappointing Euro 2015 with the England Under-21s, Harry was really looking forward to the new season. It would be his first as Tottenham's top striker. With Emmanuel gone, Harry now wore the famous Number 10 shirt. He was following in the footsteps of Spurs legends Jimmy Greaves, Gary Lineker and Harry's own hero, Teddy Sheringham.

Pochettino had strengthened the Spurs squad over the summer. They had signed Son Heung-min, a goal-scoring winger, and Dele Alli, a young attacking midfielder.

Harry and Dele clicked straight away. After a few

training sessions, Dele knew where Harry would run, and Harry knew where to make space for Dele. It was like they had been playing together for years. Soon, they were making up cool goal celebrations.

'It's like you guys are back in the school playground!' captain Hugo Lloris teased, but it was great to see them getting along so well.

Despite all of his excitement, Harry didn't score a single goal in August 2015. The newspapers kept calling him a 'one-season wonder' but that only made him more determined to prove them wrong.

'You're playing well and working hard for the team,' Pochettino reassured him. 'As soon as you get one goal, you'll get your confidence back.'

Against Manchester City, Christian's brilliant free kick bounced back off the post and landed right at Harry's feet. He was in lots of space and the goalkeeper was lying on the ground. Surely he couldn't miss an open goal? Some strikers might have passed the ball carefully into the net to make sure but instead, Harry curled it into the top corner.

Goooooooooooooooaaaaaaaaaaaaaaaaalllllllllllllllllllllll llllllll!!!!!!!!!!!!!!!!!!!!

Harry was delighted to score but most of all, he was relieved. His goal drought was over. Now, his season could really get started.

'Phew, I thought you were going to blaze that one over the bar!' Dele joked.

After that, Harry and Dele became the Premier League's deadliest double act. Between them, they had power, skill, pace and incredible shooting. By the end of February 2016, Tottenham were only two points behind Leicester City at the top of the table.

'If we keep playing like this, we'll be champions!' Pochettino told his players.

Every single one of them believed it. Spurs had the best defence in the league and were also one of the best attacking sides. Dele, Érik and Christian created lots of chances, and Harry scored lots of goals. It was one big, happy team effort. The pranks and teasing never stopped.

'How long do you have to wear that thing for?'

Dele asked during training one day. 'Halloween was months ago, you know!'

'Very funny,' Harry replied, giving his teammate a friendly punch. He was wearing a plastic face mask to protect his broken nose. 'Who knows, maybe it will bring me luck and I'll wear it forever!'

'Let's hope not!' Christian laughed.

Next up was the game that Harry had been waiting months for – the North London Derby. Could they win it again? Arsenal were only three points behind Spurs, so the match was even more important than usual.

'Come on lads, we've got to win this!' Harry shouted in the dressing room before kick-off, and all of his teammates cheered.

The atmosphere at White Hart Lane was incredible. The fans never stopped singing, even when Tottenham went 1–0 down. They believed that their team would bounce back, especially with Harry up front.

Early in the second half, Harry thought he had scored the equaliser. The goalkeeper saved his vicious shot, but surely he was behind the goal-line?

'That's in!' Harry screamed to the referee. But the technology showed that a tiny part of the ball hadn't crossed the line.

It was very frustrating but there was no point in complaining. Harry would just have to keep shooting until he got the whole ball into the net.

In the end, it was Toby Alderweireld who made it 1–1. Tottenham were playing well, but they needed a second goal to take the lead.

The ball was heading out for an Arsenal goal-kick but Dele managed to reach it and flick it back to his best friend, Harry. It looked like an impossible angle but with the supporters cheering him on, anything seemed possible. In a flash, Harry curled the ball up over the keeper and into the far corner.

Goooooooooooooooooooooaaaaaaaaaaaaaaaaaaaaaalllllll llllllllllllllll!!!!!!!!!!!!!!!

It was one of the best goals Harry had ever scored. He felt on top of the world. He took off his mask as he ran and slid across the grass. Dele was right behind him and gave him a big hug.

'Maybe you *should* keep wearing that!' he joked.

Tottenham couldn't quite hold on for another big victory. A draw wasn't the result that Spurs wanted, but Harry would never forget his incredible goal.

'We're still in this title race,' Pochettino urged his disappointed players. 'We just have to win every match until the end of the season.'

Harry and Dele did their best to make their Premier League dream come true. Dele set up both of Harry's goals against Aston Villa and they scored two each against Stoke City. But with three games of the season to go, Tottenham were seven points behind Leicester.

'If we don't beat Chelsea, our season's over,' Harry warned his teammates.

At half-time, it was all going according to plan. Harry scored the first goal and Son made it 2–0. They were cruising to victory but in the second half, they fell apart. All season, the Spurs players had stayed cool and focused but suddenly, they got angry and made silly mistakes. It finished 2–2.

'We threw it away!' Harry groaned as he walked off the pitch. He was absolutely devastated. They had worked so hard all season. And for what?

'We've learnt a lot this year,' Pochettino told his players once everyone had calmed down. 'I know you feel awful right now but you should be so proud of yourselves. Next season, we'll come back stronger and win the league!'

There was one bit of good news that made Harry feel a little better. With twenty-five goals, he had won the Premier League Golden Boot, beating Sergio Agüero and Jamie Vardy.

'And they said I was a one-season wonder!' Harry told his brother Charlie as they played golf together. A smile spread slowly across his face. He loved proving people wrong.

CHAPTER 21

ENGLAND

When Harry first joined the England squad back in 2015, he was really nervous. It was a massive honour to represent his country but there was a lot of pressure too. If he didn't play well, there were lots of other great players that could take his place. Plus, it was scary being the new kid.

'You'll get used to this,' Wayne Rooney reassured him. 'I remember when I first got the call-up. I was only seventeen and it was terrifying! Just try to ignore the talk and enjoy yourself.'

Wayne helped Harry to feel more relaxed around the other senior players. They had fun playing golf and table tennis together. They were nice guys and Harry soon felt like one of the lads.

'France, here we come!' he cheered happily.

England qualified for Euro 2016 with ten wins out of ten. Harry added to his debut goal with a cheeky chip against San Marino and a low strike against Switzerland.

'At this rate, you're going to take my place in the team!' Wayne told him.

Harry shook his head. 'No, we'll play together up front!'

When Roy Hodgson announced his England squad for Euro 2016, Harry's name was there. He was delighted. There were four other strikers – Wayne, Jamie Vardy, Daniel Sturridge and Marcus Rashford – but none of them were scoring as many goals as him.

'You'll definitely play,' his brother Charlie told him.

Harry couldn't wait for his first major international tournament. His body felt pretty tired after a long Premier League season with Tottenham, but nothing was going to stop him.

'I really think we've got a good chance of winning it,' he told Dele, who was in the squad for France too.

His friend was feeling just as confident. 'If we play

, we can definitely go all the way!'

ere both in the starting line-up

up match against Russia. With

playing in midfield, Harry was England's number-one striker. He carried the country's great expectations in his shooting boots.

'I *have* to score!' he told himself as the match kicked off in Marseille.

England dominated the game but after seventy minutes, it was still 0–0. Harry got more and more frustrated. He was struggling to find the burst of pace that got him past Premier League defences. What was going wrong? His legs felt heavy and clumsy.

'Just be patient,' Wayne told him. 'If you keep getting into the right areas, the goal will come.'

When they won a free kick on the edge of the Russia box, Harry stood over the ball with Wayne and his Tottenham teammate Eric Dier. Everyone expected Harry to take it but as he ran up, he dummied the ball. Eric stepped up instead and curled the ball into the top corner. 1–0!

'Thanks for letting me take it,' he said to Harry as

they celebrated the goal.

'No problem!' he replied. England had the lead and that was all that mattered.

But just as they were heading for a winning start to the tournament, Russia scored a late header. As he watched the ball flying towards the top corner, Harry's heart sank. He was very disappointed with the result and with his own performance in particular. It wasn't good enough. If he didn't improve, he would lose his place to Jamie or Daniel or Marcus.

'I believe in you, we all believe in you,' Hodgson told him after the game. 'So, believe in *yourself*!'

Harry tried not to read the player ratings in the English newspapers. Instead, he focused on bouncing back. If he could score a goal against Wales in the next game that would make everything better again.

But at half-time, it was looking like another bad day for Harry and England. He worked hard for the team but his goal-scoring touch was gone. The ball just wouldn't go in. When Gareth Bale scored a free kick to put Wales 1–0 up, Harry feared the worst.

'We need a quick goal in the second half,' Hodgson

told the team in the dressing room. 'Jamie and Daniel, you'll be coming on to replace Harry and Raheem.'

Harry stared down at the floor. Was that the end of his tournament? He was really upset but he had to accept the manager's decision.

Harry watched the second half from the bench and cheered on his teammates. He was a good team player. When Jamie scored the equaliser, he joined in the celebrations. When Daniel scored the winner in injury time, he sprinted to the corner flag to jump on him.

'Get in!' he screamed.

It was only after the final whistle that Harry started worrying again. Had he lost his place in the team, or would he get another chance against Slovakia?

'I'm sorry but I've got to start Daniel and Jamie in the next match,' Hodgson told him. 'Rest up and get ready for the next round. We need you back, firing!'

Without Harry, England couldn't find a goal, but 0–0 was enough to take them through to the Round of 16. He would get one more opportunity to score against Iceland, and he was pumped up for the biggest game of his international career.

It started brilliantly. Raheem was fouled in the box and Wayne scored the penalty. 1–0! It was a huge relief to get an early goal but two minutes later, it was 1–1.

'Come on, focus!' Joe Hart shouted at his teammates.

Harry and Dele both hit powerful long-range strikes that fizzed just over the crossbar. England looked in control of the game, but then Iceland scored again.

'No!' Harry shouted. His dream tournament was turning into an absolute nightmare.

England needed a hero, and quickly. Daniel crossed the ball to Harry in his favourite position near the back post. It was too low for a header so he went for the volley. Harry watched the ball carefully onto his foot and struck it beautifully. Unfortunately, it just wasn't his day, or his tournament. The goalkeeper jumped up high to make a good save. So close! Harry put his hands to his face – he was so desperate to score.

As the minutes ticked by, England started panicking. Harry's free kick flew miles wide. What a disaster! The boos from the fans grew louder.

'Stay calm, we've got plenty of time!' Hodgson called out from the touchline.

That time, however, ran out. At the final whistle, the Iceland players celebrated and the England players sank to their knees. They were out of the Euros after a terrible, embarrassing defeat.

As he trudged off the pitch, Harry was in shock. It was the worst feeling ever. He felt like he had really let his country down. Would they ever forgive him?

To take his mind off the disappointment, Harry watched American Football and focused on his future goals. With Tottenham, he would be playing in the Champions League for the first time, and trying to win the Premier League title. With England, he would be playing in the qualifiers for World Cup 2018. There were lots of exciting challenges ahead.

'I need to make things right!' Harry told himself.

CHAPTER 22

TOTTENHAM FOR THE TITLE?

'Argggghhhhhhhhhhhhhhhhhhh!' Harry screamed as he lay down on the turf. He tried to stay calm but it felt like really bad news. As he waved for the physio, the pain got worse and worse. White Hart Lane went quiet. The Spurs fans waited nervously to see whether their star striker could carry on.

'You're not singing anymore!' the opposing Sunderland fans cheered bitterly.

If only Harry hadn't slid in for the tackle. Tottenham were already winning 1–0 thanks to his goal. That was his job: scoring goals, not making tackles. But Harry always worked hard for the team. As he went to block the Sunderland centre-back, his right ankle twisted awkwardly in the grass. If the injury wasn't too serious, Harry promised himself that he would never defend again.

Unfortunately, it *was* serious. Harry tried to get up and play on but that wasn't possible. He hobbled over to the touchline and sat down again. The Spurs fans cheered and clapped their hero but Harry's match was over. He was carried down the tunnel on a stretcher.

'There's good news and there's bad news,' the doctor told him after the X-rays. 'The good news is that there's no fracture. The bad news is that there's ligament damage.'

Harry wasn't a medical expert but he knew that 'ligament damage' meant no football for a while. 'How long will I be out of action?' he asked, fearing a big number.

'It's too early to say but you should prepare yourself for eight weeks out. Hopefully, it won't be that long.'

Eight weeks! If everything went well, Harry would be back before December but it was still a big blow. His 2016–17 season had only just started. He had only played in one Champions League match. Tottenham needed him.

'Who's going to get all our goals now?' he asked.

'Without you hogging all the chances, I'll score loads more!' Dele replied.

It was good to have Katie and his teammates around to cheer Harry up. It was going to be a boring, difficult couple of months for him. He would just have to recover as quickly as possible. To keep himself going, Harry picked out a key date in the calendar: 6 November. The North London Derby – that was what he was aiming for.

'I always score against Arsenal!' Harry reminded everyone.

Thanks to lots of hard work in the gym, he made it just in time. Harry was delighted to be back on the pitch, even if he wasn't at his best. Early in the second half, Tottenham won a penalty and Harry quickly grabbed the ball. It was the perfect chance to get a comeback goal.

He took a long, deep breath and waited for the referee's whistle. As the Arsenal keeper dived to his left, Harry placed it down the middle.

*Goooooooooooooooooaaaaaaaaaaaaaaaallllllllllllllllll
llllll!!!!!!!!!!!!!!!!!!!!!*

He was back! Harry pumped his fists at the crowd
as his teammates jumped on him.

'What a cool finish!' Son cheered.

Harry didn't last the full match, but he was pleased
with his return. 'If I want to win the Golden Boot
again, I've got some catching up to do!' he told
Pochettino.

Tottenham got knocked out in the Champions
League Group Stage, but Harry still had time to grab
his first goals in the competition.

'Never mind, we've just got to focus on the Premier
League title now,' he told Dele. 'We'll conquer Europe
next year!'

After all his goals, Harry became a transfer target
for Real Madrid and Manchester United. Tottenham
wanted to keep their local hero for as long as possible,
so they offered Harry a big new contract until 2020.
Saying no didn't even cross his mind.

'I can't leave!' Harry said happily. 'This is my home
and we've got trophies to win.'

To celebrate, he went on another scoring spree. Two against Watford, three against West Brom, three against Stoke, two against Everton. By March, he was up to nineteen goals and at the top of the goal-scoring charts again.

'Congratulations, you're back where you belong,' Katie told him.

Harry was pleased but the Premier League title was his number one aim. Spurs were in second place behind Chelsea. Harry would give his all to catch them.

For Harry, winning the 2017 FA Cup was aim number two. In the quarter-finals, Tottenham faced his old club Millwall. So much had changed in the five years since his loan spell there. He would always be grateful to the Lions for their support but that didn't mean he would take it easy on them. Trophies always came first.

As soon as the ball came to him, Harry shot at goal. The Millwall keeper saved it but Harry didn't even notice. He was lying on the grass in agony.

'Is it your right ankle again?' the physio asked after rushing over to him.

Harry just nodded. Was it the same injury all over again? He couldn't bear to think about another eight weeks on the sidelines. He managed to limp off the pitch and down the tunnel. He didn't need to use the stretcher this time and that was a good sign.

'There is ligament damage,' the doctors confirmed, 'but it's not as serious as before. We'll do our best to get you back for the semi-final.'

With a target to aim for, Harry was determined to recover in time. He was back in action two weeks before their big cup match against Chelsea. There was even time for him to score a goal.

'See, I'm feeling sharp!' he promised Pochettino. There was no way that he could miss playing in the FA Cup semi-final. He was a big game player and his team needed him.

The atmosphere at Wembley was electric. As usual, Harry was the second Spurs player out of the tunnel. As he looked up, he could see big blocks of white in the crowd.

'*Tottenham! Tottenham! Tottenham!*'

If the stadium was this loud for the semi-final, what

would the final be like? But Harry couldn't get ahead of himself. He had to focus on beating Chelsea first.

The Blues took the lead but with Harry on the pitch, Spurs were always in the game. He stayed onside at the front post to flick on Christian's low cross. Thanks to his clever touch, the ball flew right into the bottom corner.

Goooooooooooooooooooaaaaaaaaaaaaaaaaaaalllllllllllll llllllllllllllllll!!!!!!!!!!!!!

'It's like you've got eyes in the back of your head!' Christian cheered as they hugged.

'Why would I need that?' Harry asked. 'The goal doesn't move – it's always in the same place!'

Despite his best efforts, Chelsea scored two late goals to win 4–2. It was very disappointing but Tottenham's season wasn't over yet.

'We've got five Premier League matches left,' Harry told Dele. 'If we can get all fifteen points, the pressure is on Chelsea.'

The first three points came at White Hart Lane in the North London Derby against Arsenal. Dele got the first goal and Harry scored the second from the

penalty spot. The dream was still alive! But at West
Ham a week later, Spurs fell apart again. Harry, Dele
and Christian tried and tried but they couldn't get
the goal they needed. In the second half, Tottenham
panicked and conceded a silly goal. The 1-0 defeat left
them seven points behind Chelsea.

'No, the title race isn't over yet,' Pochettino told his
players. 'Come on, let's finish on a high!'

There was no chance of Harry relaxing. Even if
he didn't win the Premier League, he could still win
the Golden Boot. He was only three goals behind
Everton's Romelu Lukaku with three games to go.
Harry closed the gap to two with a neat flick against
Manchester United.

'Three goals against Leicester and Hull? I can do
that!' he told Dele.

'But what if Lukaku scores again?'

Dele was right; Harry needed to aim even higher.
Against Leicester, his first goal was a tap-in, his second
was a header and the third was a rocket from the edge
of the penalty area. Harry had another amazing hat-
trick but he wasn't finished yet. In injury time, he got

the ball in the same position and scored again!

Harry was pleased with his four goals but he couldn't help asking himself, 'Why couldn't I do that against West Ham?' He was never satisfied.

Harry would have to think about that later, though. With one game to go, he was on 26 goals and Lukaku was on 24. At the final whistle in the Arsenal vs Everton game, Lukaku was up to 25 goals for Everton thanks to a penalty, but meanwhile Harry was way ahead on 29! With two fantastic finishes and a tap-in, he had grabbed yet another hat-trick against Hull.

'Wow, you were only two goals off the Premier League record,' his proud dad told him. 'And you missed eight games through injury!'

Harry was delighted with his second Golden Boot in a row but it didn't make up for another season without a trophy. Tottenham kept getting so close to glory but would they ever be crowned champions? Harry, the local hero, never stopped believing.

CHAPTER 23

ONE OF EUROPE'S FINEST

Harry jumped up in the England wall but the free kick flew past him and into the top corner. As he watched, his heart sank. Scotland were winning 2–1 at Hampden Park with a few minutes to go.

'Come on, we can't lose this!' Harry shouted to his teammates.

England were unbeaten in qualification for the 2018 World Cup and this, in June 2017, was a key match against their British rivals. It was also Harry's first match as the national captain. For all of these reasons, he refused to let it end in an embarrassing defeat.

With seconds to go, Kyle Walker passed to Raheem Sterling on the left wing. Harry was surrounded by Scottish defenders but he was clever enough to escape. The centre-backs watched Raheem's high cross sail over their heads and thought they were safe. But they weren't. They had missed Harry's brilliant run to the back post.

There wasn't enough time or space to take a touch, so Harry went for a side-foot volley. With incredible technique and composure, he guided his shot past the keeper.

Gooooooooooooooooooooooaaaaaaaaaaaalllllllllllllllllll llll!!!!!!!!!!!!!!!!

It was another big goal in a big game. Under pressure, Harry hardly ever failed.

'You're a born leader,' England manager Gareth Southgate told him after the match. 'That's why I gave you the captain's armband.'

At twenty-four, Harry wasn't a bright young talent anymore. After three excellent seasons, he was now an experienced player with lots of responsibility for club and country. Now he felt ready to take the next step and become one of Europe's finest.

'I might not have as much skill as Cristiano Ronaldo and Lionel Messi but I can score as many goals,' he told Dele.

Harry was full of ambition ahead of the 2017–18 season. It was time to shine in the Champions League as well as the Premier League. But first, he had to get August out of the way.

'Maybe I should just take the month off!' Harry joked at home with Katie.

No matter how hard he tried and how many shots he took, he just couldn't score. He was trying to ignore all the talk about his August goal curse. Their beautiful baby daughter was certainly helping to take his mind off things.

'Yes, you could stay home and change Ivy's nappies with me!' Katie replied with a smile. She knew that Harry could never stay away from football. He loved it so much.

On 1 September, he travelled with England to play against Malta. 'Don't worry, I've got this,' he told his teammates. 'August is over!'

As Dele twisted and turned in the penalty area, Harry got into space and called for the pass. The goalkeeper rushed out but he calmly slotted the ball into the net.

Goooooooooooooooooooaaaaaaaaaaaaaaaalllllllllllllllllll llllllll!!!!!!!!!!!!!!!!!!!

On the touchline, Southgate pumped his fists. Tottenham fans all over the world did the same. Their goal machine was back.

'Finally!' Dele teased him. 'What would you do without me?'

Harry was too relieved to fight back. 'Thanks, you're the best!' he replied.

Once he scored one, Harry usually scored two. He did it against Malta and then he did it against Everton in the Premier League. As always, Harry's timing was perfect. Tottenham were about to start their Champions League campaign against German giants Borussia Dortmund.

'They picked the wrong time to face me!' he said confidently.

Harry won the ball on the halfway line, headed it forward and chased after it. He wasn't letting anyone get in his way. As he entered the Dortmund penalty area, the defender tried to push him wide. Harry didn't mind; he could score from any angle! Before the keeper could react, the ball flew past him.

The Tottenham fans went wild.

> *He's one of our own,*
> *He's one of our own,*
> *Harry Kane – he's one of our own!*

Harry went hunting for another goal and he got it.

'He just gets better and better!' the commentator marvelled.

It was Harry's first Champions League double, but he wanted a third. He was always hungry for more goals. With a few minutes to go, Pochettino took him off.

'The hat-trick will have to wait until next week!' he told his star striker, patting him on the back.

The APOEL Nicosia defence was prepared for Harry's arrival but there was nothing that they could do to stop him. He made it look so easy. He scored his first goal with his left foot and the second with his right. There was half an hour left to get his third but he only needed five minutes.

Kieran Trippier curled the ball in from the right and Harry ran from the edge of the box to glance it down into the bottom corner. All that heading practice had been worth it.

Goooooooooooooooooooooooaaaaaaaaaaaaaaalllllllllll llllllllllllll!!!!!!!!!!!!!!!

Harry ran towards Kieran and gave him a big hug. He was always grateful for the assists but this one was particularly special. Harry had his first ever Champions League hat-trick.

'That was perfect!' he told Son afterwards, clutching the match ball tightly.

'Yeah, it was a good win,' his teammate replied.

'No, I mean it was a perfect hat-trick,' Harry explained. 'One with my right foot, one with my left, and one with my head. That's the first time I've ever done that!'

Son laughed. 'You score so many goals. How can you remember them all?'

Every single goal was important to Harry and he often watched videos of his matches to help him improve. He never stopped working on his game.

'Is Kane the best striker in Europe right now?' the newspapers asked. Harry had already scored thirty-six goals by September and he still had three months of the year to go!

To keep his feet on the ground, Harry thought back to his early football days. Arsenal had rejected him and Tottenham had nearly done the same. As an eleven-year-old boy, he had told his hero David Beckham that he wanted to play at Wembley for England. Thanks to lots of practice and determination, Harry had achieved that dream and so much more.

His shirt now hung next to Becks' shirt in the hallway at Chingford Foundation School. Harry had the future at his goalscoring feet. He would do everything possible to lead England to World Cup glory in Russia. But before that, Harry was still determined to win trophies with his boyhood club, Tottenham.

CHAPTER 24

FOOTBALL'S COMING HOME

Harry couldn't wait for the biggest challenge of his football career so far. Not only was he on his way to Russia to play in his first World Cup, but the England manager, Gareth Southgate, had also picked him to captain his country.

With Three Lions on his shirt and the armband on his sleeve, could Harry lead his nation to glory again, after fifty-two years of hurt? It looked unlikely. At the 2014 World Cup, England had finished bottom of their group and at Euro 2016, they had lost to Iceland in the second round. Harry, however, was full of confidence – as always.

'I believe we can win the World Cup,' he told the media. 'We're going to fight and give everything we've got.'

The England team spirit was growing stronger and stronger every day. Yes, they were young but they weren't going to let that stop them. They had the talent to succeed and they got on really well together, no matter which Premier League club they played for. Kyle was one of Harry's best friends – so what if he had moved from Tottenham to Manchester City? 'We're all playing for England now!' everyone agreed.

It was time to give the fans something to cheer about. That task began against Tunisia, one of the top African nations. After the peace and quiet of their base camp, the England players finally experienced the amazing World Cup atmosphere. All that noise, all that colour – what a buzz!

'This is it,' Harry told his teammates, 'this is what we've been dreaming about since we were kids!'

With the adrenaline pumping through their bodies, England started brilliantly. John Stones lept up high to head Ashley Young's corner towards the top corner. Surely, it was going in…no, saved! But yet again, Harry was in the right place at the right time for the rebound.

Goooooooooooooooooooooooooaaaaaaaaaaaaaaaaaaaa aaaaaaalllllllllllllllllllllllllllllllllllllllll!!!!!!!!!!!!!!!!!!!!!!

Harry had his first World Cup goal already! He ran towards the corner flag and slid gleefully across the grass. Soon, he was at the bottom of an England team bundle.

When he finally escaped, Harry stood in front of the cheering crowd and held up the Three Lions on his red shirt. 'Come on!' he roared.

Even when Tunisia made it 1–1 from the penalty spot, Harry kept believing.

'There's still plenty of time to score again!'

Even when defenders wrestled him to the ground in the box but the referee shook his head, Harry kept believing.

'We'll find a way!'

Even with seconds to go, Harry kept believing.

'We can do this!'

Harry Maguire flicked Kieran Trippier's corner towards goal. Harry Kane was waiting at the back post, totally unmarked. What a chance to become

England's World Cup hero! He calmly steered his header past the goalkeeper.

Goooooooooooooooooooooooooaaaaaaaaaaaaaaaaaa aaaaaaalllllllllllllllllllllllllllllllllllllllll!!!!!!!!!!!!!!!!!!!!!

Another game, another two goals for Harry, England's big game player. And in a World Cup, too! It was the best feeling ever.

'H, what would we do without you?' Ashley screamed.

On the bench, Southgate punched the air. What an important goal, what an important win!

England's next victory, against Panama, was a lot more comfortable.

Kieran crossed and John headed home. 1–0!

Harry smashed in an unstoppable penalty. 2–0!

Jesse curled a long-range shot into the top corner. 3–0!

John finished off a brilliant team move. 4–0!

Harry was wrestled to the ground in the box again and this time, the referee pointed to the spot. 5–0!

The England fans couldn't believe what they were seeing, but Harry could.

'This is awesome!' he laughed in the dressing room at half-time. 'More of the same!'

Harry was on a hat-trick, after all. A fifth goal would take him above Belgium's Romelu Lukaku as the top scorer at the 2018 World Cup.

With 30 minutes to go, Harry looked over at the bench and saw Jamie Vardy warming up. He was about to come off – was there time for one last shot? No, but Ruben Loftus-Cheek's shot flicked up flukily off Harry's heel.

Goooooooooooooooooooooooooaaaaaaaaaaaaaaaaaaa aaaaaalllllllllllllllllllllllllllllllllllllllll!!!!!!!!!!!!!!!!!!!

'H, that's the worst hat-trick ever!' Jesse Lingard joked.

Harry shrugged and smiled. 'Whatever, there's no such thing as a bad hat-trick!'

Every goal counted, especially for a Number 9. Harry would treasure his World Cup matchball forever. With England through to the Round of 16, suddenly the fans were full of hope and excitement:

It's coming home, it's coming home,
It's coming, FOOTBALL'S COMING HOME!

The players, however, had to keep their feet on the ground. A 1–0 defeat to Belgium in the final game of the group stage set up a second-round match against Colombia.

'This is a massive test for us,' Southgate told his players, 'but we're ready!'

Harry battled bravely against the big centre-backs. When he made a run to head Kieran's corner, Carlos Sánchez pushed him to the floor.

'Foul!' Harry cried out.

Penalty! The Colombian players argued for ages with the referee and they even tried to scuff up the spot, but nothing could stop an ice-cold striker like Harry. He just waited calmly and, when the referee blew the whistle, slotted it coolly home.

Goooooooooooooooooooooooooaaaaaaaaaaaaaaaaaaa aaaaaaalllllllllllllllllllllllllllllllllllllll!!!!!!!!!!!!!!!!!!!!!!

What a tournament he was having – that was goal number six already!

England were on their way to the World Cup quarter-finals, but in the last minute, Colombia equalised. As Harry watched the ball cross the goal-line, he put his hands on his head. Oh no, what now?

'Dig deep!' he shouted to his struggling teammates.

Could England win a World Cup penalty shoot-out for the first time ever? They had been practising for weeks. Harry could barely walk but he knew that his nation needed him. As captain, he had to lead by example.

'I'll go first,' he said firmly.

With all eyes on him and a yellow wall of Colombia fans in front of him, Harry stepped up slowly and... SCORED, of course!

He pumped his fist and re-joined his teammates on the half-way line. Even when Jordan Henderson's penalty was saved, Harry knew that it wasn't over. He trusted their other Jordan – Jordan Pickford – to make at least one super save in the shoot-out.

Carlos Bacca ran up and...there was the super save!

Now, Eric Dier just needed to keep cool and...

Gooooooooooooooooooooooooooaaaaaaaaaaaaaaaaaa aaaaaaalllllllllllllllllllllllllllllllllll!!!!!!!!!!!!!!!!!!!!!

What a moment – England were through to the World Cup quarter-finals after WINNING ON

PENALTIES! Harry raced over to hug his keeper.

'Jordan, you hero!' he screamed. It was time for an even bigger England team bundle.

Was football really coming home? The impossible now seemed possible. Harry watched all the amazing videos of the celebrations back home.

'Look what we've started, lads,' he told his teammates before their quarter-final against Sweden. 'Come on, we can't stop now!'

England weren't ready to go home yet. Harry Maguire scored a thumping header.

'If one Harry doesn't get you, the other one will!' the TV commentator screamed – and then Dele grabbed a second to send England into the World Cup semi-finals for the first time in twenty-eight years. The whole nation was going football crazy!

'Is it coming home?' a journalist asked afterwards.

Harry grinned. 'We'll have to wait and see, but hopefully!'

Against Croatia, England made another brilliant start when Kieran curled a fantastic free-kick into the top corner – 1–0!

*It's coming home, it's coming home,
It's coming, FOOTBALL'S COMING HOME!'*

Could England score a second goal to settle the
semi-final? Jesse threaded a great pass through to
Harry in the penalty area.

He just had the goalkeeper to beat...SAVED!

He got to the rebound first...OFF THE POST!

Harry couldn't believe his bad luck, and neither
could the fans. England's superstar striker was usually
so lethal!

Croatia fought their way back into the match – 1–1!
Suddenly, the England players looked nervous and
tired. Harry did his best to urge his team on but could
they hang on for penalties? No- in the 110th minute,
Mario Mandžuki´c won it for Croatia.

At the final whistle, Harry sank to his knees,
surrounded by his band of football brothers. They
had all given absolutely everything.

It was devastating to get so close to the final but
they were still a huge success story. They hadn't
brought the World Cup home but they had brought

football home: England had fallen in love with its national team again. Thousands of fans stayed behind in the stadium to clap and cheer for their heroes.

'It hurts a lot,' Harry tweeted later that night. 'We can be proud and we'll be back. Thanks for all your support. #ThreeLions.'

England lost their third place play-off against Belgium but Harry did finish his first World Cup with an individual award – the Golden Boot for top scorer! It was a great achievement, even if it wasn't the team trophy that he really wanted.

There was plenty of time for that. This was just the beginning for Southgate's England side. Harry couldn't wait to lead his country to glory at Euro 2021 and World Cup 2022.

HARRY KANE HONOURS

Individual

🏆 PFA Young Player of the Year: 2014–15

🏆 Premier League PFA Team of the Year: 2014–15, 2015–16, 2016–17

🏆 Premier League Golden Boot: 2015–16, 2016–17

🏆 World Cup Golden Boot: 2018

KANE

9 **THE FACTS**

NAME: Harry Edward Kane

DATE OF BIRTH: 28 July 1993

AGE: 27

PLACE OF BIRTH: Walthamstow, London

NATIONALITY: England

BEST FRIEND: Dele Alli

CURRENT CLUB: Tottenham

POSITION: ST

THE STATS

Height (cm):	188
Club appearances:	406
Club goals:	242
Club trophies:	0
International appearances:	48
International goals:	32
International trophies:	0
Ballon d'Ors:	0

★ ★ ★ **HERO RATING: 88** ★ ★ ★

GREATEST MOMENTS

7 APRIL 2014,
TOTTENHAM 5-1 SUNDERLAND

Harry's first Premier League goal was a long time coming. After four loan spells, he finally got his chance at Tottenham under Tim Sherwood. Against Sunderland, Christian Eriksen curled a brilliant ball into the six-yard box and Harry beat his marker to score. It was a real striker's finish and a sign of the great things to come.

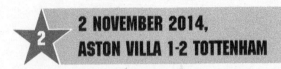

2 NOVEMBER 2014,
ASTON VILLA 1-2 TOTTENHAM

This was the goal that changed Harry's career at White Hart Lane. He has definitely scored better goals but this last-minute free kick won the match for Tottenham. Before this, Harry was a substitute. After this, he became the star striker we know and love.

7 FEBRUARY 2015,
TOTTENHAM 2-1 ARSENAL

This was the day that Harry became a true Tottenham hero. In the big North London Derby, he scored two goals to secure a famous victory. Harry's first goal was a tap-in but the second was a world-class header. He used his power and technique to direct the ball right into the corner of the Arsenal goal.

19 MARCH 2015,
ENGLAND 4-0 LITHUANIA

It was Harry's international debut at Wembley and he
had only been on the pitch for 80 seconds. Raheem
Sterling crossed from the left and, as usual, Harry was
in the right place at the right time. He scored with a
simple header at the back post and then bumped into
the match official!

6 OCTOBER 2017,
ENGLAND 1-0 SLOVENIA

On a tense night at Wembley, the new England
captain led his country to the 2018 World Cup in
Russia. In the last minute, Kyle Walker crossed from
the right and Harry stretched out his lethal right leg to
poke the ball past the keeper.

PLAY LIKE YOUR HEROES

THE HARRY KANE FINISH

STEP 1: Make a clever forward run between the defenders.

STEP 2: When you get the ball, control it perfectly. That first touch is really important!

STEP 3: Use your skill and strength to escape your marker and open up a bit of space to shoot.

STEP 4: Don't wait! Strike the ball as early as possible to surprise the keeper.

STEP 5: Keep it low! When the ball zips across the grass, it's harder for the keeper to save.

STEP 6: Aim for the corner! Picture the goal in your head and pick your spot. Go for the right or the left but never go down the middle.

STEP 7: As the ball hits the back of the net, run towards the fans in the corner with your arms out wide and a big grin on your face.

TEST YOUR KNOWLEDGE

QUESTIONS

1. Who was Harry's first Tottenham hero?

2. What position did Harry first play at Ridgeway Rovers?

3. Which other England legend also played for Ridgeway Rovers?

4. Which three clubs did Harry have trials with when he was a youngster?

5. Name three of Harry's teammates in the Tottenham youth team.

6. How many loan spells did Harry have before settling at Spurs?

7. Who was the Spurs manager when Harry made his first Premier League start?

8. Who gave Harry his Number 18 shirt when he left Tottenham?

9. Harry scored on his England debut – True or False?

10. How many goals did Harry score for England at Euro 2016?

11. How many Premier League Golden Boots has Harry won so far?

Answers below. . . No cheating!

1. *Teddy Sheringham* 2. *Goalkeeper* 3. *David Beckham* 4. *Arsenal, Watford and Tottenham* 5. *Any of Tom Carroll, Jonathan Obika, Kudus Oyenuga, Ryan Mason, Andros Townsend and Steven Caulker* 6. *Four – Leyton Orient, Millwall, Norwich City and Leicester City* 7. *Tim Sherwood* 8. *Jermain Defoe* 9. *True – Harry scored after only 80 seconds against Lithuania!* 10. *0* 11. *2*

VAN DIJK

TABLE OF CONTENTS

CHAPTER 1

EUROPEAN CHAMPION!

1 June 2019, Wanda Metropolitano Stadium, Madrid

For Virgil and his Liverpool teammates, it felt great to be back in the Champions League Final for the second year in a row. Last time, they had lost 3–1 to Cristiano Ronaldo's Real Madrid; this time, only a win would do.

Liverpool! Liverpool! Liverpool!

Although the location had changed, from Ukraine to Spain, the electric atmosphere in the stadium had stayed the same. That's because the Liverpool fans were the best in the world, and they had plenty to

cheer about, especially after the 'Miracle of Anfield'.
Their terrific team had fought back from 3–0 down
in the semi-final first leg, to beat Lionel Messi's
Barcelona 4–3! Now, with a victory over their
Premier League rivals Tottenham, they could lift the
trophy and become Champions of Europe for the
sixth time.

Liverpool! Liverpool! Liverpool!

'Are you ready, big man?' the manager Jürgen
Klopp asked his star centre-back as the players left
the dressing room before kick-off.

Virgil didn't say a word; he didn't need to. Instead,
he just gave his manager a confident nod. Oh yes,
he was ready and raring to go! Big games called for
big game players, and he was the ultimate big game
player. That's why Liverpool had paid £75 million to
sign him from Southampton, making him the most
expensive defender in the world. He was always so
calm and composed. He never got nervous and he
loved playing under pressure. He was born for this –
the biggest stage in club football.

'Right, lads,' their captain Jordan Henderson called

out from the front of the Liverpool line. 'It's time to go out there and win the Champions League!'

'YEAH!' the other ten players cheered behind him:

Alisson,

Joël Matip,

Andy Robertson,

Trent Alexander-Arnold,

Gini Wijnaldum,

Fabinho,

Roberto Firmino,

Sadio Mané,

Mohamed Salah,

and in the middle, the man at the centre of everything – Virgil!

What a talented team, and their spirit was so strong too. After the 'Miracle of Anfield', the Liverpool players felt like they could achieve absolutely anything. They were all fired up and determined to put their previous disappointments behind them – losing the 2018 Champions League Final to Real Madrid, and also losing the 2019 Premier League title to Manchester City. That one still hurt badly, but a

European trophy would help make them feel a whole lot better. This was their moment to bring glory back to Liverpool Football Club.

As he waited in the tunnel, Virgil casually reached up a long arm to touch the ceiling above him, just like he did with the 'This is Anfield' sign back home. He liked to tap it for good luck, not that they would need any of that...

When the big moment arrived, Virgil walked slowly out onto the pitch in Madrid, straight past the Champions League trophy without even looking at it.

'That can wait until it's ours to keep!' he told himself.

Virgil wasn't messing around. In the very first minute, he muscled his way past Tottenham's star striker Harry Kane to win the ball. He headed it down to Gini, who passed to Jordan, who lifted it over the top for Sadio to chase. The Liverpool attack looked so dangerous already. And as Sadio tried to chip the ball back to Jordan, it struck the Spurs midfielder Moussa Sissoko on the arm.

'Handball!' cried Sadio.

'Handball!' cried Virgil, way back in defence.

The referee pointed to the spot. *Penalty!*

Mohamed stepped up and... scored – *1–0!*

What a perfect start! Virgil jogged over to join in the team celebrations but then it was straight back to business. When there was defending to do, he was Liverpool's leader, organising everyone around him.

'That's your man, Joël!'

'Close him down, Gini!'

'Watch that run, Robbo!'

'Stay focused, Trent!'

'Come on guys, this isn't over yet!'

Virgil loved talking, and he spoke from experience. Once upon a time, he had been a talented young defender who made too many mistakes, but not anymore. He had learnt so many harsh lessons during his years with Willem II, Groningen, Celtic, Southampton and the Netherlands national team. And each one had helped to make him an even better, smarter footballer.

At half-time, Liverpool still had their 1–0 lead. They were now just forty-five minutes away from

Champions League glory...

'Come on lads, keep fighting!' Klopp urged his tired players. 'One more, final push!'

It was the end of a very long season, but Virgil wasn't going to head off on his summer holidays empty-handed. No way, this trophy belonged to Liverpool! He fought hard for every header and tackle, and he won them all.

He's a centre-half, he's a number four,
Watch him defend, and watch him score,
He'll pass the ball, calm as you like,
He's Virgil van Dijk, he's Virgil van Dijk!

Tottenham weren't giving up, though. As Dele Alli played a quick pass forward to Son Heung-min, they had two vs. two in attack. Joël was marking Kane, which meant that it was Virgil's job to stop Son Heung-min.

No problem! The South Korean had lots of speed and skill, but so did Virgil. He was the complete centre-back and not one Premier League striker had got past him all season. He knew exactly what to do in these difficult situations...

Virgil followed Son all the way into the Liverpool penalty area, keeping up but never diving in. He wasn't that kind of a defender. Instead, Virgil waited patiently and cleverly until the crucial moment. Then he used his strength and long legs to clear the ball away for a corner-kick.

'Phew!' the Liverpool fans breathed a big sigh of relief. Virgil had saved the day yet again!

'Great work!' shouted Alisson, patting him on the back.

'Keep going!' shouted Virgil, clapping encouragingly towards his teammates.

There were still fifteen minutes to go, and a second Liverpool goal would really help to calm things down. What could Virgil do to help his attackers at the other end of the field? He sliced his shot in the Tottenham penalty area, but then battled to win the second ball. Virgil's flick-on landed at Joël's feet, who set up super sub Divock Origi to score. 2–0!

As the goal went in, Virgil was racing back into defence. He turned and threw his arms up triumphantly. What would Liverpool do without him? He had played his part yet again. Now, they just had to hold on...

At last, the final whistle blew – Liverpool were the new Champions of Europe! Virgil didn't jump for joy like many of his teammates; instead, he fell to the floor. The exhaustion, the emotion, the excitement – at first, it was all too much for him to take. He had been dreaming about this moment since he was six years old. Was he still dreaming? No, it was real!

Virgil didn't stay down on the grass for long. His teammates wouldn't let him.

'We did it! We did it!' Gini Wijnaldum shouted, high-fiving his friend.

'Yes, Virg!' Alisson cheered, wrapping him in a big bear hug.

With tears in his eyes and the Anfield roar ringing in his ears, Virgil walked proudly around the pitch. He was a Champions League winner now. 'Champions League winner' – yes, he liked the sound of that.

'I told you we'd win it!' Virgil told his manager as they embraced near the halfway line.

After lots of hugs and high-fives, it was time for the Liverpool players to collect their winners' medals and then, best of all, the trophy! As Jordan the captain lifted the cup high above his head, flames shot up around the stage. Virgil, of course, was at the back of the team huddle, towering over everyone and cheering at the top of his voice:

Campeones, Campeones, Olé! Olé! Olé!

What a feeling! One by one, Virgil was achieving all his childhood football dreams. First, he had become the new captain of the Netherlands national team and now, the Boy from Breda was a European Champion too.

CHAPTER 2

BOY FROM BREDA

Hellen van Dijk had four important life lessons that she wanted to pass on to her children:

Be respectful.

Work hard.

Stay positive.

Always follow your dreams.

For her eldest son Virgil, those dreams were all about becoming a professional football player. It had been his favourite sport since the very first time he kicked a ball. It was the only thing he ever talked about, and the only thing he wanted to do, all day, every day. At the age of six, he was already out there on the local pitches, battling for the ball and battling to be the best.

'Pass it!'

'Hey, that's a foul!'

'Goooooaaaaaallllllllll!'

Virgil was far from the only youngster with those superstar dreams, however. Football was the most popular sport in the Netherlands, where he lived, and also across the whole, wide world. So, the road to the top would be a long and winding one, especially for a boy from Breda.

Breda was a city in the south of the Netherlands, more famous for its factories than for its football stars. Although they did have a local team, NAC Breda, they played down in the Dutch second division. To Virgil, the big clubs like Ajax and Feyenoord felt a long, long way away. He didn't really have many local football heroes to look up to, other than the big kids who showed off their skills on the pitches near where they lived.

Most of the best Dutch footballers either came from big cities in the north of the country:

Dennis Bergkamp, Johan Cruyff, Marco van Basten, Frank and Ronald de Boer...

Or, their families had moved to the Netherlands from a small country in South America called Suriname:

Patrick Kluivert, Edgar Davids, Clarence Seedorf, Aron Winter, Frank Rijkaard, Ruud Gullit…

And Virgil's mum! Yes, Hellen was from Suriname too, just like Seedorf and Davids! Sadly, she didn't have enough money to take her children on the long flight back to visit her birthplace. So instead, from their home in Breda, she taught them as much as she could about the history and culture of the country.

'We Surinamese like to stay calm and enjoy life,' she joked with Virgil. 'We're not as uptight as Dutch people like your dad!'

'Hey, I heard that!' Ron replied with a smile.

'Good!' Hellen laughed, before moving on to her son's favourite subject. 'And when it comes to football, our players have got it all – power, pace, and of course, that South American skill. No, you don't find that kind of natural talent in the Netherlands!'

At first having parents from different countries made Virgil feel a bit different from his friends, both those at school and on the pitch. But the older he grew, the prouder he became of his background. The Netherlands and Suriname – like all those football heroes before him, he was determined to bring together the best of both worlds.

CHAPTER 3

WDS'19

When Virgil arrived at his first training session with his local youth team in Breda, WDS'19, the coaches asked him the usual question: what position do you like to play?

'Striker,' he replied without even pausing to think.

Like most seven-year-old footballers, Virgil thought scoring goals was way cooler than stopping them.

The powerful feeling of ball hitting boot,
BANG!

The awesome sight of it flying past the keeper and into the net,
ZOOM!

And, best of all, the roar of the crowd celebrating your huge hero moment.

HURRAAAAAAY!

What could be better than that? Definitely not blocking other people's shots, that's for sure! Shooting or tackling – was that question even worth asking?! Not to young Virgil – he knew which one he preferred.

'Remember, the goalscorers get all the glory,' he taught his younger brother, who was learning fast about football. Soon, he'd be ready to go in goal and face Virgil's fierce shots. 'That's why the best players are always attackers.'

Virgil was aiming to become the next Ronaldinho, not the next Paolo Maldini. The Brazilian was always smiling and always trying out exciting new tricks. Virgil loved watching skilful players who looked like they were having lots of fun. To him, that's what football was all about.

'OK, well let's see how you get on up front then,' agreed Ferdi Hoogeboom, John van den Berg and Rik Kleyn.

They were the three coaches in charge at WDS'19. The first thing they noticed about Virgil – other than his confidence – was his size. He was easily the tallest boy on the team, and once he started playing, easily the strongest too.

Virgil started the match in the striker's role, but he didn't stay there long. He wanted to be on the ball all the time, and he wasn't just going to wait for it to eventually arrive at his feet. He dropped deeper and deeper until he was in the middle of the field, at the centre of everything.

Then calmly and cleverly, Virgil took control of the game. He used his superior size and strength to win the ball back for his team, and then pushed his team forward with his dribbling and passing.

'He looks so comfortable on the ball,' van den Berg turned to Hoogeboom, sounding impressed. 'And he's not shy, is he, for a new kid?'

Virgil was organising everything, telling his teammates where to go and what to do.

'Luuk, make the run!'

'Bas, watch the left winger!'

'Come on guys, I'm marking two players here!'

Already, at the age of seven, this kid was clearly a

leader. And he was clearly a defender or midfielder – not an attacker.

'Why do kids always say they're strikers?' Hoogeboom, van den Berg and Kleyn laughed together, rolling their eyes. 'Is that the only position they've heard of?!'

The WDS'19 coaches were delighted with their new young signing, and so were the players. Suddenly, the goalkeeper had hardly any saves to make, and the other defenders didn't need to panic anymore – because, if their opponents did get through, Virgil was always there to save the day. No-one got past Virgil – no-one. He wasn't the quickest player, but it didn't matter. He was really good at reading the game and working out what the striker would do next.

'He plays like a little professional already!' Kleyn thought to himself.

Virgil loved every minute of every WDS match. He was actually quite happy about not being the striker because it meant he got to be more involved in the action – the passing, the tackling, the battling for the ball. Maybe he would be the next Maldini after all, or the next Edgar Davids in midfield. He would just have to save all his great goalscoring for kickarounds with friends.

Virgil wore his blue-and-white shirt with passion and pride. He was playing for a proper team now, with his own special shirt number on the back, just like his heroes. It felt like the first step on his journey to the top. WDS had links with the local professional football club, NAC Breda, and then after that? Who knew! Well, Virgil had a plan, of course.

'One day, I'm going to play in a Champions League final,' he told his dad excitedly as they drove home together after another WDS win, 'and I'll be the captain of the Netherlands national team too!'

CHAPTER 4

KING OF THE CRUYFF COURT

Virgil's life was all about football. When he wasn't playing the game, he was still thinking about playing it, and imagining how it would feel to be a famous superstar in the future.

'Don't worry, I'll buy us a big, big house,' he promised his mum, 'and lots of fast, fancy cars too!'

Virgil didn't have a lot of time for thinking, however, because he was too busy playing. There was always a game going on somewhere, a chance to practise his skills. When he wasn't training or winning matches for WDS, he was taking shot after shot against his brother in the big goals near their house until it got dark. Or even better, he was winning matches on the local Cruyff court.

The pitches were named after Johan Cruyff, the greatest Dutch player of all time. In 2003, his charity had opened courts all over the country to give young kids a space to call their own where they could play football. There were two courts in Breda, and one of them was very near to where the van Dijks lived. It was a small pitch, covered in short, artificial grass, and surrounded by a high, wire fence to stop balls from flying out into the roads or through neighbours' windows. During most evenings, weekends and school holidays, that Cruyff court was Virgil's home.

'Do you want to take a sleeping bag with you?' Ron joked as his son rushed out of the door.

Virgil couldn't reply because he was still eating his breakfast, so he just waved goodbye instead.

'Well, at least we know where to find him if we need him!' Hellen said to her husband with a smile. They were just happy to see their son outside, having fun, getting exercise and staying out of trouble.

Well, Virgil was staying out of trouble off the football pitch anyway. The five-a-side games on the

Cruyff court were so competitive that there were often arguments and angry challenges. Although Virgil tried to stay away from the fighting, he was always fearless in the tackle. You had to be brave and confident if you wanted to keep playing. Most days, there was a tournament with lots of different teams and it was 'winner stays on'. If you lost, you had to wait ages on the sidelines before it was your turn again. No-one wanted that. They were too young to get tired; everyone just wanted to play football for as long as possible.

'Come on, let's do this!'

On the Cruyff court, Virgil wasn't a defender or a midfielder. He was usually one of the younger kids there, and so, unlike at WDS, he was smaller and weaker than the others. Instead, he played on the wing or in attack, where he could try out all his Ronaldinho tricks.

The aim of the game was to win, but also to out-skill your opponent – the cooler the move, the louder the cheer from the crowd. Providing entertainment was key, especially with so many people watching.

There wasn't much space on the small Cruyff court, though, and the level of football was always really high. Sometimes, professional players from NAC Breda would even come down for a bit of extra training. So Virgil's first touch had to be really good, and his fancy footwork had to be really fast. Practice made perfect.

'Skills, Virg!'

'Woah, Jordy will never come back after you embarrassed him like that!'

Virgil enjoyed his fun Cruyff Court battles, and he learned a lot from them. After all, quick thinking and close control were really useful weapons on a bigger, eleven-a-side pitch too.

As Virgil grew older – and taller and stronger – he was making a name for himself as one of the best young players in Breda. But could he go on from being King of the Cruyff Court to become a football legend and the future captain of the Netherlands national team?

They were big dreams to have, but Virgil believed in himself.

CHAPTER 5

A WARM WELCOME AT WILLEM II

The next step in Virgil's football career was a trial
at the top local team. The pressure to perform
well made some of the young players panic, but
not Virgil. He was as calm and confident as ever
as his dad dropped him off at the NAC Breda
training ground.

'Good luck!' Ron called through the car window.

'Thanks!'

Virgil was excited about the opportunity that lay
ahead of him. If he did well at the trial, he might
get the chance to move on from WDS to bigger and
better things. He was going to work his way up to
the top, one step at a time.

He understood that things would be more serious at a proper, professional football club like Breda, but the transition was still quite shocking to him.

'What are you doing?!' the youth coach yelled at his players. 'No, no, NO – you're getting it all *WRONG!*'

It was mostly silent during the session, and the Breda youngsters seemed very serious. Wasn't football supposed to be fun? The atmosphere was so different to WDS, where everyone enjoyed themselves and shouted encouragement at each other. Could Virgil see himself staying somewhere that was so different to WDS?

'So, how did it go?' Ron asked when he arrived to pick his son up.

Virgil knew it was best to tell the truth: 'Dad, it was horrible, I hated it!'

'I'm sorry it didn't suit you, son,' Ron comforted him. 'Don't worry, there are plenty of other football clubs around. We'll find the right one for you.'

The next week, they drove twenty miles to Tilburg, the home of Willem II.

'This team is even better than Breda,' Ron explained on the journey. 'They finished second in the Dutch League last season, ahead of Ajax and PSV. And now, they're playing in the Champions League!'

Virgil's ears pricked up at the sound of those two wonderful words. Wow, Willem II must be really good if they were playing in the Champions League! By the time they got to the training ground, Virgil couldn't wait for the trial to start. He was ready to shine at a Champions League club.

This time, there was no shouting from the coaches as he arrived. Instead, there was a warm welcome from the Willem II youth coach, Jan van Loon.

'Thanks for coming, Virgil – it's great to have you here.'

Wow, what a difference! As he walked out onto the training field, Virgil could tell that he was going to like the atmosphere at Willem II. The players were laughing and joking as they warmed up, and once the session started, they worked hard while also having fun. Much better!

'Excellent, Virgil!' van Loon clapped and cheered

when he stopped one of the strikers in a one-on-one situation.

The coach watched as Virgil won the ball again… and again… and again. The Willem strikers tried and tried, but no-one could get past the powerful new defender.

It wasn't just Virgil's strength that impressed van Loon; it was also his understanding of the game. Just when it looked like a striker was about to get past him, he would stretch out a leg and steal the ball at the crucial moment. Other players were quicker, but Virgil always seemed to know where to be, when to act and what to do next. He made it all look so easy, but it was very rare to see such a natural defender at such a young age.

'Some of that stuff can take years to teach!' van Loon thought to himself.

And some of it you couldn't teach at all; it was just instinct. You either had it, or you didn't, and Virgil definitely had it. The Willem II youth coach knew straight away that he had to sign this special talent.

'So, how did it go?' Ron asked at the end of the

session. He had been watching from the car with his fingers crossed because he didn't want to put his son off on his big day.

'Dad, this is Jan, the coach,' Virgil replied, trying to control the smile spreading across his face.

'Nice to meet you, Jan.'

'Nice to meet you too, Mr van Dijk.'

'Please, call me Ron.'

'Ron, I'll keep it short – your son has a very special talent! Our strikers spent ages trying to beat him today, but no-one managed it – not a single one. We'd love for Virgil to join us here at Willem II. We think with some extra coaching, he could be a real star. Would you like some time to think about it first?'

Ron looked across at Virgil, who was shaking his head violently. He didn't want to wait; he wanted to play for Willem straight away.

'No, I think my son has made up his mind already!' Ron laughed. 'Thanks, he'd love to join the team.'

CHAPTER 6

DISHWASHING DAYS

At first, Virgil moved smoothly through the ranks
of the Willem II academy. He made each new age
group look as easy as the last. With the right kind
of coaching, he was developing into a top young
defender. But things began to change when he
reached the Under-17s.

Until then, Virgil had always been one of the
biggest and strongest players on his team.

But now that he was sixteen, everyone else but
him had grown. Even his younger brother was taller
than him now! Virgil had to play at right-back instead
because his coach didn't think he was fast enough,
or good enough, to be a centre-back anymore. There

were also questions about his attitude.

'Come on Virgil – *FOCUS!* You look like you're not even trying today.'

It was often his calm playing style that got him into trouble. When Willem were winning a game comfortably, Virgil sometimes switched off and made silly mistakes. But the problem was that even when he was fully focused, he just looked really relaxed.

'I can't help it,' he complained to his teammates after another telling-off from his coach, 'that's just who I am!'

Until then, Virgil had always believed that Willem II would give him his first professional contract.

But now that he was sixteen, that was all in doubt. At that age, the coaches were looking to see who had what it took to become a top professional player, and who didn't. Only the most talented young footballers would make the next step-up to the Willem II Under-19s. And even then, they might not start earning money for another year or two.

So, as Virgil finished high school, he searched for a part-time job that he could fit in around his busy football schedule. Fortunately, he found one, washing dishes at the Oncle Jean restaurant.

'When can you work, kid?' asked the owner, Jacques Lips, when he went along for an interview.

Virgil had checked this carefully. 'Wednesdays and Sundays are the only nights I don't have training or a match.'

'Perfect, those are our busiest times – you've got yourself a job!'

So after day-time practices with Willem II, Virgil would get the train back to Breda station, pick up his bike and cycle fifteen minutes to the restaurant. Then, after finishing his five-hour shift, he would cycle home if he still had any energy left. If not, he would get his dad to come and pick him up.

It wasn't fun, but it was the only way for Virgil to keep his football dream alive. To start with, he didn't say much to anyone at Oncle Jean. He just got on with his boring job in the back of the restaurant.

'You're earning money so that you can go out on Saturday nights with your mates,' he had to keep telling himself during those long, dull hours at the dirty kitchen sink.

But the longer Virgil worked there, the more he got to know his new boss. It turned out that he was a really nice guy and they got on well.

'How would you like to do more shifts and earn some extra money?' Lips suggested one day. 'We need good, hard workers like you.'

'Thanks, but I really don't have time. Sorry, I have to be at the Willem academy every da—'

'I get it – football comes first!' Lips interrupted with a smile. 'That's fine, but are you sure it's worth all this effort? Do you really think you're going to be a professional player one day?'

Virgil nodded confidently. 'Yes, I do. I'm going to be a star!'

'Okay, well if you change your mind and want to earn some extra money, just let me know. Good luck, kid, I hope you make it!'

Virgil really hoped so too. He couldn't give up now, not when he had worked so hard to get this far. And not when the Willem II first team was in sight, training only metres away from them.

'Look, there's Jens Janse. He's a defender like me and he's only twenty-one!'

Virgil was determined to achieve his football dream, but for that to happen, something significant had to change. Thankfully, it soon would.

CHAPTER 7

ONWARDS AND UPWARDS

'Oh my, where has my cute little boy gone?' Hellen teased Virgil as he sat down for breakfast. Suddenly, her eldest son was starting to tower over her.

'I swear you're getting taller and taller every day!'

His mum was right about that. In 2008, Virgil finally had his growth spurt, and it went on and on all summer. He shot up from a pretty average five-foot nine to a gigantic six-foot four.

'You could be a basketball player now!' suggested his brother, who was back to being the smaller one again.

Virgil smiled but shook his head. 'No, I can be a big, powerful centre-back now!'

Hopefully, his days as a right-back were over.
He was ready to become the deadliest defender in
the world.

When Virgil returned to Willem II for preseason
training, the staff just stood there staring at him in
shock. Was this really the same kid they had been
coaching for years? And Virgil's teammates were
just as surprised.

'Woah mate, what happened to you this summer?'

'Watch out, giant coming through!'

'Hey, what's the weather like up there?'

Virgil was delighted with his new-found height,
but his body didn't cope well with the changes.
At first, he found playing football really painful.
Running, kicking, tackling – nothing felt right
anymore. It was like he was playing in someone
else's body. He had problems with his knees, his
hamstrings, his ankles...

Argghhhhh!

'Don't worry, these things are normal at your age,'
the coaches reassured him. 'Soon, you'll be better
than ever!'

Soon? That was no good – Virgil needed to be better than ever now! Otherwise, he would never move up from the Willem Under-17s to the Under-19s. It was so frustrating for him, but in the end, the only answer was to stop playing and listen to the physio's advice:

'You need to rest and then recover. If you don't, you'll do yourself some serious damage.'

Over the next six weeks, Virgil had to show all of his patience and dedication. He spent hours in the gym, doing the same exercises over and again. It was slow progress, but eventually his body started to feel right again.

'At last!' Virgil cheered with relief. He was finally pain-free, and ready to return to action.

When he made his big comeback, Virgil really was better than ever. The Willem coaches had been right about that. He was still the same calm defender with excellent decision-making skills, but now he had that extra height for winning headers. And an extra burst of speed too, thanks to the physio.

What a complete package! No-one was getting past him now.

An attacker raced down the right wing and tried to pull the ball back to his partner in the middle. Virgil saw it coming and calmly stepped in to deal with the danger. *INTERCEPTION!*

A forward twisted and turned on the edge of the box, looking for a way through. In desperation, he decided to go for goal. It was a decent shot, but Virgil bravely got his big body in the way. *BLOCK!*

A speedy striker chased after a long pass over the top. Although he had a head-start, Virgil got back, and he got the ball too. *RECOVERY!*

A skilful playmaker dribbled his way through the Willem defence. Finally, he was one on one with Virgil, who waited and waited until he was ready to pounce. *TACKLE!*

Their opponents curled a corner into the crowded penalty box, and up jumped Virgil, head and shoulders above the rest. *HEADER!*

With this new and improved version of Virgil in defence, the Willem Under-17s picked up clean sheet after clean sheet. It wasn't long before his performances attracted attention from the age group above.

'This kid could be the next Jaap Stam!' some people predicted. Stam was a top Dutch defender who had spent a season at Willem in the 1990s before moving on to play for Manchester United, Lazio and AC Milan.

Fortunately, Virgil could handle these new high expectations. Soon after joining the Under-19s, he became their captain. He loved the extra responsibility of the role. He was already a leader on the pitch anyway.

'The armband just makes it more official!' Virgil told himself as he organised and encouraged the teammates around him.

After a frustrating few years, suddenly everything was going right for Virgil again. He was even playing some matches for the Under-23s. And from there, it was only one giant leap to the Willem first team. His football dream was alive and kicking.

CHAPTER 8

GOING TO GRONINGEN

Despite all of Virgil's excellent defending, there were some people at Willem who still weren't convinced. Mostly, it came down to the same old issues: his concentration and his calm playing style.

'At this level, he can make a mistake or two and nothing happens,' the reserve team coach Edwin Hermans argued. 'But if he does that stuff in the Dutch League, he'll get destroyed!'

His assistants agreed. 'It's like he switches off and stops trying sometimes when it looks like the game is won. There's no question that he's got the talent to play for the first team, but the attitude? I just don't know.'

To make matters worse for Virgil, the Willem first team was fighting relegation from the Dutch First Division. In that tricky situation, the manager turned to his most experienced professionals, not 'the next big thing'.

But did Virgil really have that much potential anyway? In the end, the club's conclusion was that he was a good young player but not a stand-out future star. So, should they offer him that first contract he was hoping for?

Hermans said yes, but Willem waited too long. While they were still thinking, another club came along who were much more willing to take a risk on Virgil's rising talent.

Groningen were a team in the northern Netherlands with a great record of developing young players and giving them a chance to shine. Several Dutch national team stars had started their careers at Groningen, including Arjen Robben and legendary centre-back Ronald Koeman.

Koeman's dad, Martin, had played for the club too, and he still worked there as the chief scout.

When his colleague Henk Weldmate recommended a tall, athletic defender in the Willem reserves, he went along to take a look for himself.

By half-time, Martin Koeman was both impressed and confused. Why wasn't this kid already playing for the first team? He was classy on the ball, brave in the air, and strong in the tackle. No-one had got past him at all during that half of the match. What else did Willem want from a young centre-back?

'Yes, he's still a bit raw, but he could be a real superstar one day!'

Koeman was even more confused when he found out that Willem hadn't even offered Virgil a first team contract yet. What were they waiting for?

'Right, we've got to move fast,' Koeman explained to the Groningen chairman, 'before they realise their big mistake!'

But if they really wanted to sign Virgil, they would need to give the boy from Breda a very good reason to move 200 miles away from his home:

'We believe in you and we want to help you become an even better player,' the Groningen team told him in a meeting with his agent.

Virgil had heard all that before but, unlike Willem, they were offering him a proper professional contract to prove it. This changed everything! His football dream would be safe, at least for the next few years.

'Thanks, but can I have a few days to think about it?' Virgil asked. He had a difficult decision to make, and just like when he was out there playing on the football pitch, he preferred to take his time.

It was only when Willem found out about Groningen's offer that they tried to persuade Virgil to stay. But by then, it was too late. Virgil wanted to be at a football club where he felt wanted and valued. His mind was made up; he was going to Groningen.

CHAPTER 9

LEARNING UNDER LUKKIEN

'This is it – I'm a professional footballer now and I'm on my way to the top!'

That's what Virgil was thinking as he arrived at his new club. So what if Willem hadn't wanted him? He didn't need them; he was going to become a world-class defender anyway. First at Groningen, then after that, who knew? Maybe even at Ronaldinho's Barcelona!

However, Virgil didn't get off to the smooth start that he was expecting at Groningen. He was hoping to go straight into the first team squad, but instead, he found himself training with the Under-23s. And when match day came, he was only one of the substitutes.

'What's going on?' Virgil thought to himself as he sat there sulking in angry silence. 'I didn't travel all that way to waste my time like this!'

At Willem, he was hardly ever on the bench. Even during Virgil's worst spell, when the coaches thought he was too small and slow to be a central defender, they had just moved him across to right-back. He was better than the bench! Had he made a massive mistake by going to Groningen? Should he have stayed at home after all?

Virgil wasn't the type of person who kept quiet when something was troubling him. He believed in speaking his mind. So once the game finished, he went straight up to the Under-23s manager and asked him:

'Why am I not playing?'

'Because you're not ready to play,' Dick Lukkien replied simply.

'Yes, I am!' Virgil protested.

'No, you're not.'

Stubborn Virgil had met his match. Lukkien wasn't backing down. Although the Under-23s manager had been impressed by Virgil's talent in training, he had also noticed something else that wasn't so positive. The defender's body was in a really bad way.

'You need to work on building up your fitness first,' Lukkien explained. 'Otherwise, you're going to get a bad injury. How many matches were you playing per week at Willem?'

Virgil shrugged casually. 'Two, sometimes three when they called me up to the Under-23s...'

'I thought so – that's far too much football for a youngster like you! I know you want to reach the first team as quickly as possible, but you can't rush these things. You'll get there, I promise, but right now you need to be patient.'

On the football field, Virgil could wait ages for the perfect moment to make a tackle. But that was because it was fun. Doing lots of boring fitness work in the gym, on the other hand, was not fun at all.

'Keep going, keep going!' the Groningen coaches encouraged him.

That wasn't easy for Virgil, especially as he was so far away from all his friends and family in Breda.

There was no-one to drive him to training, so he had to cycle everywhere. He was on his own now, which meant growing up fast and doing things that he didn't want to do. But through all the challenging and lonely times, Virgil stayed determined about one thing. No matter what, he was going to make his football dream come true...

'Excellent, Virgil!' Lukkien applauded on the touchline. He was delighted with his defender's progress. He looked so much stronger and sharper now. At last, he was ready to play.

And that was just the start of Virgil's learning under Lukkien. In matches, the manager didn't let his star defender relax for a second.

'Virgil, stay focused!'

'I am!'

'No, you're not!'

Lukkien knew how good Virgil could be, but he still got a bit lazy whenever Groningen were winning comfortably. That had to stop. Losing concentration wasn't acceptable anymore, not even for a moment, not if Virgil wanted to move up to the first team.

By pushing him hard, Lukkien got the best out of his classy centre-back. And it worked. In the final weeks of the 2010/11 season, Virgil was called up to the senior Groningen squad for an away game against ADO Den Haag.

'Congratulations, I told you you'd get there in the end!' Lukkien said with a handshake and a smile.

'Thanks, Coach!' Virgil replied, trying his best not to burst with pride. 'Thanks for everything, for believing in me. I know I haven't always showed it, but I'm really grateful for all your help.'

'You deserve it – you've worked hard for this. Good luck, kid, and remember – STAY FOCUSED!'

CHAPTER 10

GRONINGEN'S EMERGENCY EXTRA STRIKER

So, was Virgil about to make his Dutch league debut at the age of just nineteen? When the manager Pieter Huistra announced the starting line-up, he was there on the list of subs:

48 van Dijk.

Wow, it was really happening! And there was a green-and-white shirt waiting for him, with his name and number on the back. Virgil wanted to take a photo to send to his friends and family, but at the same time, he didn't want to embarrass himself in front of his new teammates. He was sharing a dressing room with experienced professionals now. Forward Dušan Tadić was a Serbian international,

while defenders Andreas Granqvist and Fredrik
Stenman both played for Sweden.

'Just act cool,' Virgil kept telling himself as the
clock ticked down to kick-off.

On this occasion, he didn't mind being on the
bench. It gave him time to soak up the atmosphere
in the stadium and get a sense of the speed and
style of the game. By half-time, however, he was
getting restless.

'Bring me on, I'm ready!' Virgil wanted to tell
his manager, but for once, he kept his thoughts to
himself during the team-talk.

Groningen were drawing at that point, but early
in the second half, they took the lead again. 3–2!
Brilliant, a win would lift them up to fifth place;
they could still qualify for the Europa League! What
would Huistra do next – go for another goal or
strengthen the defence?

Virgil, of course, was hoping for the second option.
With twenty minutes to go, he got the call he was
waiting for:

'Get ready, you're coming on!'

Virgil wasn't nervous as he ran onto the field for his Groningen debut, just excited. On the outside, he looked as calm and composed as ever, like it was just another average football match.

'You're gonna be great, kid! Just mark him tightly,' Fredrik called out, pointing to one of the ADO strikers.

No problem! At the centre of the defence, Virgil didn't have that much to do, but the whole time he could hear Lukkien's words playing in his head:

'STAY FOCUSED!'

No, there would be no silly mistakes today. No-one was getting past him. At the final whistle, Groningen were 4–2 winners and Virgil walked off the pitch with his head held high. It was a strong start to his professional football career. Fredrik was the first of many teammates and coaches to come over and congratulate him.

'Well done, mate – you're a star in the making!'

Virgil was delighted with his debut performance, and desperate for more game-time straight away. Two weeks later, he came on for the last fifteen minutes against PSV Eindhoven. This time, though, he was playing in a very different position.

In order to finish fourth and qualify for the Europa League, Groningen had to win. A 0–0 score would not be enough. So Huistra turned to his subs bench, looking for another attacking option. What about Virgil? With his height, strength and skill, the manager decided that he could be an excellent emergency extra striker.

'I want you to go up front and win every header,' his manager explained to him.

Virgil's childhood dream was coming true! He did his best to flick balls on for Dušan and Tim Matavž, but sadly Groningen just could not find that winning goal.

Noooooooooo! Many of the players collapsed to the floor in disappointment, but Virgil stood tall and strong. It wasn't over yet; Groningen could still qualify for the Europa League through the play-offs.

'Come on, we can do this!' Virgil urged his teammates. Even at such a young age, he wasn't shy about speaking up.

Together, they battled their way past Heracles
Almelo to set up a final against… ADO Den Haag
again! Groningen were feeling confident; too
confident, it turned out. In the first leg, they were
thrashed 5–1. 5–1! Was that their Europa League
dream over?

No way! Virgil still believed. In the second leg
at home at the Noordlease Stadium, he started his
first ever game for Groningen. Huistra picked him
to play at right-back, but before long, he was on
the attack again…

Early in the second half, Groningen won a free
kick on the left side of the ADO box. Three players –
Petter Andersson, Leandro Bacuna and Virgil –
stood around the ball, discussing who would take it.

'Trust me, I've got this,' Virgil assured the others.

As well as being a top defender, Virgil was also a
free kick king. He could strike the ball with lots of
power, swerve and accuracy. BANG! His shot curled
around the wall and then dipped down into the
bottom corner.

Gooooooooooooooaaaaaaaaallllllllllllllllll!!!!!!!!!!!!!!!!

What a time and what a way for Virgil to score
his first Groningen goal! He got hugs and high-fives
from his teammates, but they didn't have time to
celebrate properly. It was now 3–6 on aggregate –
Groningen had forty minutes left to score another
three goals at least.

'Come on, we can do this!'

Leandro fired in a long-range rocket. 4–6!

Virgil was now playing as an emergency extra
striker again. When Petter dribbled forward, he
timed his run perfectly and then, with his weaker left
foot, squeezed a shot under the ADO keeper. 5–6!

*Goooooooooooooooooooooaaaaaaaaaaaaaaaaallllllllllll
lllllllllllllllll!!!!!!!!!!!!!!!!!!!!*

Two goals on his full Groningen debut – Virgil was
a club hero already!

'Are you sure you're a defender?' Petter joked as
they rushed back for the restart.

Virgil smiled and shrugged. 'I can play anywhere!'

Groningen, however, still needed one more goal.

Virgil flicked a header on to Tim, who shot just
wide. *CLOSE!*

Tim was through one-on-one with the keeper, but his chip hit the crossbar. *EVEN CLOSER!*

Groningen weren't giving up. In the eighty-ninth minute, Dušan curled one last corner into the ADO box. As the ball bounced down, Tim reacted first. His shot was going in, until it struck a defender on the arm.

'Penalty!' cried Virgil, along with all his teammates and the thousands of supporters in the stadium.

The referee pointed to the spot and Tim stepped up and scored. 6–6!

What an incredible game! Virgil was desperate to keep playing, but he was absolutely exhausted after his goalscoring efforts. As he hobbled off in extra time, the Groningen fans gave him a standing ovation.

Virgil! Virgil! Virgil!

'What a performance, kid!' Huistra said, giving him a great big hug.

Virgil slumped down in his seat on the bench to watch the rest of the drama unfold: twenty tense minutes of football and then a penalty shoot-out.

'I should be out there taking one!' Virgil thought

to himself. He loved the pressure, and he could strike
a penalty just as well as he could strike a free kick, if
not better.

But there was nothing Virgil could do now, except
hope and cheer. He could feel his heart pounding in
his chest as one by one his teammates stepped up to
take a spot-kick.

'Go on, Andreas!'

'Yes, Thomas!'

'Nice one, Dušan!'

After nine penalties, ADO were 4–3 up. It was all
up to Tim now – could he score from the spot again?

'Come on, come on,' Virgil muttered under
his breath.

The keeper dived the wrong way, but Tim's
powerful shot smacked against the crossbar.

Noooooooooo! Again, the Groningen players
collapsed to the floor in disappointment. This time,
their Europa League dream really was over.

Virgil felt their pain and frustration, but he also
felt a lot of pride too. His football career had come
a long way in such short period of time. Only a

month before, he had been training with the
Under-23s, and learning under Lukkien. Now,
Virgil was a first team regular, a classy young
defender, a free kick king, a club hero and
Groningen's emergency extra striker.

CHAPTER 11

A HORRIBLE TIME
IN HOSPITAL

Soon after the 2011/12 season kicked off, Virgil's
days as Groningen's emergency extra striker came
to an end. That's because he was now the club's
first-choice centre-back. With Andreas and Fredrik
both gone, he was the new leader in defence.

Virgil loved the responsibility of the role. Out
on the football field, he was always talking, always
organising his teammates:

'Kees, that's your man!'

'Tim, drop deeper!'

'Johan, get tighter!'

Virgil still made a few silly mistakes now and then
when he got too comfortable, but when he stayed

fully focused and read the game well, no-one could get past him. And it was in the biggest games that Virgil shone the brightest. With him at the heart of their defence, Groningen beat Ajax 1–0 and then Feyenoord 6–0.

That day, Virgil was head and shoulders above everyone else. In the very first minute, he intercepted a through-ball and then launched a beautiful long pass from right to left to set Dušan away and score. *1–0!*

'What a ball!' his goalscoring teammate thanked him with a double-five.

Eighty-eight impressive minutes later, Virgil made it 5–0 with an unbelievable shot from nearly forty yards. As the ball flew past him, the Feyenoord goalkeeper just sat down and gave up. He had no chance of stopping a thunderstrike like that.

Goooooooooooooooooooooaaaaaaaaaaaaaaaalllllllllllll llllllllllllllll!!!!!!!!!!!!!!!!!!

'Mate, you're amazing!' Leandro cheered, leaping into his tall teammate's arms.

Virgil stood there smiling and beating his chest

with pride. Not bad for his first goal in the Dutch league! He would never forget his man-of-the-match performance, and neither would the Feyenoord manager, Ronald Koeman.

'My dad was right about that big Groningen centre-back,' Koeman muttered to himself. 'If he keeps improving, he could be the next superstar Dutch defender.'

But just when everything seemed to be going so well for Virgil, disaster struck. It all started with a bad stomach ache in the days before the big local derby against Heerenveen.

'It's a sign that you need to start eating more healthily,' the club doctor Henk Hagenauw warned him. 'When was the last time you had a proper meal?'

Virgil shrugged. He was living with his young teammate, Tim Keurntjes, and neither of them had a clue about cooking. 'Does McDonald's count?' he asked, knowing the answer.

Hagenauw rolled his eyes. 'I'm serious – you can't keep filling your body with junk food all the time. You're a professional footballer now and diet is really important. Look, eat lots of fruit and vegetables and see if it gets any better.'

But a few days passed, and Virgil's pain grew worse. Would he have to miss the big derby match? It got so bad that in the end, he had to wake Tim up in the middle of the night and ask him to drive him to the hospital.

'Arggghhhh!' Virgil screamed out in agony. 'Are we there yet? How much further?'

When he got to the hospital, the news wasn't good. Virgil had ruptured his appendix and that was just one of many medical problems.

'You're lucky to be alive,' the doctors told him, 'and you're going to need major surgery.'

Major surgery? Virgil couldn't believe it. It was the first day of April – April Fool's Day – but this was no time for joking, no laughing matter. This was serious.

Like most twenty-year-olds, Virgil had thought that he was invincible. Until now. Now, he was lying in a hospital bed, unable to do anything, and his body was in a really bad way. Now, he wasn't just fighting for his football career; he was also fighting for his life.

'How are you feeling?' his mum asked anxiously from the chair next to his bed. As soon as she got the phone call, Hellen had rushed up from Breda to be by his side. She couldn't let her eldest son go through this alone.

'Not great,' Virgil replied honestly.

For two long, slow, boring weeks, that hospital became his home. During much of that time, Virgil couldn't do anything except sit, sleep, rest and pray that he would get better. But slowly, after days of rest, his body grew stronger and stronger, until eventually he was able to walk again. Those first steps were so tiring, but Virgil was determined to get back on his feet and back out on the pitch as soon as possible.

'So, when can I start playing football again?' he asked, crossing all his fingers and toes.

'Virgil!' Hellen said, sighing loudly. How could he even think about that yet, when he had only just had major surgery?

'Your mum's right – I'm afraid that football will have to wait,' the doctor explained. 'Remember, you've lost a lot of weight and strength. It'll take time to build you back up. But if everything goes well with your recovery, you could be back fit for next season.'

'Next season' – it wasn't the answer that Virgil had been hoping for, but it was still a whole lot better than 'Never'. In fact, it was only a few months away. Yet again in his football career, he would just have to be patient and work hard. But after his horrible time in hospital, Virgil didn't mind so much. He felt lucky to be alive at all.

Those two weeks were the wake-up call that Virgil needed. From now on, he decided, he was going to be a disciplined, dedicated professional. He would take good care of his body and eat a balanced, healthy diet.

No, Virgil wasn't going to let anything like that get in the way of his football dream again.

CHAPTER 12

SAYING YES TO CELTIC

After his horrible time in hospital, Virgil came back stronger, faster, more determined and more unbeatable than ever. Groningen's new Number 6 only missed two league matches during the whole 2012/13 season, and that was only because of suspension.

With their best defender back, Groningen became much harder to beat. They finished the season in seventh place, just missing out on the Europa League again.

So close! Sadly, Virgil knew that was probably as good as it would ever get for him at Groningen. Most talented players at mid-table Dutch clubs eventually moved up to one of the country's top three teams: Ajax, Feyenoord or PSV Eindhoven.

'I'm ready for that next step now,' Virgil told his agent confidently.

During the summer of 2013, two of those top clubs were looking to sign new young centre-backs: Ajax and PSV. And there were three names at the top of both of their lists:

Mike van der Hoorn from FC Utrecht,

Jeffrey Bruma from Chelsea,

and Virgil van Dijk from Groningen.

So which one would they choose? Virgil had a positive meeting with Ajax's Director of Football, Marc Overmars, but in the end, the club signed van der Hoorn instead. PSV, meanwhile, went for Bruma, and Feyenoord stuck with Stefan de Vrij and Bruno Martins Indi.

What about Virgil? Well, he had nowhere left to go in the Netherlands.

'Why don't they want me?' he asked himself. Virgil thought back to his performances against the top teams that season. Yes, he had made a few silly mistakes, but nothing too serious. And for every error, there were loads of examples of excellent defending...

Or perhaps it was the same old issue: Virgil's casual playing style. He wasn't a typical big, brave centre-back who threw himself into every tackle. Instead, he read the game well and got into the right positions to win the ball in other ways. Did the top Dutch clubs really think that he didn't care when he was on the football pitch?

'Forget about it,' his agent told him, 'there are plenty of other clubs in other countries.'

What about Brighton, who had just missed out on promotion to the English Premier League?

'No, I want to play in one of the top leagues in Europe,' Virgil decided.

What about FC Krasnodar, a Russian team who were offering Virgil a big money move?

'No, I want to play in one of the top leagues in Europe.'

What about Celtic, the Champions of Scotland?

'You'd get the chance to play in the Champions League,' his agent added as an extra fact to tempt him.

It worked – that was Virgil's football dream. If there was the chance to play in Europe's greatest club competition, then he was in!

'And they really want to sign me?' he asked his agent.

Yes! Having sold Kelvin Wilson to Nottingham Forest, Celtic needed a new star centre-back. After months of searching, their chief scout, John Park, handed a shortlist to the manager, Neil Lennon. There were two names at the top:

Mike van der Hoorn from FC Utrecht.

Virgil van Dijk from Groningen.

They were both brilliant defenders, but Park preferred Virgil. He had the confidence to try things that others didn't, especially when he brought the ball out from the back. He was different, special.

'Right, well I better go and take a look at him in action then,' Lennon declared.

By half-time, the Celtic manager was both impressed and confused. Why wasn't Virgil already playing for one of the top clubs in Europe? He had amazing composure, strength, speed and technique.

What else could you want from a young centre-back?

'Wow, this guy's got everything!' he thought to himself.

And best of all, Virgil was available to buy for less than £3 million. What a bargain! Lennon couldn't believe his luck – what were Celtic waiting for?

'Right, we've got to move fast,' he explained to the chairman, 'before the big Premier League clubs come looking at him!'

When he met with Celtic, Virgil was impressed immediately. It was a famous club with an incredible history. The chance to play in the Champions League was a key factor, of course, but most of all, he just wanted to be at a football club where he felt wanted and valued. That's why he had gone from Willem II to Groningen, and that's why he said yes to Celtic.

'It feels very good and I'm very excited to be here,' Virgil told the Scottish media as he held up a green-and-white hooped shirt with the Number 5 on the back.

The Celtic manager was very excited too, and soon, so were the players. The first thing they noticed about Virgil was his size. At six-foot four, he looked like a basketball player, but once the training session started, it was clear that Virgil was a football superstar. The club's strikers all lined up to test their new Dutch defender: Georgios Samaras, Teemu Pukki, Kris Commons, Anthony Stokes, Leigh Griffiths… But as hard as they tried, no-one could get past him.

'What is this guy doing here?' his new teammates wondered. 'He should be playing for Real Madrid or Manchester United, not Celtic!'

And no-one could get the ball off him either. Wouldn't he be wasted in defence? With his touch and technique, Virgil could easily move into midfield instead. Whatever position he played, Celtic would need to make the most of his time at the club.

'Enjoy yourself,' Lennon told his new star signing. 'I've got a feeling that you won't be here for long!'

CHAPTER 13

A STRONG START IN SCOTLAND

Virgil's first year at Celtic was an all-round success. Not only did he become the club's rock at the back, but he also showed his quality in attack.

Before all that, however, Virgil needed a bit of time to get used to life in Scotland. He had to adapt to a new country, a new league, the sometimes dreary weather and the always difficult accent. When he first arrived, he thought that he spoke English pretty well. But when his Scottish teammates started talking, he found that he could hardly understand a word!

'Could you say that again,' Virgil asked politely at first, 'and a little more slowly this time?'

But when he still didn't understand, he decided it was easier to just nod instead.

On the pitch, Virgil settled in quickly at Celtic. His class was clear right from his debut – a 2–0 win against Aberdeen – but he had to wait three long months to score his first goal for his new club. Finally, away at Ross County, he went forward for a free kick and jumped the highest to meet Emilio Izaguirre's cross. His header bounced down, hit the post and then the back of the net.

Goooooooooooooooooooooaaaaaaaaaaaaaaaalllllllllllll lllllllllllllll!!!!!!!!!!!!!!!!!!!!!

There was no big celebration from Virgil, just a casual jog towards the Celtic fans near the corner flag. He was a cool guy, after all.

'At last, big man!' his captain Scott Brown cried out.

Virgil only had to wait another twelve minutes to score his second Celtic goal. As Charlie Mulgrew curled a corner into the box, he made a late sprint from the edge of the area to the six-yard box and flicked the ball down into the bottom corner. He was a brilliant attacking defender, especially for a centre-back. *2–0!* On the touchline, Lennon clapped and smiled. What a signing!

Now that Virgil was off the mark, there was no stopping him. Against St. Johnstone, he got the ball in his own half and dribbled forward, through one tackle, then another, then another. What a run! He made it look so easy. He was into the penalty area now, and he calmly poked the ball past the keeper.

Goooooooooooooooooooooaaaaaaaaaaaaaaaallllllllllll llllllllllllllllll!!!!!!!!!!!!!!!!!!!!

It was a wondergoal, the best that Virgil had scored since his days on the Cruyff court in Breda. Even Ronaldinho or Messi would have been proud of a solo run like that. As he ran past the celebrating Celtic fans, Virgil made a heart symbol with his hands. He was having so much fun playing for this football club.

'Put van Dijk up front!' many of the supporters suggested after that.

But if they did that, Celtic would lose their best centre-back! When he played in defence, Virgil could star at both ends of the field. Against Hibernian, he kept the strikers quiet and then fired an unstoppable free kick into the top corner. The shot was so good that Lennon got up off the bench to give him a standing ovation.

'Is there anything this guy can't do?' his manager wondered to himself.

Celtic still hadn't lost a single league match all season. And as the games went by, they became even harder to beat. Virgil formed a formidable centre-back partnership with Efe Ambrose, a powerful defender from Nigeria. Once they got used to playing together, no-one could get past them. And if they ever did, they had keeper Fraser Forster to beat. From December until late February, Celtic's defence didn't concede a single goal. The clean sheets just kept coming and coming:

5–0, 1–0, 2–0, 1–0, 1–0, 1–0, 4–0, 3–0...

After an amazing 1,256 minutes of Scottish Premier League football, Celtic finally let a goal in against Aberdeen, but that was only because Virgil had been sent off for a late, last-ditch tackle.

'Sorry, guys, I let you down there,' he apologised

to his fellow defenders in the dressing room afterwards. Although they had set a new club record together, he still felt bad about bringing their brilliant run to an end.

'Hey, just don't do it again, okay?' Fraser said with a reassuring smile. 'We need you out there on the pitch!'

It was true; what would Celtic do without their star centre-back? Virgil returned from suspension just in time for their trip to Partick Thistle in late March 2014. With a victory, they would be crowned the Champions of Scotland again, with a whopping seven games to spare. The title hadn't been won that early since 1929.

'Come on, let's do this!' Scott roared as the players left the dressing room.

Virgil couldn't wait to win his first major trophy as a professional footballer. He had waited a long time for this moment. In the fourth minute, he passed the ball forward to Kris Commons, who played it out wide to Emilio, who crossed it into Anthony Stokes. *1–0!*

By the end of the game, it was 5–1 to Celtic, the perfect way to win their third title in a row. At the final whistle, Virgil and his teammates hugged and celebrated their success. Yes, glory was expected when you played for a top team in Scotland, but they had worked really hard all season long to reach their target.

When the players returned to the dressing room, Virgil was one of the first to put on a special green T-shirt with '14 CHAMPIONS' written on the back. He wrapped a Celtic scarf around his neck, and jumped up on the benches to sing along with all the others:

Campeones, Campeones, Olé! Olé! Olé!

For the proper trophy presentation, however, Virgil had to wait until after Celtic's final league game of the season, at home against Dundee United. Following a comfortable 3–1 victory, the pitch was cleared, and a green-and-white stage was set up in the centre circle.

Then one by one, the players walked up to collect their winners' medals. When it was Virgil's turn, he waved to the supporters and to his family and friends in the crowd. It was lovely to share this special day with them all.

At last, it was time for the main event.

'10, 9, 8, 7…,' the Celtic fans counted down, '…3, 2, 1… HURRAAAAAAAYYY!'

As Scott lifted the SPFL trophy high into the sky, Virgil was right behind him with his arms up in the air. Winning was simply the greatest feeling in the world.

Virgil had really enjoyed his first season at Celtic. Not only had he lifted the league title, but he had also been selected for the Scottish Team of the Year and named on the shortlist for the Player of the Year award. All at the age of only twenty-one.

Hopefully, there would be plenty more success to come. Although it sometimes looked like it was all too easy for him, Virgil was still learning lots. And best of all, he was gaining valuable European experience.

CHAPTER 14

EUROPEAN EXPERIENCE

With a cheeky nutmeg, Andrés Iniesta escaped past Efe and into the Celtic six-yard box. 'Uh-oh,' the fans thought, but out of nowhere, another defender slid across to make the saving tackle. Who was it? Virgil, of course!

Celtic Park let out an almighty roar. The atmosphere in the stadium was always great, but on big European nights like this one in October 2013, it was electric. Thanks to their top Dutch defender, they were still drawing 0–0 with Barcelona.

Come on, Celtic!

Virgil felt another rush of adrenaline flow through his body. This was what playing professional football was all about – the crowds, the competition, the pressure to perform. He was born to play on the biggest stage.

The Champions League was proving to be just the challenge that Virgil needed. Despite a strong performance against AC Milan at the San Siro, Celtic had conceded two cruel, late goals. Arghhhhh! That was a painful learning experience for all of them.

But now, they had the chance to bounce back against Barcelona. Although Messi was missing through injury, the Spanish side still had Iniesta, Neymar Jr, Cesc Fàbregas and Pedro, plus Alexis Sánchez on the bench.

Not one of them could get past Virgil, though. He was having one of his greatest games in a Celtic shirt. He had too much speed and strength for the Barcelona forwards, and he always seemed to know what they would do next. He won every header and intercepted every through-ball.

From start to finish, the Celtic fans cheered their beloved defender on.

Olé, Olé, Olé, Olé, Virgil van Dijk, Dijk!

With him at the back, they believed they could beat any team in the world.

Celtic looked pretty comfortable for the first sixty minutes, but then Scott got sent off. Suddenly, that changed everything. Could they really hold on against Barcelona, with only ten men? Virgil did his best. He blocked shots from Xavi, then Pedro, and then Neymar Jr.

Olé, Olé, Olé, Olé, Virgil van Dijk, Dijk!

But the Barcelona attacks kept coming. In the seventy-fifth minute, Sánchez got the ball out wide on the right wing and crossed it into the box. The Celtic defence thought they had it covered, but no, somehow Fàbregas had a free header at the back post. 1–0!

As the ball landed in the back of the net, Virgil turned away in anger. For once, he was lost for words on the football pitch. Who was meant to be marking Fàbregas, and why had they let him escape? One mistake and all their hard work was wasted!

It was another painful Champions League learning experience for Celtic, and there were more to come.

In the away game at the Nou Camp two months later, Barcelona thrashed them 6–1, even without Messi. And it could have been even worse if it wasn't for Virgil.

Against the best attackers in the world, the Dutch defender raised his game to the highest level. Neymar Jr dribbled forward, with Xavi to his right. It was two against one, but Virgil waited for the Brazilian to make his move. On the edge of the Celtic penalty area, Neymar Jr played the pass, but Virgil read the situation superbly. In a flash, he turned and stretched out a leg to beat Xavi to the ball.

'Yes, that's it!' the Celtic supporters cheered.

Again and again, Virgil dealt with the Barcelona danger. But he couldn't do it all on his own.

'Come on, help me out here!' he screamed at his struggling teammates, as yet another goal went in.

Even in a 6–1 defeat, Virgil put on a one-man defensive masterclass. He didn't deserve to be on the losing team, and he definitely didn't deserve to score an own goal. But football could be a cruel game sometimes. Virgil had learnt that a long time ago. And if he wanted to be the best, he had to battle against the best. As frustrating as it felt, it was all good European experience for him.

'You were magnificent tonight,' Virgil's manager told him after the match. 'You should be really proud of that performance.'

Unfortunately, that was the end of Celtic's Champions League adventure. The next season, they entered the Europa League instead. Virgil and his teammates still got to play against quality opponents, though. After getting through the group stage, they travelled to the San Siro Stadium again, this time to take on Inter Milan.

Could Virgil put on another excellent European performance? He was up against Mauro Icardi, one of the top young strikers in the world.

'Let the battle begin!' Virgil thought to himself.

He was usually so composed in defence, but for once, he lost his cool.

In the twenty-seventh minute, Virgil rushed into a challenge on Inter's second striker, Rodrigo Palacio, and fouled him from behind. The referee blew his whistle – free kick and a yellow card!

Although Virgil thought a booking was a bit harsh, he didn't argue. He just got on with the game, knowing that he had to be more careful now...

But in the thirty-sixth minute, Icardi got to the ball first and flicked it on. As Virgil tried to outmuscle him, he tripped the Inter striker, who fell to the floor. The referee blew his whistle again – another free kick and another yellow card!

As the official reached for the red card in his pocket, Virgil shook his head in disbelief. 'No way, you can't send me off for that!'

But he could and he did. Celtic battled on without their star centre-back, but it was no use, and Inter scored a late winner to knock them out of the Europa League. As the goal went in, Virgil's shoulders slumped.

'It's all my fault,' he thought to himself. 'Why didn't I wait like I usually do? Only fools rush in!'

Oh well – it was another European experience for Virgil to learn from.

CHAPTER 15

SIGNING FOR SOUTHAMPTON

As Virgil relaxed in the sun on his summer holidays,
he thought again about his footballing future. He had
just turned twenty-four, which felt like an important
age. He was no longer a promising young player; he
was now in his prime. So, was it time to move on
and test himself in one of Europe's top leagues?

'With your talent, you could go anywhere you
want!' his friends and family reminded him.

Virgil had really enjoyed his two seasons at Celtic.
He had won his first professional trophies there:
two Scottish League titles and a League Cup too.
He had scored his best ever goal and played some
of his greatest games, especially in Europe.

Virgil loved the club dearly: the coaches, the players and, of course, the fantastic fans. It really felt like one big family. Celtic were the team who had taken a chance on him when others wouldn't, and he was so grateful for that. He had learned so much, in the Champions League in particular.

'But now I want to play in the Premier League,' Virgil admitted to his best friends at the club.

They all understood. As Lennon had said to him when he first arrived from Groningen, no-one expected a superstar like Virgil to stay at Celtic for long.

'Well, let's wait and see whether we make it to the Champions League Group Stage,' he decided eventually.

In the qualifying rounds, Celtic stormed past Stjarnan from Iceland and then squeezed past Qarabağ from Azerbaijan.

'Yeess!' Virgil shouted, pumping his fists at the fans. After another strong defensive display, they had secured a win *and* a clean sheet.

Celtic were now just one round away from reaching the Champions League group stage.

The last team standing in their way were Malmö.
Celtic won the first leg 3–2 at home at Celtic Park,
but in the second leg in Sweden, they threw it away.

'Nooo!' Virgil groaned, swiping angrily at the air.
'Come on, we're better than that!'

Sadly, Celtic would be playing in the Europa
League instead. But would their star centre-back still
be there? It looked very unlikely because Virgil had
received an interesting offer from England.

Southampton weren't in the Champions League,
or the Europa League, but they were doing well in
the Premier League. The Saints had finished eighth
and then seventh in the last two seasons. And their
manager? The ex-Feyenoord manager and Dutch
defensive legend, Ronald Koeman, who was also the
son of Martin, the man who had first scouted Virgil
at Groningen!

It was simply meant to be. Southampton needed a
new defender because their Belgian centre-back Toby
Alderweireld had moved to Tottenham. And when
the club scouts showed him their shortlist, Koeman
knew instantly which one he wanted: Virgil!

The Saints manager thought back to that awful day when Groningen thrashed his Feyenoord side 6–1. Despite the team's attacking quality, it was their tall, classy centre-back who had been the standout player.

'If he keeps improving,' Koeman had said to himself, 'he could be the next superstar Dutch defender.'

Well now, three years later, it was time for Koeman to help turn Virgil into a Premier League superstar. In early September 2015, Celtic accepted Southampton's offer of £13 million. That was a lot of money for a player arriving from Scotland, but it was worth it, the Saints were sure.

'This is the perfect step for me right now,' Virgil told the journalists when his transfer was announced. He knew all about the club's reputation for developing top young players – Gareth Bale, Theo Walcott, Adam Lallana, Luke Shaw. Hopefully, he would be next. 'I just want to play as much as possible and show everyone what I'm capable of.'

Although the season had already started, Virgil was able to settle in quickly at Southampton, just like he had at Celtic. It helped that he had a Dutch manager and some Dutch teammates too.

'Welkom!' said midfielder Jordy Clasie, who had arrived from Feyenoord.

'Hallo!' said defender Cuco Martina, who had arrived from FC Twente.

Plus, there was also a familiar face from Virgil's Groningen days.

'Dušan!' he shouted, giving his old friend a big hug.

It also helped that Virgil was a confident character and a very talented footballer. Yes, he was the new kid at the club, but that didn't mean he was going to keep quiet and show too much respect to his new teammates. He wanted to impress everyone with his all-round game: his strength, speed, skill and positioning. It didn't take long. By the end of his first training session, the Southampton players were delighted with their new signing.

'I'm so glad he's on our team,' the Saints attackers said to each other. 'It must be horrible playing against him in a real match!'

Salomón Rondón and Rickie Lambert found that out for themselves when Virgil made his

Southampton debut against West Brom. As hard as
the strikers tried, they couldn't find a way past him,
and the game finished 0–0. Virgil was delighted
to get a clean sheet straight away. He had passed
his first Premier League test with top marks. He
felt comfortable already, as if he had been playing
alongside José Fonte for years.

'What a start!' his centre-back partner cheered as
they high-fived.

And two weeks later, Virgil gave the Saints fans
even more to cheer about. At home at the St Mary's
Stadium, he went forward for an early corner against
Swansea City. As James Ward-Prowse's cross came
in, Virgil made his move towards the front post.
Then he leapt up and guided a header down into
the bottom corner. He was so good at that attacking
header. *1–0!*

*Goooooooooooooooooooooaaaaaaaaaaaaaaaaallllllllllll
llllllllllllllll!!!!!!!!!!!!!!!!!!!!!*

Virgil had his first Premier League goal! He ran
over to the Saints fans behind the goal with his arms
out wide – he was becoming a club hero already!

Usually he was so calm and composed out on the football pitch, but this was a very special moment. By the corner flag, Virgil jumped up and punched the air with passion.

'Come on!'

In the second half, Dušan made it 2–0 and Sadio Mané made it 3–0. Southampton were flying, just like their new star centre-back.

CHAPTER 16

DUTCH DEBUT AT LAST!

In the autumn of 2015, a few weeks after his move to Southampton, Virgil finally got the phone call that he had been waiting years for – he had been selected to play for the Netherlands national team!

'Thank you very much, it's a real honour,' he told the new coach, Danny Blind, trying to sound as calm and polite as possible.

As soon as the call was over, however, Virgil danced around the room, yelling at the top of his voice. 'I'm going to be an international!'

It was his childhood dream come true. Although he was very proud of having family from Suriname, he had always wanted to play football for the

Netherlands. It was his home, the country where he had lived for most of his life. He couldn't wait to pull on the famous orange shirt again, and this time, for the senior team.

Back in 2011, when he was first starting out at Groningen, Virgil had played for the Netherlands Under-19s and then the Under-21s. His international career had been going well, until one terrible game against Italy.

That day, Lorenzo Insigne and Ciro Immobile destroyed the young Dutch defence. The humiliating defeat was far from just Virgil's fault, but he did miss a few crucial tackles. And so when the next Netherlands Under-21 squad was picked, his name wasn't there.

'Never mind,' Virgil thought, trying to stay positive. He would just focus on his club football instead.

Three years later, there had been talk of a call-up to the Netherlands senior squad for the 2014 World Cup. At that time, Virgil was playing well at Celtic and the national coach, Louis van Gaal, needed new defenders.

'Take a look at van Dijk,' his coaches suggested. 'The kid's got real quality.'

But in the end, van Gaal decided that starring in the Scottish League didn't mean that Virgil was good enough to go to the World Cup. He picked Terence Kongolo and Bruno Martins Indi instead.

'Never mind,' Virgil thought, trying to stay positive. It hurt, but he believed that if he kept focusing on his club football, one day his international call-up would come.

And now, at last, in October 2015, it had arrived. He was going to make his Dutch debut! For the first time in ages, Virgil was a little nervous as he joined up with the squad for the UEFA Euro 2016 qualifier against Kazakhstan. Would the senior players like Robin van Persie and Wesley Sneijder welcome him into the team?

Virgil didn't need to be nervous, though. He was one of many new, young players in the squad, and he was already friends with Gini Wijnaldum and Daley Blind from the Under-21s. They were all part of the Netherlands' exciting next generation.

'Let's show we're ready to shine!' the young Dutch stars declared.

Virgil started at centre-back alongside Jeffrey Bruma, the defender that PSV had chosen to sign instead of him. There were no hard feelings, though; they were national teammates now and they had to work together.

'That's your man, Jeff!'

'Step up, Virg!'

For the first ninety minutes, however, they didn't have much to do in defence. Georginio scored the first goal and Wesley scored the second. The Netherlands were cruising to a comfortable victory on Virgil's debut.

But comfortable could be dangerous for Virgil. That's when his concentration slipped, and he made silly mistakes. Sadly, he didn't have his old coach Liekken's words playing in his head:

'STAY FOCUSED!'

In the last minute, a cross came in and Virgil got caught in the middle between the two Kazakhstan strikers. One headed the ball across to the other. *GOAL!*

'Noooooo!' Virgil shouted, kicking the air in frustration. It was not the way that he wanted his first game to end. That was the end of their clean sheet, but at least he still had a victory on his Dutch debut.

Three days later, Virgil's second cap ended in a disappointing defeat. At half-time against the Czech Republic, the Netherlands were already 2–0 down.

For the first goal, Virgil got dragged out of defence and dived into a tackle. He didn't get the ball and he couldn't get back in time to stop Pavel Kadeřábek from scoring either.

'Why did I do that?' Virgil screamed up at the sky. He was usually so cool and composed.

That mistake was still on his mind ten minutes later, when Josef Šural dribbled into the box. This time, Virgil didn't dive in. He waited, blocking the passing option, but the Czech forward dribbled past him easily instead and scored.

Oh dear, what a disaster! This time, Virgil kept his eyes fixed down at his feet. He was furious with himself and he couldn't bear to see the looks that the other Netherlands players were giving him. It was such a horrible feeling to know that he was the one to blame.

'Hey, these things happen,' his manager tried to comfort him at half-time. 'Don't worry about it, just learn from it.'

In the second half, however, Blind decided to take Virgil off and bring on a striker. The Netherlands fought back after that, but they still lost 3–2.

Uh oh, was Virgil's international career about to end before it had even started? No, he was a confident character; he could come back from this. The Dutch team was going through a difficult time and he was determined to play an important part in turning things around. With the team failing to qualify for Euro 2016, its coaches were looking to the future.

CHAPTER 17

SHINING AT SOUTHAMPTON

Back in the Premier League, Virgil was doing a great job at Southampton of stopping the top strikers from scoring. At first, he watched videos to work out their weaknesses, but mostly, he just focused on using all of his own strengths.

He outmuscled Arsenal's Olivier Giroud,

He outran Everton's Romelu Lukaku,

He stuck tight to Tottenham's Harry Kane,

And he read the clever moves that Manchester United's Wayne Rooney tried to make.

Then once he had the ball, Virgil coolly dribbled forward or passed it to a teammate. Everything he did looked so effortless and classy, even the tough tackles.

'We love you, Virgil!' the Saints supporters cheered. The Dutch defender had to be one of their best signings ever.

Virgil's calm confidence was rubbing off on the rest of the Southampton team. From January 2016 onwards, they won twelve of their last eighteen league games, against the likes of Manchester United, Manchester City, Tottenham – *and* Liverpool.

'Come on you Saints!' Virgil cheered crazily when Sadio scored the winning goal against The Reds at St Mary's. From 2–0 down, they had fought their way back to a famous 3–2 victory.

Southampton now had a strong team spirit and big game players at both ends of the pitch – Sadio in attack and Virgil at the back. Together, they led their team up the table and all the way to sixth place. It was Southampton's best league finish since 1985.

For Virgil, it was the best possible start to life in the Premier League. Some critics had suggested that the step-up from Celtic would be too big for him, but he had proved them all wrong. At the club's end of season awards ceremony, he was voted the

Players' Player of the Year and the Fans' Player of the Year.

As Virgil made his way up to the stage, wearing a smart black suit and tie, the whole room began to sing:

We've got Van Dijk,
Virgil Van Dijk,
I just don't think you understand,
He's Ronald Koeman's man,
He's better than Zidane,
We've got Virgil van Dijk!!

Wow, what was he supposed to say after an amazing welcome like that? At first, all he could do was laugh and smile. He was used to hearing his song in the stadium, but not at a fancy awards ceremony!

'I want to thank everyone who voted for me,' Virgil managed to say eventually. 'I'm lost for words – I'm just very happy!'

Virgil couldn't wait for his second Premier League

season to start, but meanwhile, in the summer of 2016, Southampton said goodbye to their manager, Koeman, and more of their best players. Graziano Pellè went to China, Victor Wanyama went to Tottenham, and even Virgil's friend Sadio went to Liverpool.

'No, not you too!' Virgil joked, but really, he was happy for his friend.

Sadio smiled, 'Hey, you'll be joining me there soon – I'm sure of it!'

That sounded awesome, but to make his dream move happen, Virgil needed to keep shining at Southampton a little longer. Once again, he set about stopping the top strikers in the Premier League: Leicester City's Jamie Vardy, Manchester City's Sergio Agüero, and now Liverpool's Sadio Mané.

'Man, I hate playing against you!' his friend complained as they hugged after a hard-fought 0–0 draw at St Mary's. 'It's like you can read my mind every time!'

Virgil laughed. 'That's a shame, mate, because I love playing against you!'

And thanks to their sixth-place finish, Southampton were also through to the Europa League group stage. There, they would face Sparta Prague, Hapoel Be'er Sheva, and Virgil's old enemy, Inter Milan.

Yes, it was time for his rematch with Mauro Icardi, Inter's ace Argentinian striker. Virgil had lost their last battle by getting sent off before half-time.

'Not this time,' he told himself. 'I'm ready to get my revenge!'

However, Inter won 1–0 at the San Siro and they went 1–0 up at St Mary's too, thanks to a goal from Icardi.

'Noooooooo!' Virgil groaned, swiping the air angrily. He had been too busy stopping Inter's other striker to block the shot.

But after that goal, Virgil went into big game mode. He was determined to get Saints back into the match. In the second half, he pushed forward at every opportunity. It was like his old days as Groningen's emergency extra striker all over again.

Virgil's powerful header was saved and then Oriol Romeu's looping shot crashed against the crossbar.

Was it just Southampton's unlucky day? No, Virgil stayed in the six-yard box, waiting for the rebound. It felt like whole minutes passed by as the ball dropped… down… slowly… onto Virgil's boot. *1–1!*

Goooooooooooooooooooaaaaaaaaaaaaaaaaalllllllllllllll llllllllllllll!!!!!!!!!!!!!!!!!!!!

Yes, he had his revenge at last! Virgil ran towards the Saints supporters with one arm up in the air and a calm look on his face, like he scored goals every game.

'Let's go and win this now!' Virgil urged his teammates on. José was on the bench, so he was proudly wearing the Southampton captain's armband.

Five minutes later, Dušan's dangerous cross from the left flicked off one Inter defender, then another, and into the bottom corner. *2–1!*

Southampton were beating Inter Milan! And with Virgil leading from the back, they held on for another famous victory.

'Well done, lads, we deserved that!' he cheered at full time.

Sadly, their Europa League adventure didn't last much longer, but at least Saints had that one massive win over Inter Milan to remember forever.

And at least they had Virgil. Because in January 2017, José became the latest Saints star to leave. Not only had Virgil lost his trusty centre-back partner, but Southampton had lost their captain. Luckily, the manager Claude Puel didn't have to look very far to find the club's new leader.

'Virgil will be the new captain of the team,' he announced.

CHAPTER 18

INJURY ISSUES

Could life get any better? Virgil was now the official captain of a Premier League club and he was also one game away from playing in the League Cup final at Wembley Stadium.

'Come on, we've got to get there,' Virgil kept telling his teammates. 'We've worked so hard for this!'

Their semi-final first leg against Liverpool had been one of his greatest games in a Saints shirt. Once Nathan Redmond gave them an early lead, Southampton had lots of defending to do. But Virgil dealt with every danger superbly.

He used his size against Daniel Sturridge,

He used his strength against Adam Lallana,

He used his pace against Philippe Coutinho, and

he used his football brain against Roberto Firmino.

When Virgil played that well, no-one could get past him. The match finished 1–0 – Southampton were so close now.

'Well done, guys,' he walked around the pitch shouting, 'but we're not in the final yet!'

And before that big second leg at Anfield, Virgil and his teammates had a Premier League game to win. It was never easy against a team like Leicester City. They were solid in defence and in attack, they had Jamie Vardy, one of England's best finishers.

In the first half, Southampton looked unstoppable. Virgil kept Vardy quiet, and at the other end, James Ward-Prowse and Jay Rodríguez got the goals. 2–0 – it was looking like the perfect preparation for the Liverpool second leg.

But early in the second half, Virgil tangled with Vardy as he cleared the ball away.

'Arghhhh!' he cried out as he collapsed to the ground.

The striker's studs had caught him on the left ankle. It was an accident, but Virgil was in agony.

He sat there, wincing and waiting for the physio.

'What's wrong?' Ryan Bertrand asked. 'Do you reckon you can run it off?'

Virgil just shook his head. He didn't need to be a doctor to know that it was a serious injury.

The longer he stayed down, the more worried the Southampton fans grew. Uh oh, would their incredible captain be able to continue?

Eventually, Virgil got up and tried to play on through the pain. But it was no use; his ankle was really throbbing now. With a frustrated flail of the arm, he sat down again and started unlacing his boot.

Virgil's game was over, but what about his Wembley dream? The semi-final second leg against Liverpool was only three days away...

'No chance,' the Southampton physio told him straight away. 'I'm sorry, but it's a bad injury.'

Virgil's heart sank. 'How long will I be out for?' he asked, dreading the answer. The final was just over a month away...

'Two months, at least, I'm afraid.'

Two months? There was no way that he would

be fit in time for Wembley!

Virgil had to watch the second leg against
Liverpool from the sidelines. It wasn't easy but
Southampton did their injured captain proud. The
defence stayed strong and in the last minute, Shane
Long scored a winner. Saints were through to the
League Cup Final!

At the final whistle, Virgil clapped and cheered
and tried to keep a smile on his face. He was really
happy for his teammates, of course, but he hated
not being out there on the pitch with them.

'Don't worry, we'll win the trophy for you!'
Ryan promised.

With ten minutes to go, it was still Southampton
2 – Manchester United 2. Virgil could hardly bear
to watch as United attacked the Saints goal again
and again. Up in the stands, he headed and kicked
every ball.

'Keep going!' he muttered under his breath,
shaking his restless legs.

But just when it looked like the final would go to
extra time, Ander Herrera crossed the ball into the

box and there was Zlatan Ibrahimović, in between the Southampton centre-backs and completely unmarked. *3–2!*

Noooooooo! It was a goal that Virgil was sure that he could have stopped. If only he'd been out there captaining his team instead of recovering from injury.

Oh well – hopefully there would be other opportunities in the future. For now, Virgil had to focus on getting back to full fitness. Unfortunately, however, that took much longer than expected. Two months passed, then three, then four, and he still wasn't ready to return.

'I can't believe it's taking so long,' Virgil complained to his mum on the phone. 'At this rate, I'll probably miss most of next season too!'

It was September 2017 when he finally made his Premier League comeback, eight long months after his ankle injury. With Saints winning 1–0 with five minutes to go at Crystal Palace, the manager Mauricio Pellegrino brought Virgil on for Dušan to add some extra calm in defence.

As he ran onto the field, the Southampton supporters let out an almighty cheer. Their captain had returned at last! And even though he'd been out of the team for ages, it was like Virgil had never been away. He was still the same superstar centre-back, with the same speed, strength and great positioning. But before Virgil could really show off his full range of skills, the final whistle blew.

'Ah, it feels good to be back!' he told Ryan with a big smile as they celebrated the victory.

Virgil, however, wouldn't be staying at Southampton for long.

CHAPTER 19

WORLD'S MOST EXPENSIVE DEFENDER

Turning Liverpool into a trophy-winning team was a long-term project for their manager, Jürgen Klopp. The German couldn't just buy all the players that he wanted in one go. That would cause chaos, and besides, the club didn't have that much money to spend. So instead, he had to build his squad up slowly and smartly, summer after summer.

In 2016, Klopp had signed Sadio, Virgil's friend from Southampton, and Gini, his Dutch international teammate.

Then in 2017, Klopp signed Mohamed Salah to play in attack, Andrew Robertson to play at left-back, and Alex Oxlade-Chamberlain to play all over the pitch.

They were all brilliant buys, but there was still one key position that Liverpool were desperate to fill that summer – a star centre-back. They had Dejan Lovren, Joël Matip and Ragnar Klavan, but something was still missing. The team had conceded over ninety league goals in the last two seasons. That was way too many.

'Come on Klopp, we need a star centre-back!' their fans cried out.

What Liverpool needed was a world-class defender, a real leader at the back who could help make everyone around him better. And their manager knew exactly who he wanted.

Klopp had watched Virgil shine so many times, against his Liverpool team but also against AC Milan and Barcelona in the Champions League for Celtic. He really admired the Dutch defender's composure and confidence, as well as his speed and strength. He had it all.

'Virgil's the perfect fit for us,' the Liverpool manager declared. 'We need the best, and that's him!'

But the problem was that he wasn't available at

the right price. During the summer of 2017, it looked certain that Virgil would leave Southampton, either to go to Liverpool or to Chelsea. Both clubs were willing to pay a massive £60 million, but Saints said no. They wanted even more for their incredible captain.

'What?' Virgil responded in disbelief. 'That's not fair – they're making sure that no club can afford me!'

He loved Southampton and he would always be grateful to the club for giving him his first experience of Premier League football. But now, Virgil was ready to take his next step. Liverpool were offering him the chance to play in the Champions League again. He was twenty-six years old; what if he didn't get that chance again?

Earlier that summer, Virgil had travelled to Cardiff with friends to watch the 2017 Champions League Final between Real Madrid and Juventus. As he soaked up the amazing atmosphere and the fantastic football, he had dared to dream that one day, he might still get to play in a big game like that. And as he left the stadium that night, he met a group of Liverpool fans who wanted him to join their club.

Surely that wasn't just a coincidence? It was meant to be!

'I'm sorry but I want to leave,' Virgil told his manager, Pellegrino, firmly.

But Southampton wouldn't budge, and Liverpool didn't have enough money to make a bigger offer. So when the new Premier League season started, Virgil had no choice but to stay where he was. He wasn't happy about it, but he got on with being the club captain. What else could he do? After a long injury, he just wanted to play football again.

Virgil's Liverpool dream wasn't over yet, though. Klopp could have signed another, cheaper centre-back instead, but no, he waited patiently for his first choice. He was building the best squad possible to challenge for all the top trophies. They would just have to find the money for Virgil somewhere, somehow…

In the end, it came from Philippe Coutinho's £130-million move to Barcelona. Once they knew it was a done deal, Liverpool went back with a much bigger, final offer for Virgil, one that Southampton couldn't say no to – £75 million!

Wow, when the new transfer window opened on 1 January 2018, Virgil would be the new most expensive defender in the world.

'What a waste of money!' some supporters argued. 'In his last game for Southampton, they let in four goals. Against Leicester!'

'Yeah, and he's only ever played six games in the Champions League. For Celtic! Is he really that good?'

Even Alan Shearer wasn't so sure: 'Van Dijk is a good player, yes, but for £75 million? No, he's not worth it at all.'

Virgil knew that he had a lot to prove at Liverpool, but he believed in himself. He always had, even when he wasn't doing well at Willem II, and when he got ill at Groningen. Now that he had arrived at one of the biggest clubs in the world, it was time to show that he belonged there.

'I'm delighted and honoured to become a Liverpool player,' Virgil announced proudly. 'I can't wait to pull on the famous red shirt for the first time in front of the Kop.'

But what number would he wear on the back of

that shirt? Virgil had chosen '17' at Southampton, but that was already taken. Gini was '5' and Dejan was '6'.

'I'll take 4,' he decided.

That was the number worn by the Liverpool centre-back, Sami Hyypiä. And like Virgil, Hyypiä had also started his career at Willem II. It was meant to be.

From day one, Virgil felt right at home. Liverpool was one big family, like Celtic. He already knew Gini from the Netherlands national team, plus Sadio from Southampton and Andy from his time in Scotland. He also shared an agent with Jordan Henderson. It was meant to be.

Everyone was so friendly! And at the end of Virgil's very first training session, he found a club legend waiting for him.

'Welcome to the greatest team in the world!' Kenny Dalglish greeted him warmly. 'Here's my phone number. If you need anything, just call.'

Virgil wanted to get his Liverpool career started straight away. His ankle injury was gone, and he was raring to go. Their next match was only a few days

away. And it wasn't just any old match; it was the
Merseyside derby against Everton.

CHAPTER 20

MERSEYSIDE DERBY DEBUT

5 January 2018, Anfield

Virgil was desperate to make his Liverpool debut in the Merseyside derby. It was the third round of the FA Cup rather than a Premier League fixture, but still, playing against their local rivals Everton was always one of the most important matches of the season.

'Hmm, I'm not sure that's a great idea,' Klopp told him. 'You've only just arrived, and you need time to settle in. Look, I'll put you on the bench and we'll see how the game goes.'

Virgil accepted his manager's decision, but suddenly everything changed during the warm-up.

Dejan had a tight hamstring, so he moved to the bench. That meant Virgil would be starting alongside Joël instead.

'Thanks, boss – I'm ready!'

He couldn't wait. Virgil wasn't nervous about his Merseyside derby debut – he was never nervous. He was just super-excited. He gave the 'This is Anfield' sign a quick tap as he walked down the tunnel and out onto the pitch.

Wow, the noise was incredible! It was great to hear 'You'll Never Walk Alone' again, a song the fans also sang at Celtic. Looking up, Virgil could see the red and white of Liverpool all around him – shirts, scarves, flags and banners. And some of them had his name on already! It was a very proud day for him and his family.

'Look, Mum, I made it!' he wanted to shout out. 'Just like I always said I would!'

By the time the game kicked off, Virgil felt calm and focused again. He kept talking to his teammates, pointing and organising them into position. It didn't matter that he was the new kid; it was his job to lead the Liverpool defence. That's why they had paid £75 million for him.

It wasn't a perfect performance, but as the game went on, Virgil grew in confidence. He won his battles with Dominic Calvert-Lewin and worked well with Joël. Playing for a top team like Liverpool, he had more of the ball than ever. It was a fun chance for him to show off his skills. Most of the time, he kept his passing pretty simple, but sometimes, he dared to play long diagonal balls out to Roberto or Sadio on the wings.

'Excellent!' Klopp encouraged him from the sidelines.

By half-time, Liverpool were winning 1–0 thanks to a James Milner penalty. They looked pretty comfortable, but Virgil knew that he couldn't relax. He didn't want to make any mistakes, especially not against Everton. He was aiming to become a Liverpool hero, not a villain.

Early in the second half, Virgil went up for a free kick. Although Klopp had signed him for his defending, he could be dangerous in attack too. At

six-foot four, he was the tallest player in the box.
How amazing would it be if he could score on
his Merseyside derby debut?

Virgil made a late run towards the six-yard box,
watching Alex's cross all the way. It was coming
straight towards him! At the right moment, he
leapt up high and headed the ball downwards.
The power was perfect, but sadly it flew straight
at Jordan Pickford.

'Ahhhhh!' the Liverpool supporters sighed in
disappointment.

'That was your chance and you blew it!' Virgil
scolded himself as he raced back into position.
Hopefully, there was still time left to get another...

But from Liverpool's next corner, Everton
launched a lightning-quick counter-attack. Virgil
and his fellow defenders sprinted back as fast as
they could and managed to stop Phil Jagielka from
shooting. Problem solved? No, because no-one had
spotted Gylfi Sigurdsson's run from deep. Except
Jagielka, who played the ball back for Sigurdsson to
strike first time into the bottom corner. *1–1!*

Virgil was annoyed at himself for following
the ball, but most of all, he was furious with his
midfielders: 'Why wasn't anyone tracking that run?'
he shouted up into the Anfield air.

Virgil could already see that he had lots of work
to do if he was going to turn Liverpool into a mean
defensive machine. But for now, he had a Merseyside
derby to win. Every time he went forward for a free
kick or a corner, he was causing problems for the
Everton defence. He could feel a goal coming...

However, time was running out for Virgil to
become a Liverpool hero on day one. With five
minutes to go, he waited in the crowded box for
Alex's curling cross. It was another good one and
this time, Pickford came off his line to try to punch
the ball away. Virgil, however, was much bigger and
stronger. He beat the Everton keeper to the ball and
steered a glancing header down into the bottom
corner. *2–1!*

*Goooooooooooooooooooooaaaaaaaaaaaaaaaallllllllllll
lllllllllllll!!!!!!!!!!!!!!!!!!!!*

Anfield exploded with noise and emotion. What a

football fairy tale – Virgil had scored the winning goal on his Merseyside derby debut! He ran towards the corner flag, roaring at the fans, and then slid across the grass on his knees. It was the new greatest feeling in the world.

'Yes, Virg, you beauty!' Alex screamed, wrapping him in a big bear hug.

Soon, Virgil was at the centre of a huge team huddle. At the final whistle, he looked up at the sky with an enormous grin on his face. Debuts didn't get any better than that. Even in his wildest dreams, he hadn't imagined scoring the winner in the Merseyside derby.

As he punched the air with both fists, Virgil thought to himself, 'I've got a really good feeling about playing for this club!'

CHAPTER 21

SO CLOSE IN THE CHAMPIONS LEAGUE

After that amazing Merseyside derby debut, Virgil travelled to Dubai with the Liverpool squad for a warm weather training camp. It was a great chance for him to get to know his new teammates and to adapt to the new team tactics.

At his previous clubs, Virgil had played in defences that dropped deeper and deeper when their opponents were on the attack. There would be no sitting back at Liverpool, though. Klopp wanted his team to press high up the pitch, starting with Sadio, Roberto and Mohamed in attack and ending with Virgil in defence on the halfway line. That way, when they won the ball back, they would be in a better position to counter-attack and score goals.

'I know it feels risky right now,' the manager explained, 'but I believe in you. You read the game so well and even if you do make mistakes, you're quick enough to chase down any striker. And don't forget you've still got a sweeper keeper behind you!'

At first, it did feel a bit dangerous, but Virgil soon got used to Liverpool's high defensive line. It turned out that he was the perfect man for the job – calm, clever and excellent at decision-making. He very rarely got things wrong these days.

'How did you know I was going to do that?' Sadio moaned as Virgil made yet another tackle in training.

He laughed, 'I can read you like a book, mate!'

Virgil was already loving life at Liverpool and soon it was time for his Champions League return. He couldn't wait to hear the anthem again and feel the excitement of the big European nights. That was why he had said goodbye to Southampton and hello to a new life at Liverpool.

With Virgil leading from the back, the team was

on fire. In the Round of 16, they thrashed Porto 5–0 and then in the first leg of the quarter-finals, they beat their Premier League rivals Manchester City 3–0 at Anfield. It was one of the best team performances that Virgil had ever been a part of. Could Liverpool go all the way in the Champions League?

'We can't get carried away,' Klopp warned his players. 'First of all, we need to stay strong in the second leg. City aren't finished yet!'

At Anfield, Virgil didn't have that much defending to do, but he was much, much busier at the Etihad. As soon as the match kicked off, City pushed forward on the attack with Raheem Sterling, Gabriel Jesus, Leroy Sané, Kevin De Bruyne, and David and Bernardo Silva.

Wow, it was going to be a very long night for the Liverpool defence. As Virgil went to clear the ball down the left wing, Sterling rushed in and shoved him over.

'Hey, that's a foul!' Virgil cried out on the floor, but the referee signalled, 'Play on!', and City had the ball.

Uh oh, with their star centre-back out of position, Liverpool were in big trouble. In a flash, Fernandinho passed to Sterling who crossed to Jesus, who was in exactly the place where Virgil would have been. *1–0 to City!*

Virgil waved his arms furiously at the linesman and then the referee. 'No way, that has to be a free kick to us!'

But it was no use; the goal had been given. Virgil had to calm down quickly and focus on stopping City from scoring again.

He won every header against Jesus and Sterling, and every tackle too. He had the speed as well as the strength; that's what made him such a world-class centre-back. And with the pressure on, he always played his best football. The fans trusted him to lead them into the Champions League semi-finals.

In the second half, City pushed further and further forward, looking for another goal. They left big gaps at the back and Liverpool's front three took full advantage.

Mohamed reacted first to a loose ball in the box

and chipped it over the diving defender. *1–1!*

Roberto pounced on Nicolás Otamendi's mistake and slid a shot past Ederson. *2–1!*

Even when Sergio Agüero came on, City still couldn't score past Virgil and the rest of the team. They stood together, united, a strong wall of red shirts. Game over – Liverpool were into the Champions League semi-finals!

Next up: Roma. Liverpool won the first leg 5–2 and, despite some tense moments in the second leg in Italy, they eventually made it through… to the final! Virgil couldn't believe it; in his first half-season at the club, he was going to play in a Champions League Final.

'Bring it on!' he roared.

Liverpool's opponents would be Real Madrid, who had won the trophy for the last two years in a row. It was going to be their toughest challenge yet, but Klopp's players were full of confidence. They had got this far, so why not believe?

'We have nothing to fear!' their manager told them in the dressing room in Kiev. 'We deserve to be here, and when we're at our best, we can beat anyone!'

There would be fascinating battles at both ends of the pitch.

At one end:

MOHAMED VS SERGIO RAMOS, one of Virgil's rivals as the best defender in the world. His style was very different, though; he was all about aggression and tough tackling.

And at the other:

VIRGIL VS CRISTIANO RONALDO!

He couldn't wait to test himself against one of the greatest footballers of all time. Just like on his Liverpool debut, Virgil felt excited, not nervous.

'I wouldn't miss this for the world!'

Whenever the pressure was on, Virgil liked to think back to his younger days on the Cruyff court in Breda. Yes, football was about winning, but it was also about having fun. He played the beautiful game because he enjoyed it. And although the Champions League Final was really important, it was just another match. It was nice to know that there were more important things in life, especially his wife, Rike, and his daughter, Nila. Family came first, even before football.

'But I'd really love to lift that trophy!' Virgil thought to himself in the tunnel.

That feeling grew stronger and stronger as he walked out onto the pitch, past the trophy. Yes, he was ready to make his family proud, and all the Liverpool fans too, of course. They held up their red scarves with hope and excitement, bringing the Anfield roar all the way to the Ukraine.

Liverpool! Liverpool! Liverpool!

For the first fifteen minutes, The Reds were on top. The Madrid defenders were really struggling to cope with the speed and skill of Roberto, Mohamed and Sadio. But every time they got a goalscoring chance, their shot was blocked, or saved, or missed the target.

So close! With each wasted opportunity, the Liverpool supporters grew more and more restless in their seats. 'We *have* to take one of these soon!'

If not, Real Madrid had players who could really punish them on the counter-attack...

Ronaldo raced down the right wing at top speed, and into the penalty area. Uh oh, Robbo was out of position, so it was all up to Virgil now. No problem!

Calmly, he jogged over towards Ronaldo, trying to push him as wide as possible.

'Whatever you do,' Virgil kept telling himself, 'don't dive in!'

Just as the Real Madrid striker was about to shoot, he slid in front of him. He didn't manage to block the shot, but he didn't have to. Ronaldo blazed it high over the bar.

'Come on, concentrate!' Virgil urged his teammates. Ronaldo might miss once, but he hardly ever missed twice.

A few minutes later, Liverpool's job became a whole lot harder. Their top scorer Mohamed had to go off with a shoulder injury after an awkward challenge from Ramos. In the stands, some of the fans stood there with their hands on their heads, as if they'd already lost the match.

'Keep going, we can still win this!' Virgil called out as inspiration.

At half-time, the score was still 0–0. Liverpool were playing well; they just had to stay focused and not make any silly mistakes...

It all started with a simple long ball over the top. Virgil jogged back casually, knowing that his goalkeeper would reach it long before Real Madrid's Karim Benzema. The next part, however, was totally unexpected. As Loris Karius tried to throw it out to Dejan, Benzema stuck out a leg and deflected the ball into the net. *1–0!*

Virgil didn't see the first part because he was too busy organising his teammates, but he turned around in time to see the ball roll slowly over the goal line. He stood there, frozen in shock. In all his years of football, he had never seen anything like it. What on earth had just happened?

Ultimately, it didn't matter; all that mattered was that Liverpool were losing and they had forty minutes left to fight back.

'Let's go, let's go!' Virgil encouraged from defence.

With Mohamed missing, who was going to step up and score the equaliser? Virgil was there in the box for the corner, but this time, it was Dejan who headed it goalwards and Sadio who tapped it past the keeper. *1–1!*

'Yes, Sadio!' Virgil screamed as he chased after his friend. Thanks to him, it was game on again!

Unfortunately, Liverpool's joy lasted less than ten minutes. Marcelo crossed from the left and Gareth Bale scored a breathtaking bicycle-kick. *2–1!*

For Virgil, it was another horrible moment where he could only stand still and watch the goal go in, as if in slow motion. It was an unstoppable strike, worthy of winning any football match.

Was there still time for Liverpool to fight back once more? No, but there was time for another bad mistake. Bale hit a swerving shot from thirty yards out and somehow it slipped straight through poor Loris's hands. *3–1!*

Until that moment, Virgil had kept believing. However, as the ball hit the back of the net, he felt his last bit of hope fade away. His head dropped and his shoulders slumped. Liverpool had come so close, they had fought so hard, but ultimately, their 2018 Champions League dream was over.

CHAPTER 22

KOEMAN'S CAPTAIN

It was a long and difficult flight home for the Liverpool players after losing the 2018 Champions League Final. No-one knew what to say – what could they say? It was over and they were all too devastated for words.

Luckily for Virgil, he soon had other football to focus on. Two days later, he was off to Slovakia to play for the Netherlands national team.

Although they had failed to qualify for the 2018 World Cup as well as Euro 2016, things were starting to look a bit better under their new manager, Ronald Koeman. Virgil was delighted to be working with his old Southampton boss again, who had a very special job for him to do:

'I want you to be the new captain of the Netherlands national team.'

Wow, another childhood dream come true! It was the new proudest moment of Virgil's life. There was no greater honour in football than wearing the armband and leading your country.

'Thank you so much, I won't let you down!' Virgil promised.

It felt like the start of a new era for the Dutch team. Old stars like Robin van Persie, Rafael van der Vaart, Arjen Robben and Wesley Sneijder were all gone, and now it was up to the next generation. They had plenty of quality players – Memphis Depay, Quincy Promes, Ryan Babel, Daley Blind, and, of course, Gini and Virgil. It was Koeman's job to get the best out of them and turn them into a winning team, with a little help from his new captain.

The Netherlands could only draw their friendlies against Slovakia and Italy, but their performances were improving ahead of the first-ever UEFA Nations League. When Virgil saw the other two teams in League A Group 1, his eyes lit up:

The new World Cup winners France,
and the Netherlands' big local rivals, Germany.

'Four nice, easy games there!' Virgil joked with Gini.

Yes, they had some tough tests ahead, but that's exactly what the national team needed. The Dutch players couldn't wait to play against Germany in particular. There had been many famous matches between the two countries in the past – at the 1974 World Cup, at Euro 1980, and especially at Euro 1988 when the Netherlands had won 2–1 to make it through to the final. Since then, Germany had won the 2014 World Cup, but as for the Netherlands? They had won nothing.

'They think they're going to thrash us,' Virgil told his teammates, 'but we'll show them!'

Before the Germany game, however, the Netherlands faced France. For Virgil and his brilliant young centre-back partner Matthijs de Ligt, that meant defending against the skill of Antoine Griezmann, the strength of Olivier Giroud... and the speed of the next world superstar, Kylian Mbappé.

'Bring it on!' Virgil declared confidently. He loved a challenge.

In the very first minute, Mbappé dribbled into the box and nearly scored. He made up for his near-miss thirteen minutes later, and scored a goal after a mix-up in the Dutch defence. Virgil was marking Giroud, but who was marking Mbappé? It was a question that no-one could answer.

'Come on, concentrate!' Virgil urged the players around him. To succeed at international level, they had to learn their lessons quickly.

After that early error, the Netherlands did improve. Gini shot just wide, and then Ryan scored an equaliser. *1–1!*

'Yes, that's more like it!' Captain Virgil clapped and cheered.

Could they now hold on for the draw? As the cross came in, Virgil was marking Giroud in the middle again. He thought he had everything covered, but at the last second, the French striker snuck in front of him, stretched out his left leg and volleyed the ball into the net.

'Nooooooo!' Virgil groaned, turning away in anger. He was supposed to be the team leader now! It was another harsh lesson for him to learn at international level.

Although the match ended in defeat for the Netherlands, there were plenty of positives to take into the next game. The Germans were in for a surprise.

As the match kicked off at the Johan Cruyff Arena in Amsterdam, it was clear that the Dutch players were really pumped up. They were faster to the ball, and fiercer in the tackle.

'Yeahhhhhhhhh!' the fans roared them on.

In the thirtieth minute, Virgil went forward for a Dutch corner-kick. He had scored one international goal already, but that was in a friendly. This was a big game, against their biggest rivals. If he scored here, he would become a true national hero...

Ryan won the header at the back post, but the ball bounced off the crossbar and down inside the six-yard box...where Virgil was waiting to nod it in. 1–0!

Gooooooooooooooooooooaaaaaaaaaaaaaaaalllllllllllll llllllllllllll!!!!!!!!!!!!!!!!!!!!

'Come on!' Virgil shouted passionately as he leapt up and punched the air. It was a moment that he would never ever forget.

That goal gave the Netherlands so much confidence. This time, they were going to win, no matter what. They battled and battled until eventually Memphis and Gini scored to secure the victory.

It was 3–0 against Germany – what a result! Under Virgil's leadership, the Netherlands were officially back in business. With a wonderful 2–0 win over France, they moved to the top of the table. As long as they didn't lose their away game in Germany, they would be on their way to the UEFA Nations League finals...

The Germans, however, were out for revenge. In the first twenty minutes, they stormed into a 2–0 lead. When the second goal went in, Virgil looked around him. He could see that his teammates were losing hope. What could he do? He was the captain of his country now; it was his job to lead the fight-back. Virgil kept talking, organising, encouraging, and pushing his players forward. It wasn't over until it was over. With time running out, Quincy scored a screamer. *2–1!*

'Game on!' Virgil called out. 'Come on, I know we can get another one!' His country was counting on him as captain. Virgil loved the responsibility of his role; it only made him stronger. For the last minutes, he stayed up front as an emergency extra striker, just like in his old days at Groningen. And it turned out that Virgil hadn't lost his scoring touch...

In injury time, Tonny Vilhena curled one last cross into the box. A German defender flicked it on and in a flash, Virgil struck the sweetest volley of his life. The ball flew past Manuel Neuer before he could even react. *2–2!*

Gooooooooooooooooooooaaaaaaaaaaaaaaaaalllllllllllll llllllllllllllll!!!!!!!!!!!!!!!!!!!

What an emotional moment! Virgil had helped take the Netherlands national team to the UEFA Nations League finals. He stood in front of the Dutch fans and roared like a lion, like a leader.

'Yesssssssss!' Frenkie de Jong screamed out as he jumped on Virgil's back.

Six months later, in June 2019, the team travelled to the final tournament with high expectations. In the semis, hosts Portugal faced Switzerland, while the Netherlands were up against England. For Virgil and Gini, that meant going head-to-head with their Liverpool teammates Jordan Henderson and Trent Alexander-Arnold.

'May the best country win!' they teased each other in the build-up to the game.

After 120 minutes of football, that country turned out to be the Netherlands. Once again, they showed amazing team spirit to fight back, after Matthijs had conceded an early penalty. The Dutch players never gave up; Virgil wouldn't let them.

Matthijs made up for his mistake with a powerful header. *1–1!*

Then in extra time, the Netherlands forced the England defenders into two sloppy errors. *2–1, 3–1!*

Virgil was now just one game away from winning

his first international trophy. And as captain, he would be the one who got to lift it! That thought spurred him on as he led the Dutch team out in the UEFA Nations League Final against Portugal.

It was a re-match of the 2018 Champions League Final clash – Virgil vs Ronaldo. Who would win Round Two?

Unfortunately, it was Cristiano's team who came out on top again. In the sixtieth minute, Gonçalo Guedes hit a shot that was too hot for Jasper Cillessen to handle. 1–0! And that turned out to be the only goal of the game. As hard as they tried, the Netherlands couldn't quite pull off another comeback.

'Unlucky guys,' Captain Virgil comforted his teammates at the final whistle. 'Well played – we gave it everything.'

He was disappointed, but not devastated. After all, the Dutch had done so well to get past France, Germany and England to the UEFA Nations League Final. Along the way, the new Netherlands national side had proved a lot of people wrong. Now, Virgil and his talented teammates were

ready for their next major challenge: qualifying
for Euro 2020.

CHAPTER 23

PREMIER LEAGUE PLAYER OF THE YEAR

Back at Liverpool, Virgil was feeling very confident about the 2018/19 season ahead. Over the summer, the club had added what Klopp hoped were the four final pieces of the puzzle that was his best possible squad:

Stoke City's skilful winger Xherdan Shaqiri,

RB Leipzig's box-to-box dynamo Naby Keïta,

Monaco's classy passer Fabinho,

and Roma's sweeper keeper Alisson.

In Virgil's opinion, Alisson was the star signing of the summer. Yes, £55 million was a lot of money for a goalkeeper, but he was worth every penny. Having played against him in the Champions League, Virgil knew that the Brazilian was exactly what they needed: a brilliant shot-stopper, who could also tackle and pass like an outfield player.

Liverpool now had the most expensive defender in the world and the most expensive goalkeeper too.

'No-one's going to get past us now!' Joe Gomez said with a smile during preseason training.

Virgil was like a big brother to him, and a second coach when they were out on the pitch together. He was always talking to him, offering praise and advice. For youngsters like Joe and Trent, Virgil made everything seem so simple and easy.

'That's it – you've just got to read the situation. What's your best option? What's the striker going to do next?'

Virgil liked helping other players to make the most of their abilities. Football was all about working together as a team and he was determined that Liverpool would win something this season. One trophy would be good; two would be great.

The Champions League was top of Virgil's wish-list, especially after losing last year's final against Real Madrid. But he was desperate to win the

Premier League title too. In England, that's what made you a legend, and becoming a legend was what playing football was all about.

'Hey, we're definitely good enough to go for both!' Virgil discussed with Gini.

It certainly looked that way as the 2018/19 season started. Liverpool won each of their first six league games, scoring fourteen goals and only letting in two. The first came from an Alisson error, and the second was an unstoppable strike from Tottenham's Érik Lamela. Other than that, their defence looked unbeatable.

Especially Virgil – no-one could get past him. All Premier League season long, not one single player managed to get past him. He was so talented that he could stop every type of attacker:

Speedy ones like Marcus Rashford and Pierre-Emerick Aubameyang,

Strong ones like Christian Benteke and Glenn Murray,

Skilful ones like Gerard Deulofeu and Eden Hazard, and even the sharp-shooting ones like Harry Kane and Sergio Agüero.

Suddenly, £75 million seemed like a bargain for the best defender in the world!

But Virgil knew that all his hard work would be for nothing, unless Liverpool won a trophy. At the start of January 2019, they were top of the Premier League table and through to the Champions League Round of 16.

'So far so good,' Virgil thought to himself.

It was all going according to plan, but their next opponents, Bayern Munich, would be a tough team to beat. Their Polish Number 9, Robert Lewandowski, was one of the smartest strikers around.

Away at the Allianz Arena, however, Virgil was victorious. Not only did he do his job in defence, but he also assisted the Liverpool attack.

In the twenty-fifth minute, Virgil looked up and spotted Sadio sprinting down the left wing. PING! He delivered a long, perfect pass, straight onto Sadio's right boot. He controlled the ball brilliantly, turned past Neuer and then chipped it over the Bayern defenders. 1–0! Southampton's old stars had done it again.

But with twenty minutes to go, the match was tied at 1–1. There could only be one winner...

As James Milner's corner looped into the Bayern box, Virgil moved into the right position. Then he leapt high off the ground and threw his head bravely towards the ball. BOOM!

Goooooooooooooooooooooaaaaaaaaaaaaaaaalllllllllllll llllllllllllllll!!!!!!!!!!!!!!!!!!!!!

Scrambling to his feet, Virgil raced over to the cheering Liverpool fans near the corner flag. He was so happy to score another important goal and send his team through to the Champions League quarter-finals.

He's a centre-half, he's a number four,
Watch him defend, and watch him score,
He'll pass the ball, calm as you like,
He's Virgil van Dijk, he's Virgil van Dijk!

One of the great things about him was that the biggest games were his best games. Virgil loved nothing more than playing under pressure.

That was lucky for Liverpool because every game was now a big game. In the Premier League, they had slipped one point behind Manchester City after a series of disappointing draws. The defending wasn't the problem; thanks to Virgil, they were keeping clean sheet after clean sheet. No, now it was the attacking that was the issue.

'Come on, we've got nine games left,' Klopp tried to motivate his players, 'and we have to win them all. Otherwise, the title race is over, and City will be champions again.'

Challenge accepted! Liverpool started scoring goals again and beat Burnley, Fulham and Tottenham.

They couldn't have done it without their star defender, though. With the score at 1–1, Lucas Moura launched a quick Tottenham counter-attack. Uh oh, Virgil was two-on-one against Son Heung-min and Moussa Sissoko.

No problem! In a flash, he read the situation superbly. Sissoko had the ball and he was the player who was less likely to score. So Virgil backed away and let him run forward, while also blocking the path of a pass to Son. As he entered the penalty area, Sissoko had no choice but to shoot himself. *BANG!* He fired it high over the bar.

What clever, world-class defending! And a few minutes later, Liverpool went up the other end and scored the winning goal. It was Virgil, however, who had saved the day in the first place.

'What would we do without you?' Klopp asked at the final whistle, giving his star centre-back a big hug.

Virgil shrugged and smiled. With his manager's help, he had become one of the best defenders in the world. And at the PFA awards ceremony a few weeks later, he was named the new Premier League Player of the Year.

'I'm very proud and honoured,' Virgil thanked the audience, holding the huge trophy in his hands. It wasn't the one he really wanted, though...

The Premier League title race between Manchester City and Liverpool went on and on, and neither team dropped a single point. Every time one of them won, so did the other. It was incredible!

Manchester City 2 Cardiff City 0,
Southampton 1 Liverpool 3,
Crystal Palace 1 Manchester City 3,
Liverpool 2 Chelsea 0,
Manchester City 1 Tottenham 0,
Cardiff City 0 Liverpool 2,
Manchester United 0 Manchester City 2,
Liverpool 5 Huddersfield Town 0…

Virgil refused to give up until the very last minute of the very last match. He scored his team's first goal in a 3–2 win at Newcastle United. Right, the pressure was back on Manchester City now, but two days later, their star centre-back Vincent Kompany scored the winner against Leicester.

'Nooooooo!' Virgil groaned when he saw the scoreline.

The title race went all the way down to the final day in May 2019. Liverpool were at home against Wolves, while City were away at Brighton. If City won, the title was theirs. But if they drew or lost,

Liverpool could lift the trophy instead.

There was a glimmer of hope for Liverpool when Brighton took the lead, but it only lasted for one minute. After that, City stormed ahead – *1–1, 2–1, 3–1, 4–1!*

Despite beating Wolves and finishing with an amazing ninety-seven points, Liverpool would not be crowned the new Champions of England. It was a crushing blow to come so close to winning their first-ever Premier League title. The Anfield crowd still treated the players like heroes, however. What a successful season it had been, their best for nearly thirty years.

'We must be the greatest team to ever finish second!' they all agreed proudly.

Virgil found it hard to believe and painful to accept, but at least his trophy hunt wasn't over yet – because just five days earlier, Liverpool had pulled off another of the greatest comebacks in Champions League history, against Barcelona.

Despite a decent performance at the Nou Camp, the first leg had finished in a 3–0 defeat for

Liverpool. That was largely due to the brilliance of Lionel Messi. Virgil had done his best to win the battle against the Argentinian, but he could create chances out of nothing.

'Look, we didn't deserve that,' Klopp told his disappointed players at full-time. 'But remember, there's still ninety minutes to go – anything could happen!'

Anfield was full of hope as the two teams walked out for the second leg. The Liverpool supporters had seen their club fight back from 3–0 down in the 2005 Champions League Final against AC Milan. They called that 'The Miracle of Istanbul', so why not a 'Miracle of Anfield' now?

The Liverpool players felt positive too, and they showed it by attacking from the start. In the sixth minute, Jordan's shot was saved, but Divock Origi scored the rebound. *3–1!*

'Come on!' Virgil shouted, punching the air passionately. Now, they just needed two more – could they really do this? They had to believe, otherwise what was the point of playing at all?

Even as the minutes ticked by without a second goal, the players didn't panic. A football match could change in a flash...

And this one did. Gini came on and scored two goals in two minutes. 3–3 – Liverpool were level!

Virgil wanted to go wild like the fans above them in the stands, but no, he had to keep calm. At the moment, the match was going to extra-time. And with Messi and Luis Suárez still on the pitch, Barcelona were always in the game.

At the same time, however, one more Liverpool goal would take them through to their second Champions League Final in a row...

Trent was about to walk away and let Xherdan take the corner, when he suddenly spotted Divock unmarked in the middle. Surely, it was worth a try? Trent quickly whipped the ball into the box and Divock smashed it into the top corner. *4–3 to Liverpool!* The miracle was complete.

Somehow, despite the deafening Anfield roar, Virgil stayed calm in defence until the final whistle. But as soon as it blew, he ran towards Alisson, who jumped into his arms.

'We did it! We did it!' they shouted again and
again together.

Unbelievable – there were no words to describe
what they were feeling. It was simply the greatest
game that they'd ever played in.

'Right, we really have to win the Champions
League after that!' Virgil declared.

And they did. Liverpool were given a penalty in
the very first minute in the final against Tottenham.
Mohamed stepped up and… scored – *1–0!*

It was simply meant to be. Spurs' strikers tried
and tried to score an equaliser, but there was no
way past Virgil and Joël. They were too strong, too
quick and too clever. Then with time running out
for Tottenham, Liverpool went up the other end and
scored a second. 2–0 – game over – they were the
new Champions of Europe!

For Virgil, it was the perfect end to a sensational
season. After overcoming so many setbacks and
disappointments during his younger years, he was
officially now one of the best defenders – no, one of

the best footballers in the world.

Now finally, Virgil had a team trophy to go with all those individual awards – Premier League Player of the Year, PFA Players' Player of the Year, Man of the Match in the Champions League Final… And it wasn't just any old team trophy that he had won; it was the greatest club trophy in the world.

'Can life get any better than this?' Virgil asked himself as he stood there on the pitch in Madrid. He had a smile on his face, a winners' medal around his neck, his orange boots in one hand, and the Champions League trophy in the other.

Despite all that, the answer was still 'Yes!'. Once the excitement wore off, Virgil still had ambitions in his sights: to win the Premier League title with Liverpool, and then to lead the Netherlands to Euro 2020 glory. Was there anything that the Dutch defender couldn't do?

VIRGIL VAN DIJK
HONOURS

Celtic

🏆 Scottish Premiership: 2013–14, 2014–15

🏆 Scottish League Cup: 2014–15

Liverpool

🏆 UEFA Champions League: 2018–19

🏆 UEFA Super Cup: 2019

🏆 Premier League: 2019–20

Individual

🏆 PFA Players' Player of the Year: 2018–19

🏆 Premier League Player of the Season: 2018–19

🏆 Liverpool Players' Player of the Season Award:
2018–19

🏆 Liverpool Fans Player of the Season Award: 2018–19

🏆 UEFA Men's Player of the Year Award: 2018–19

🏆 UEFA Defender of the Season: 2018–19

VAN DIJK

4 THE FACTS

NAME:
Virgil van Dijk

DATE OF BIRTH:
8 July 1991

AGE: 29

PLACE OF BIRTH:
Breda

NATIONALITY: Netherlands

BEST FRIEND: Gini Wijnaldum

CURRENT CLUB: Liverpool

POSITION: CB

THE STATS

Height (cm):	**193**
Club appearances:	**395**
Club goals:	**43**
Club trophies:	**8**
International appearances:	**34**
International goals:	**4**
International trophies:	**0**
Ballon d'Ors:	**0**

★ ★ ★ **HERO RATING: 90** ★ ★ ★

GREATEST MOMENTS

30 OCTOBER 2011,
FC GRONINGEN 6–0 FEYENOORD

After starting out as an emergency extra striker, Virgil
soon settled back into the centre of the Groningen
defence. In this Dutch league match, he made a
huge impression at both ends of the field. As well as
a clean sheet, Virgil also got an assist for a beautiful
long pass to Dušan Tadić, and a brilliant long-range
goal. It was an all-round performance that the furious
Feyenoord manager, Ronald Koeman, never forgot.

1 OCTOBER 2013, CELTIC 0–1 BARCELONA

At Celtic, Virgil enjoyed his first taste of Champions League football. He raised his game brilliantly against the likes of AC Milan and Barcelona. In this match at Celtic Park, Virgil kept out Andrés Iniesta, Cesc Fàbregas, Pedro, Alexis Sánchez and Neymar Jr for seventy-five minutes. It was the perfect practice for all those big games ahead at Liverpool.

5 JANUARY 2018, LIVERPOOL 2–1 EVERTON

Virgil made his Liverpool debut in this Merseyside derby in the FA Cup. Jürgen Klopp didn't want his new signing to start, but in the end, he had to because of other injured players. Virgil showed no fear as he jumped high to score the winning goal and become an instant Anfield hero. It was a sign of great things to come.

19 NOVEMBER 2018, GERMANY 2–2 NETHERLANDS

In March 2018, Virgil's old Southampton boss Ronald Koeman made him the new captain of the Netherlands national team. It turned out to be a very wise move indeed, as Virgil led his country to the final of the first-ever UEFA Nations League. Along the way, he scored two goals against their rivals Germany, including this late and very important equaliser.

1 JUNE 2019, TOTTENHAM 0–2 LIVERPOOL

It was second time lucky for Virgil in the Champions League Final. A year after Liverpool's disappointing defeat to Real Madrid, he helped lead them to victory over Tottenham. It was skill, rather than luck, however, that helped him keep out Harry Kane and Son Heung-min in the second half. At the final whistle, Virgil also got a second prize to go with his winner's medal: the man of the match award.

PLAY LIKE YOUR HEROES

VIRGIL VAN DIJK'S DEADLY DEFENDING

STEP 1: Keep talking and organising your teammates, from the first kick until the final whistle.

STEP 2: Deal with any attacks as calmly as possible. You want to make defending look like a casual walk in the park.

STEP 3: Don't rush in and make a clumsy tackle. Watch carefully and wait patiently. Be smart and make the striker make the next move.

STEP 4: Slow striker? Use your super-speed to outsprint him.

STEP 5: Small striker? Use your super-strength to outmuscle him.

STEP 6: If all else fails, stretch out your long leg at the last, crucial second, and clear the ball out for a corner.

STEP 7: Right, back to the talking. Clap and shout and wave angrily at your teammates; 'Where were you?' 'Get back!'

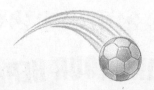

TEST YOUR KNOWLEDGE

QUESTIONS

1. What position did Virgil want to play at his first club, WDS'19?

2. Which Brazilian star inspired Virgil's skills on the Cruyff Court?

3. What was the name of Virgil's local professional club?

4. What job did Virgil do while he played for the Willem II youth team?

5. Why did Virgil have to miss Groningen's big derby match against Heerenveen?

6. How many trophies did Virgil win at Celtic?

7. Virgil was part of the Netherlands' 2014 World Cup squad – true or false?

8. How much money did Southampton pay to sign Virgil in 2015?

9. How much money did Liverpool pay to sign Virgil two-and-a-half years later?

10. Name at least two countries that Virgil's Netherlands team beat in the UEFA Nations League.

11. How many Premier League strikers got past Virgil during the 2018–19 season at Liverpool?

Answers below. . . No cheating!

1. *Striker* 2. *Ronaldinho* 3. *NAC Breda* 4. *He washed dishes at a local restaurant called Uncle Jean.* 5. *He was in hospital, having major surgery on his appendix.* 6. *Three – two league titles and one league cup* 7. *False – The national team coach Louis van Gaal decided that he wasn't good enough!* 8. *£13 million* 9. *£75 million!* 10. *Any of Germany, France and England* 11. *None!*

MBAPPE

CONTENTS

CHAPTER 1

FROM RUSSIA WITH LOVE

On 14 July 2018, Kylian sent a message to his millions of social media followers, from Russia with love: 'Happy French national day everyone. Let's hope the party continues until tomorrow night!'

'Tomorrow night' – 15 July – the French national team would be playing in the World Cup final at the Luzhniki Stadium in Moscow. It was the most important football match on the planet and Kylian's country was counting on him.

So far, he hadn't let them down at all. In fact, Kylian had been France's speedy superstar, scoring the winning goal against Denmark, and then two more in an amazing man-of-the-match performance against Argentina. That all made him the nation's best 'Number 10' since Zinedine Zidane back in 1998.

That was the year that France last won the World Cup.

That was also the year that Kylian was born.

Thanks to their new young superstar, '*Les Bleus*' were now the favourites to lift the famous golden trophy again. They had already beaten Lionel Messi's Argentina, Luis Suárez's Uruguay in the quarter-finals, and Eden Hazard's Belgium in the semi-finals. Now, the only nation standing in their way was Luka Modrić's Croatia.

'You've done so well to get this far,' the France manager, Didier Deschamps, told them as kick-off approached and the nerves began to jangle. 'Now, you just need to go out there and finish off the job!'

A massive 'Yeah!' echoed around the room. It was one big team effort, from captain Hugo Lloris in goal through to Kylian, Antoine Griezmann and Olivier Giroud in attack. Everyone worked hard and everyone worked together.

By the way, those jangling nerves didn't

belong to Kylian. No way, he was the coolest character around! He never let anything faze him. When he was younger, he hadn't just hoped to play in a World Cup final; he had expected it. It was all part of his killer plan to conquer the football world.

Out on the pitch for the final in Moscow, Kylian sang the words of the French national anthem with a big smile on his face. As a four-year-old, some people had laughed at his ambitious dreams. Well, they definitely weren't laughing now.

'Right, let's do this!' Paul Pogba clapped and cheered as they took up their positions. His partnership with Kylian would be key for France. Whenever Paul got the ball in midfield, he would look to find his pacy teammate with a perfect pass.

Kylian's first action of the final, however, was in defence. He rushed back quickly to block a Croatia cross.

'Well done!' France's centre-back Samuel Umtiti shouted.

Once that was done, it was all about attacking.

Even in a World Cup final, Kylian wasn't afraid to try his tricks and flicks. They didn't always work but it was worth the risk.

It was an end-to-end first half, full of exciting action. First, Antoine curled in a dangerous free kick and Mario Mandžukić headed the ball into his own net. 1–0 to France! Kylian punched the air – what a start!

Ivan Perišić equalised for Croatia but then he handballed it in his own box. Penalty! Antoine stepped up... and scored – 2–1 to France!

The players were happy to hear the half-time whistle blow. They needed a break to breathe and regroup. Although France were winning, they still had work to do if they wanted to become World Champions again.

'We need to calm things down and take control of the game,' Deschamps told his players. 'Stay smart out there!'

Kylian listened carefully to his manager's message. He needed to relax and play to his strengths – his skill but also his speed. This was his chance to go down in World Cup history:

Pelé in 1958,

Diego Maradona in 1986,

Zidane in 1998,

Ronaldo in 2002,

Kylian in 2018?

In the second half, France's superstars shone much more brightly. Kylian collected Paul's long pass and sprinted straight past the Croatia centre-back. Was he about to score in his first World Cup final? No, the keeper came out to make a good save.

'Ohhhh!' the supporters groaned in disappointment.

But a few minutes later, Paul and Kylian linked up again. From wide on the right wing, Kylian dribbled towards goal. Uh oh, the Croatia left-back was in big trouble.

With a stepover and a little hop, Kylian cut inside towards goal but in a flash, he fooled the defender with another quick change of direction.

'Go on!' the France fans urged their exciting young hero.

What next? Kylian still had two defenders in front

of him, so he pulled it back to Antoine instead. He couldn't find a way through either so he passed it on to Paul. Paul's first shot was blocked but his second flew into the bottom corner. 3–1!

Kylian threw his arms up in the air and then ran over to congratulate his friend. Surely, France had one hand on the World Cup trophy now.

Antoine had scored, and so had Paul. That meant it must be Kylian's turn next! He would have to score soon, however, in case Deschamps decided to take him off early…

When he received the pass from Lucas Hernández, Kylian was in the middle of the pitch, at least ten yards outside the penalty area. Was he too far out to shoot? No, there was no such thing as 'too far' for Kylian! He shifted the ball to the right and then BANG! He tucked the ball into the bottom corner before the keeper could even dive. 4–1!

Gooooooooooooooooooooaaaaaaaaaaaaaaaaaalllllllllll llllllllllllllll!!!!!!!!!!!!!!!!!!!!

As his teammates rushed over to him, Kylian had just enough time for his trademark celebration. With a little jump, he planted his feet, folded his arms across his chest, and tried to look as cool as he could. That last part was really hard because he had just scored in a World Cup final!

The next thirty minutes ticked by very slowly but eventually, the game was over. France 4 Croatia 2 – they were the 2018 World Champions!

Allez Les Bleus! Allez Les Bleus! Allez Les Bleus!

Kylian used the last of his energy to race around the pitch, handing out hugs to everyone he saw: his sad opponents, his happy teammates, his manager, EVERYONE! In that amazing moment, he would have hugged every single French person in the world if he could. Instead, he blew kisses at the cameras. From Russia with love!

And Kylian's incredible night wasn't over yet. Wearing his country's flag around his waist, he walked up on stage to collect the tournament's Best Young Player award from Emmanuel Macron.

'Thank you, you're a national hero now!' the French President told him proudly.

'My pleasure, Sir!' Kylian replied.

Would his smile ever fade? Certainly not while he had a World Cup winners' medal around his neck and the beautiful World Cup trophy in his hands. He didn't ever want to let go. Kylian kissed it and raised it high into the Moscow night sky.

'Hurray!' the fans cheered for him.

At the age of nineteen, Kylian was already living out his wildest dreams. The boy from Bondy had become a World Cup winner and football's next great superstar.

CHAPTER 2

A SPORTY FAMILY IN A SPORTY SUBURB

'What if he doesn't like sports?' Wilfried Mbappé whispered to his wife, Fayza Lamari, as they watched their new-born son, Kylian, sleeping peacefully in his cot. He was a man who loved to laugh but at that moment, he had a worried look on his face.

Fayza smiled and spoke softly so as not to wake the baby. 'Does it really matter? Kylian can do whatever he wants to do, and we're going to love him no matter what!'

Her husband nodded but she could still see the frown lines on his forehead.

'Relax, Wilfried, he's our son, so of course he's going to LOVE sports!'

With parents like his, Kylian was always destined

to be a sporting superstar.

Wilfried's favourite sport was football. When he was younger, he had moved to France from Cameroon in order to find a good job. As well as that, Wilfried had also been lucky enough to find the two loves of his life – his wife, Fayza, and his local football club, AS Bondy. His playing days were now over, but he had become a youth team coach instead.

Fayza's favourite sport was handball. She was a star player for AS Bondy in France's top division. Ever since she was a kid, Fayza had been racing up and down the right wing, competing fiercely with her rivals. She couldn't wait to get back out on the court, now that Kylian was born.

'No-one messes with your mum!' Wilfried always told his sons proudly.

Not only were the Mbappés a very sporty family, but they also lived in a very sporty suburb of Paris. Over the years, so many successful athletes, basketball players and footballers had grown up in Bondy. There was top talent on display wherever you turned!

The sports club, AS Bondy, was at the heart of the local community, right in the middle of all the shops and tower blocks. Growing up, Kylian could see the local stadium from the windows of their apartment. It was an inspiring sight.

AS Bondy was a place where people from lots of different French-speaking backgrounds – Algeria, Morocco, Tunisia, Haiti, Togo, Mali, Senegal, Ivory Coast – could come together and enjoy themselves. That was really important because life wasn't easy for the local people. They had to work long hours in order to feed their families and strive towards a brighter future.

For the young people of Bondy, the sports club was particularly special. It was their home away from home, where they could develop their skills, while at the same time staying out of trouble. Coaches like Wilfried taught them three simple rules to live by:

1) Respect each other.

2) Stay humble.

3) Love sport.

At AS Bondy, youngsters could forget about their

problems and just focus on their sporting dreams.

In years to come, the local kids would look up at a big mural showing Kylian's face under the words, 'Bondy: Ville Des Possibles'. No, it wasn't the wealthiest part of Paris, but it was a 'City of Possibilities' where, with hard work and dedication, you could achieve your dreams.

So, what was Kylian's sporting dream? To play handball like his mother, or football like his father? His adopted older brother, Jirés Kembo Ekoko, was already the star of Wilfried's Under-10s football team. Would Kylian follow in his footsteps?

Or perhaps Kylian would choose to play a different sport...

'He can do whatever he wants to do,' Fayza reminded Wilfried, 'and we're going to love him no matter what!'

Growing up, Kylian enjoyed playing tennis and basketball with his friends, but there was really only one sport for him. To his dad's delight, that sport turned out to be football!

CHAPTER 3

THE LITTLE PRINCE OF BONDY

Little Kylian didn't know the meaning of the word 'slow'. He was a football hero in a hurry.

By the age of two, he was already a familiar face in the AS Bondy dressing room. Just as the players were preparing for the match ahead, a little boy would race in with a football tucked under his arm.

'Look who it is – our mascot, the Little Prince of Bondy!' the club president, Atmane Airouche greeted him. 'You're just in time for the team-talk!'

Even if Wilfried wasn't there with him, Kylian was never any trouble. When the manager was talking, he just sat there quietly next to the Bondy players and listened. Before they went out onto the pitch, they all high-fived him. He was their good luck charm.

'Are we going to win today?' the captain asked Kylian.

He nodded eagerly. 'Yeah!'

Kylian would then go out and watch the games with a football at his feet.

By the age of six, Kylian already had his own future all planned out.

'What do you want to be when you're older?' Wilfried asked, recording his son's reply.

'I want to be a footballer,' Kylian said, looking confidently at the video camera. 'I'm going to play for France and I'm going to play in the World Cup too.'

Fayza tried very hard not to laugh at the serious expression on her son's young face. He had such amazing ambition! As the French national anthem played, Kylian sang along with his hand on his heart, just like the players he saw on TV.

'Great, and what club would you like to play for?'

'Bondy!'

Kylian was already training with the juniors. His coach, Antonio Riccardi, was one of Wilfried and

Fayza's closest friends, and so he had been kicking balls around with their sons for years. However, this was the first time that he would see Kylian playing a proper match against kids his own age.

'Wow!' was Antonio's response.

He looked so tiny in his baggy green shirt and shorts, but boy, could Kylian play football!

Even during the warm-up, Antonio could see the difference. He was so much better than everyone else. For a young kid, he really seemed to understand the game. Kylian didn't just kick and chase, like the others; he thought about what he wanted to do with the ball, and then did it. All those weekends at Bondy, spent watching and listening to the adults around him... Kylian had been taking everything in.

'Right, let's practise our dribbling!' Antonio called out.

The coach had set up a line of cones for them to weave through before taking a shot at goal. It looked easy but it wasn't. The first four kids either took it too fast or too slow. They either bumped the ball off cone after cone, or crawled their way down the line like a sleepy tortoise.

'At that speed, you're going to get tackled every time!' Antonio told them as kindly as he could.

At last, it was Kylian's turn and he couldn't wait to show off his skills. He had been working hard on his dribbling at home with his dad and Jirés. It was now time to test himself in front of a bigger audience.

One, two, three, four – as Kylian raced through the cones, the ball stayed stuck to his right foot. His control was so good that he didn't knock a single one of them.

'Excellent!' Antonio called out. 'Now shoot!'

But by then, Kylian was already rushing over to collect his ball from the back of the net. His shot hit the top-left corner of the net before the goalkeeper had even moved.

Kylian was the standout player in the passing practice too. The touch, the movement, the accuracy – it was like he was a professional already! Antonio was blown away by the Little Prince of Bondy. He had coached a lot of impressive kids in Paris, but he had never seen a six-year-old with that much footballing talent. Never!

'Surely he's too good to play with kids his own age?' the coach was thinking, and that was before the match at the end of the session had even started.

'Wow!' Antonio was soon saying again.

To go with his silky ball skills, Kylian also had electrifying pace. It was a winning combination that the poor Bondy defenders just could not cope with. Every time he got the ball, it was goal-time. ZOOM! Kylian was off, sprinting down the right wing, just like his mum on the handball court. Sometimes, he set up goals for his teammates and sometimes, he scored himself.

1, 2, 3, 4, 5, 6–0!

'Okay, let's switch the teams around a bit. Kylian, put on an orange bib!'

6–1, 6–2, 6–3, 6–4, 6–5, 6–6, 6–7, 6–8!

In the end, Antonio had to stop the game early because he didn't want his players to get too down-hearted. Kylian was simply in a league of his own. He was better, faster and more consistent than anyone else.

Once practice was over, Antonio went to find Wilfried.

'I don't think Kylian should be playing for the Under-7s,' he explained.

'Why not?' Wilfried replied, looking surprised. 'Did my son play badly today?'

'NO!' the coach replied, laughing at the idea. 'Quite the opposite; he was absolutely incredible! He's the best I've ever seen at that age. The Under-7s league would be a walk in the park for him; he would just get bored. He needs a challenge!'

By the age of eight, Kylian was playing for the Bondy Under-11s, skilling left-backs all game long. He was on a fast track to the top. His killer plan to conquer the football world was going very well indeed.

CHAPTER 4

FOOTBALL, FOOTBALL, FOOTBALL

'No way, Thierry Henry is the best French player ever!' Kylian argued on the walk home with Antonio. 'Did you not see his goal in the 2006 World Cup semi-final against Brazil? And he hit that on the volley too!'

If the Bondy training session finished before Wilfried and Fayza got home from work, Antonio would often go around to look after Kylian for a few hours. The coach didn't do much babysitting, though. Really, it was just two people talking football, football, football.

'Okay, but who set him up with the free kick in the first place? Zinedine Zidane, without doubt the greatest French footballer of all-time!'

'What about the final, though? France were

drawing 1–1 with Italy when Zidane got himself sent off. He let the whole team down!'

'That's true but who scored France's goal in that final? Zizou!'

'It was a penalty! Henry could have scored that.'

'Maybe, but Zizou won the World Cup for France back in 1998,' Antonio argued back. 'Those two headers in the final against Brazil – unbelievable! Wait, what year were you born?'

Kylian laughed. 'Nineteen ninety-eight!'

The Bondy coach just rolled his eyes. Sometimes, he forgot that he was talking to someone so young. That was easy to do because Kylian wasn't your average nine-year-old. He didn't just play football; he also spent hours watching it, and knew a *lot* about it. He could talk passionately about his heroes for hours.

When they got back to the apartment, they watched football on TV in the living room, while they had some snacks and drinks. After a short sit-down, however, Kylian was back up on his feet again, moving the furniture.

'Hey, what are you doing?' Antonio asked.

'Just getting the football pitch ready!' he replied.

The Bondy coach shook his head. 'No way, your parents will be furious if we break something! Can't you just wait until tomorrow to play outside?'

It was Kylian's turn to shake his head. 'No, it'll be fine. I've got a soft ball and I play here all the time! But you've got to promise that you won't tell Mum and Dad, okay? Promise?'

Antonio found it very hard to say no to Kylian. He let out a loud sigh: 'Fine, I promise, but only for ten minutes!'

Those 'ten minutes' soon turned into thirty entertaining minutes of 'Henry vs Zidane'. It was a miracle that they didn't break anything. One goal was the sofa and the other was the table. There wasn't much space, so it was all about quick feet and quick thinking. Kylian had both of those, plus home advantage. He knew the living room obstacles to watch out for, and the best angles to shoot from.

Time flew until Antonio suddenly looked at his watch and panicked. 'Okay, final whistle!'

'So, I win?' Kylian asked with a smirk. The score

was 10–8 to 'Henry'.

'Yes, this time, but we need to have a rematch soon. Come on quickly, your mum will be home any minute now! You put all the furniture back in the right place, while I clear things up in the kitchen.'

By the time they heard the sound of Fayza's key in the front door, Kylian and Antonio were sitting innocently on the sofa again, as if nothing had happened. They had moved on to their fourth football-based activity of the night – playing FIFA on the PlayStation.

'Hi, Mum!' Kylian called out as the door swung shut.

'Hi darling, how was your day?' she asked, dropping her bag down in the kitchen. When there was no reply, she tried again. 'Kylian, how was your day?'

'Sorry, can't speak right now,' her son replied, tapping the controller furiously. 'Thierry Henry is too busy teaching Zinedine Zidane a lesson!'

CHAPTER 5

CRISTIANO CRAZY!

Thierry Henry was brilliant, but he wasn't Kylian's favourite footballer in the world for long. From 2008 onwards, that was Cristiano Ronaldo. That year, the Portuguese superstar won the Champions League with Manchester United, and Kylian watched every single match on TV.

Like him, Ronaldo was a right winger with lots of speed and skill. He loved to fool defenders with his magical dancing feet. Kylian had never seen anyone do so many stepovers in a proper match. It looked so cool.

'I'm going to do that too!' he decided.

On top of that, Ronaldo was also big and strong. He battled for every ball and his headers were really powerful. That was an area of the game that Kylian needed to work on, and by the time United took on Chelsea in the final, he was Ronaldo's biggest fan.

'What a goal!' Kylian cheered when his hero scored an excellent header in the first half. He jumped up and down on the living room sofa with his T-shirt up over his head.

'Noooooooo!' Kylian groaned two hours later when Ronaldo's penalty was saved in the shoot-out. By then, the boy's T-shirt was back down on his chest, and he buried his face in it.

But no, John Terry missed for Chelsea and then so did Nicolas Anelka. Ronaldo and Manchester United were the winners!

'Yeeeeeesss!' Kylian screamed. His T-shirt was off and he was whirling it above his head like a cowboy's lasso.

Other than AS Bondy, Kylian didn't really have a favourite football team. Paris Saint-Germain were the biggest club in Paris but they were struggling near the bottom of the French league. Instead, he had lots of favourite football players: Henry, Didier Drogba,

Ronaldinho, Lionel Messi, and best of all, Ronaldo.

'Here he comes, "The New Henry"!' Airouche, the Bondy club president, made the mistake of saying one day.

Kylian shook his head firmly. 'No, I don't play like Thierry! I'm a dribbler and a creator, as well as a goalscorer. I'm "The New Ronaldo"!'

'The striker who played for Brazil?'

'No, Cristiano!'

Kylian wanted to know everything about his number one hero. Where did Cristiano grow up? What was he like when he was younger? How did he get so big and strong? Did he have a massive house now, with a cinema room and a swimming pool? What football boots did he wear? What fancy cars did he drive, and how many?

'Once I become a top professional player, I'm going to buy myself TEN beautiful cars!' he told his dad excitedly.

Wilfried rolled his eyes. 'One step at a time, son – you can't get carried away. You'll need to keep improving your skills and you'll need a driving licence too! But football's not about fame and money; it's about success and glory. Has AS Bondy taught you nothing? What's rule number two?'

'Stay humble.'

'That's right!'

Kylian's dad was right; he did still have a long way to go. But Wilfried was wrong about his son's ambition. Kylian's main aim was simple – always to be the best:

The best footballer at AS Bondy...

Then the best footballer in Paris...

Then the best footballer in France...

Then the best footballer in the world, even better than Ronaldo!

The Champions League, the World Cup, the Ballon d'Or – Kylian was going to win them all. The sports cars would just be a nice bonus, a reward for all his record-breaking work.

To keep himself inspired, Kylian decided to decorate his bedroom wall. He pulled out posters from football magazines and cut out images from newspapers too. The action poses changed and so did the kits, but the player in the picture never did.

'It's like a Ronaldo *museum* in here!' Jirés joked. 'You're obsessed, bro!'

Kylian's obsession grew even stronger in 2009 when Ronaldo signed for Real Madrid – for £80 million! It was a new world record transfer fee. After the red of Manchester United and Portugal, Cristiano would now be wearing the famous white shirt worn by the likes of Zizou and the Brazilian Ronaldo.

Kylian had a new favourite football team, and he spent hours watching YouTube videos of his hero's Spanish highlights. Tricks, flicks, free kicks, headers, long-range rockets – there were so many of them! If he kept progressing out on the pitch, Kylian hoped that he too would be worth that kind of money one day. Maybe even more.

CHAPTER 6

CLAIREFONTAINE

By the time Kylian turned nine years old, people in Paris were already talking about 'that amazing boy from Bondy'. At every match he played, there was always a group of scouts watching him.

By the time he turned thirteen, Kylian was ready to take the next big step – joining a top football academy. Playing for AS Bondy was fun, but it was time for a new challenge. After a tough three-day trial, he was one of twenty-two young players from the Paris area selected to attend Clairefontaine.

'You got into Clairefontaine? Wow, that's so cool!' his school friends said enviously.

It was the most famous academy in France and

one of the most famous in the whole world, because that's where French stars Nicolas Anelka, William Gallas and Thierry Henry had all started their careers. For Kylian, joining Clairefontaine felt like a giant leap towards greatness. He was following in Thierry's footsteps!

For the next few years, Kylian would live at the academy from Monday to Friday and then return home to visit his family at the weekends. That sounded good to him, especially when he got to explore the Clairefontaine facilities. It was like a football palace!

They were thirty miles outside Paris in the middle of the French countryside. From his dormitory window, Kylian looked out on beautiful football pitches stretching into the distance for as far as the eye could see. And that was only the start of it. They also had:

An indoor pitch,

A full stadium,

A gym,

And tennis courts too!

'Can I just stay here forever?' he joked with the Clairefontaine coaches.

That was the other amazing thing about the academy. As good as the training had been at AS Bondy with Antonio and his dad, this was ten times better. Kylian was working with France's best youth coaches now, and testing himself against France's best young defenders. Was he good enough to achieve his dream of becoming a professional footballer? That was what he was there to find out.

When Clairefontaine's Director, Jean-Claude Lafargue, watched Kylian in action, he could see the amazing raw talent straight away – the fancy footwork and the incredible pace. However, he knew that talent would need polishing in order to really sparkle at the highest level.

'He's not the best yet,' Lafargue believed, 'but with the right help, he could be!'

The Clairefontaine coaches helped Kylian to improve his weaker foot, so that his dribbling was even more dangerous. If he could take off in either direction, it was so much harder to tackle him.

Stepover to the left, stepover to the right, a little hop, and then GO!

They also helped Kylian to improve his running style so that he was even faster. He still looked a little funny with his long arms swinging, but his teammates weren't laughing when he turned and hit top speed.

'Come on, keep up!' he teased.

Most of all, however, the coaches encouraged Kylian to think about his movement. That was one of the big differences between good players and *great* players. They didn't want Kylian to tire himself out by racing around the pitch. Instead, they wanted him to save his energy for making the *right* runs.

'Look for the gaps!' they shouted.

'What are you going to do when you get the ball?' they asked. 'You've got to be one step ahead of the game!'

'If you can't find space, make space for someone else!' they told him.

Kylian was learning so much, both in the classroom and on the training field, and he was then putting it into practice on the pitch. He scored more and more goals for Clairefontaine and back home at AS Bondy too.

'Watch this!' he told his teammates when he played for them at the weekends. One touch to control the ball and then he was off. *ZOOM – GOAL!*

Kylian was determined to become the best. He was playing more matches than ever but sometimes, that still wasn't enough. He wanted his life to be football, football, football, and even more football!

If he couldn't sleep, Kylian would sneak outside for some extra training. He always kept a ball under his bed just in case. At night, the academy switched their big floodlights off but he used the torch on his mobile phone to guide himself down the stairs and onto the tarmac.

Ahhh! Out in the fresh air, with a ball at his feet, Kylian always felt more relaxed. And with no-one watching him, he could finally practise the latest Ronaldo goal in peace:

'Mbappé has it on the left wing for Real Madrid.

Gerard Piqué and Dani Alves are waiting for him on the edge of the Barcelona penalty area, but he fools them both with one simple stepover. Mbappé dummies to go right, but shifts the ball on to his left foot instead for the shot. BANG! Straight through the goalkeeper's legs....

Gooooooooooooooooooooooaaaaaaaaaaaaaaaaaalllllllllll lllllllllllllllll!!!!!!!!!!!!!!!!!!!!!

He had to whisper all this because he would be in big trouble if the Clairefontaine coaches found him out of bed.

Kylian loved his time at the Clairefontaine academy, but it couldn't last forever. At the age of fifteen, it was time for him to move on to bigger and better things.

Word had spread about Kylian's talent and all the biggest clubs in Europe were queuing up to sign him. He could take his pick, but which one would he choose?

CHAPTER 7

WHICH CLUB TO CHOOSE?
PART I

One team hoping to sign Kylian was Rennes. They
weren't one of the biggest or richest clubs in France
but they had one major advantage – his older brother
was already playing for their first team.

'You and me in the same amazing attack,' Jirés
tried to persuade him. 'Think how many goals we
could score together!'

It was certainly a tempting idea. Kylian knew
the club really well. When he was seven, he used
to practise his skills on the pitch next door, while
Jirés played for the youth team. Everyone at Rennes
remembered the little boy from Bondy who always
had a football at his feet.

Six years on and people were calling that boy the 'next Henry'. Would he sign for Rennes? Perhaps not, but it was definitely worth a try.

'Would your son like to play for us in a tournament?' one of the coaches asked Wilfried.

'Sure!' said Kylian. He never said no to football.

Wearing the red Rennes shirt, Kylian was head and shoulders above the rest. Once he got the ball, he was simply unstoppable.

'What a player!' the club's coach said enthusiastically. 'We'd love to sign your son for our youth team.'

Wilfried, however, was in no rush to decide. He wanted to make sure that Kylian chose the right club where he would be happy, as well as successful.

'Thank you, we have a lot of offers to consider,' he replied politely.

One of those other offers came from the 2010 Premier League Champions, Chelsea. They sent their scouts all over Europe, looking for the top young talent around. Kylian was soon on their radar and they invited him to come to London for a trial.

'Sure!' he said. He never said no to football.

Kylian loved his time at Chelsea. It was his first experience of being at a big club, and he walked around in a daze.

Wow, the training ground was amazing!

Wow, the Stamford Bridge stadium was really cool!

Wow, there was Didier Drogba, one of his childhood heroes!

Kylian got to meet Drogba, and he got to play some football too. He starred for the Chelsea youth team as they beat Charlton Athletic 8–0.

'You and me in the same amazing attack,' their striker Tammy Abraham tried to persuade him. 'Think how many goals we could score together!'

It was certainly a tempting idea.

'What a player!' the Chelsea coaches said enthusiastically. 'We'd love to sign Kylian for our youth team.'

But still, Wilfried was in no rush. 'Thank you, my son has a lot of offers to consider,' he replied politely.

Kylian left London with happy memories and a

blue Chelsea shirt with his name and Number 10 on the back. That was soon on display on his bedroom wall, next to all the Cristiano posters.

So, what other offers did Kylian receive? Well, every single club in France wanted to sign him, plus Bayern Munich, Manchester City, Manchester United, Liverpool, and even Real Madrid!

The Spanish giants were one of the biggest and richest clubs in the whole world and they had two other major advantages:

1) French legend Zinedine Zidane was their manager

and

2) Cristiano Ronaldo was their star player.

Zidane invited Kylian to come and spend his fourteenth birthday at Real Madrid.

'Sure!' he said. He never said no to football.

It was the best birthday present ever! When Kylian arrived at Real, Ronaldo didn't say to him, 'You and me in the same amazing attack. Think how many goals we could score together!' However, the boy did get his photo taken with his hero.

It was a moment that Kylian would never, ever forget. Wearing a white Real Madrid tracksuit, he stood there smiling next to Cristiano Ronaldo. The superstar even put his arm around his shoulders. No, it wasn't a dream – he had the picture to prove it!

Kylian spent a week at the Real Madrid academy, training with some of the best young players in the world. It was another amazing experience, and it confirmed what he and his family had known all along – that he could compete at the highest level. One day, he was going to be the best.

'What a player!' Zidane said enthusiastically. 'We'd love to sign your son for our youth team.'

Kylian had an offer from Real Madrid, but still, Wilfried was in no rush. 'Thank you, my son has a lot of offers to consider,' he replied politely.

It was going to be the biggest decision of Kylian's young life. Was he really ready to leave France behind? During his time at the Clairefontaine academy, he could go home to Bondy every weekend. If he moved to Madrid, however, Kylian would be much further away from his friends and family. That was a lot for a fourteen-year-old to deal with. But at the same time, could he really say no to Real, Ronaldo's team?

'Remember, it's not "now or never",' Fayza reassured her son. 'There'll be other opportunities. If you don't want to go there yet, no problem. Maybe you'll go there when you're a bit older!'

CHAPTER 8

MOVING TO MONACO

Kylian's mind was made up. For now, he was going to
say no to Real Madrid and stay close to his friends and
family in France. He was going to sign for a top team
with an amazing academy, where he would have the
best chance of progressing quickly into the first team.

For all of those reasons and more, Kylian chose
Monaco.

The Monaco youth system was the best in the
whole of France. The Red and Whites had more scouts
in Paris than any other Ligue 1 club, including the
local team, PSG! And the Mbappé family had known
those scouts for years, ever since Kylian's early days
at AS Bondy. They were friendly people, who really

seemed to care about his footballing future.

'Your son could be Monaco's next superstar!' they kept telling Wilfried and Fayza.

Kylian's parents had no doubts about that, but was it the right club for their son? Yes! When Kylian visited the Monaco academy centre, 'La Turbie', he was very impressed. The facilities were as big and modern as Chelsea or Real Madrid.

It was also an academy with lots of history. In the past, La Turbie had produced four of France's 1998 World Cup winners – right-back Lilian Thuram, central midfielder Emmanuel Petit, plus strikers David Trezeguet and, you guessed it, Thierry Henry!

'We want to make Kylian the next famous name on that list,' the Monaco academy director told the Mbappé family during their tour. 'This is the best place for him to develop that incredible talent.'

Sold! Kylian loved the sound of that plan. It was the offer that he had been hoping for.

'Welcome to France's greatest football club!' the academy director said, shaking his hand.

At the time Kylian joined their academy, however,

Monaco hadn't won the French league title for thirteen years. In fact, in 2011, they had even been relegated down to Ligue 2. Thankfully, a Russian billionaire called Dmitry Rybolovlev had bought the club and taken them back to the top flight.

'I'm going to lead Monaco to glory again!' Kylian declared confidently.

The club had just spent nearly £100 million on Colombian stars Radamel Falcao and James Rodríguez, but that didn't mean that they didn't care about their young stars. Layvin Kurzawa, Yannick Carrasco, Valère Germain and Anthony Martial had all made the step up from Monaco B to the Monaco first team.

'That'll be me next!' Kylian announced as soon as he arrived.

He couldn't wait to impress his new coaches and teammates. He had a lot to live up to, especially that nickname – 'The New Henry'. Kylian didn't mind the pressure, though. He was sure that he could handle it, even at a higher level.

He wasn't going to let anything stop him from achieving his goals. He always wanted to be the best.

Every time he got the ball in training, he attacked at top speed. ZOOM! He wasn't a show-off, but what was the point in having such silky skills if he wasn't going to use them?

'Excellent, Kylian!'

Leaving his marker trailing behind, he lifted his head up and looked for the pass, just like they had taught him to do at Clairefontaine. If someone was in space, he set them up to score.

'Cheers, Kylian!'

If not, he took the shot himself, and he hardly ever missed.

'Great goal, Kylian!'

Was the Monaco manager, Claudio Ranieri, watching? Kylian hoped so. His masterplan was simple but highly ambitious. He didn't want to sit around and wait patiently. By the end of his three years in the academy, he aimed to be playing for the first team. That seemed realistic to him; it was why he had chosen Monaco in the first place.

If Thierry could do it at seventeen years old, then so could Kylian.

CHAPTER 9

FIRST-TEAM FOOTBALL

After a strong start, however, Kylian's Monaco masterplan was in danger of falling apart. The last of his three
academy years had started, and his first-team dream
still seemed miles away. Did Monaco's new manager,
Leonardo Jardim, even know that he existed? Every
day, Kylian grew more and more impatient.

'I don't get it!' he moaned to Jirés. 'What am I
doing wrong?'

For years at AS Bondy and Clairefontaine, Kylian
had been the coach's favourite and the star player,
but not anymore. The Monaco Under-18s manager
didn't seem to rate him at all. He was always
criticising Kylian for something.

'Track back and help your team!'

'Stop giving the ball away. Pass!'

'Think about what you're doing!'

Kylian was doing his best to improve his game, but his coach's comments were affecting his confidence. At this rate, Monaco might not even offer him a professional contract anyway. He knew that Jirés would understand his frustrations.

'All you can do is try to ignore it and keep working hard,' his older brother told him. 'Everything will work out in the end!'

Those turned out to be very wise words. Kylian's time was coming, and sooner than even he could have predicted.

By 2015, Monaco had stopped spending lots of money on foreign players. That plan wasn't working because the club couldn't compete with PSG in the transfer market. So instead, the club's vice-president Vadim Vasilyev and technical director Luis Campos decided to focus on developing their young French talent. Local players were a lot cheaper and, potentially, a lot better.

One day, while Vasilyev was working on this new idea, he had a visit from a Monaco academy coach, who looked troubled.

'What's wrong?' the vice-president asked.

'We have a talented kid in the youth team, and I think he's going to be a star,' the coach explained.

'Great, what's his name?'

'Kylian Mbappé.'

'Okay, so what's the problem?' Vasilyev asked, looking confused. 'Let's give him a contract!'

Unfortunately, it wasn't that easy because Kylian wasn't very happy at Monaco. He didn't feel wanted by the club and he could no longer see a clear path to the first team.

Plus, he was in high demand once again. He had lots of offers to consider before he signed his first professional contract. PSG were desperate to steal him away from Monaco, and so were Arsenal and RB Leipzig.

Vasilyev went to La Turbie to find out what all the fuss was about. It didn't take him long. Within five minutes, the Monaco vice-president could see that Kylian had phenomenal talent. It wasn't just the speed and the skill; it was also the confidence, the competitive spirit, the fire in the young man's eyes. He seemed to have everything that a young player needed to succeed, and more.

'Wow, why am I only just hearing about this wonderkid?' he thought to himself.

That didn't matter now; what mattered was keeping Kylian happy at Monaco. They couldn't let him leave, especially for free! Vasilyev and Campos went to speak to Wilfried and Fayza about what they could do to help.

'Kylian wants to play first-team football,' his dad said. 'It's as simple as that. I know he's only sixteen, but my son is very ambitious. And very talented!'

Vasilyev and Campos nodded. 'Absolutely, he's one of the most talented young players we've ever seen. Leave it with us; we'll arrange for him to start training with the first team as soon as possible.'

Kylian's first chance came in November 2015. A lot of Monaco's stars were away on international duty, so Jardim needed to call up extra players to take part in the first-team training sessions.

'Get Mbappé,' Vasilyev told him. 'Trust me, you'll be impressed!'

Kylian was so excited when he heard the good news. At last! He didn't feel nervous at all as he walked into the first-team dressing room, and then out onto the first-team training pitch. He believed in himself. This was where he belonged. He couldn't wait to show Jardim what he'd been missing.

ZOOM! Kylian flew past Monaco's experienced defenders in a flash. Now, he had to make sure he finished his run with either a goal or an assist. He had to be more consistent; that was what the Under-18s coach was always telling him. Kylian lifted his head up – did he have a teammate to pass to? No, they couldn't keep up. He would have to go it alone.

The last man backed away, wondering which way Kylian would go...

Stepover to the left, stepover to the right, a little hop, and then GO!

Kylian sprinted into space and fired the ball past the keeper.

Goooooooooooooooooooooaaaaaaaaaaaaaaaaallllllllllll llllllllllllllllllllll!!!!!!!!!!!!!!!!!!!!!

Jardim was blown away by Kylian's performance. 'Wow, why am I only just hearing about this wonderkid?' he asked Vasilyev.

The vice-president laughed, 'I asked exactly the same question when I first saw him play!'

'Well, he's not going back to the youth team,' Jardim decided straight away. 'He's a Monaco first-team player now.'

CHAPTER 10

"THE NEW HENRY"

Some young players spend a long time, training with the first team, before they make their senior debut, but not Kylian. He was a hero in a hurry, and who was going to stop him? In December 2015, less than a month after his first training session, he was taking his seat on the Monaco subs' bench!

They were playing at home against AS Caen at the Stade Louis II. The stadium could hold up to 18,000 supporters but it was only ever full for the big games against rivals like PSG. There were only 5,000 in the crowd to watch Kylian's debut against Caen. Well, that was if Jardim brought him on...

'Man, you could make history tonight!' his

teammate, Tiémoué Bakayoko, told him as they watched the first half.

Kylian just smiled and nodded. It was what he had always wanted to do – break records. If he did get onto the pitch, he would become Monaco's youngest-ever first-team player. He was still eighteen days away from his seventeenth birthday. And whose record would he be breaking? Yes, Thierry Henry! That would make it extra special.

Monaco had been struggling to score goals all season. They took the lead against Caen but with five minutes to go, Ronny Rodelin grabbed an equaliser. 1–1!

A draw wouldn't do, though; Monaco needed to win. Jardim turned to his bench. He had already brought on his Portuguese winger, Hélder Costa. Who else did he have?

Paul Nardi – a goalkeeper,

Andrea Raggi – a defender,

Gabriel Boschilia – a midfielder,

Tiémoué – another midfielder,

And Kylian!

Playing a sixteen-year-old was always a risk, but Jardim reasoned that Kylian's speed and skill could be deadly against the tired Caen defence. He was the best option that Monaco had.

'Kylian, get ready,' one of the coaches shouted, passing on the manager's message. 'You're coming on!'

On the touchline, Kylian tucked his red-and-white 33 shirt into his shorts and waited for the fourth official to put the numbers up. Monaco were going all-out attack. Kylian would play on the left wing in place of the left-back, Fábio Coentrão.

'Good luck, kid,' Fábio said as they high-fived. 'Go cause some trouble!'

'I'll try!'

Within seconds, Kylian was on the ball. He controlled Bernardo Silva's pass and then thought about taking on the Caen right-back. Surely he could speed straight past him? No, not quite yet. He decided to play it safely back to Bernardo instead.

'Next time!' Kylian thought to himself.

When Bernardo passed to him again, Kylian faked to cut inside but then – ZOOM! – he dribbled

down the wing instead with his dancing feet flying.
Eventually, a defender tackled him, but the Monaco
fans were impressed already.

'That kid looks brilliant!'

Kylian kept moving and calling for the ball. He
wanted it every time. He had the composure to pick
out good passes, and the strength to go shoulder to
shoulder with his opponents. He was totally fearless.
In the end, Kylian couldn't grab the winning goal but
that night against Caen, his potential was recognised,
and a superstar was born.

'Nothing fazes you, does it?' Tiémoué laughed
as he congratulated Kylian at the final whistle. 'You
were awesome out there!'

Monaco's wonderkid wasn't getting carried away,
though.

'Yes, but we didn't win,' he replied, 'and I didn't
score.'

Kylian had been dreaming about his first senior
goal since he was four years old. How would it feel?
How would he celebrate? And what kind of a goal
would it be?

It turned out to be a left-foot shot from near the penalty spot. In the last minute of a home match against ESTAC Troyes, Hélder crossed from the left. There were two players waiting for it – Tiémoué and Kylian. He had sprinted all the way from the halfway line to get there first in a blur of orange boots. He was so determined to score.

Goooooooooooooooooooooaaaaaaaaaaaaaaaaaallllllllllll llllllllllllllllll!!!!!!!!!!!!!!!!!!!!

3–1! As his shot hit the back of the net, Kylian turned and threw his arms up in the air. Not only was it his first goal but he had made Monaco history again. Seventeen years and sixty-two days – he was now the club's youngest-ever goalscorer. And whose record had he be broken? You guessed it, Thierry Henry! That made it extra special.

'Fair enough, you finished that well,' Tiémoué laughed as they celebrated, 'but next time, it's my turn!'

Although Kylian was clearly enjoying himself out on the pitch for Monaco, he still hadn't signed his first professional contract. That was a major worry for Vasilyev. Had the club done enough to persuade Kylian to stay? Or would PSG steal him away by offering more money and fame?

No, on 6 March 2016, Kylian sat down to sign a three-year deal with Monaco. He was where he wanted to be – playing regular first-team football. He wasn't yet playing every minute, but he *was* playing lots of minutes.

'I'm very happy and very proud to sign my first professional contract,' Kylian told the club's website. 'This is the club that has helped me grow. I feel good here.'

'Right, let's start winning some trophies!' Kylian told his teammates.

Monaco finished the 2015–16 season in third place in Ligue 1, a massive thirty-one points behind the champions, PSG. Still, the good news was that they qualified for the Champions League. Kylian was super-excited about that. Even in the thirty-five minutes of Europa League football he had played against Tottenham, he had managed to set up a goal for Stephan El Shaarawy.

Kylian couldn't wait for the challenge of the Champions League. It was the ultimate test for any football superstar. Who knew, maybe he would even get to play against Cristiano Ronaldo's Real Madrid!

Kylian's youth team days at Monaco weren't quite over yet, though. The Under-19s were through to the final of the Coupe Gambardella against Lens, and they needed their seventeen-year-old wonderkid.

'Sure!' said Kylian. He never said no to football.

Back in Paris at the Stade de France, he was Monaco's matchwinner. He set up the first goal for his strike partner Irvin Cardona with a wicked, no-look pass. 1–0!

The second half, however, was The Kylian Mbappé Show. He used his pace and power to get past the Lens defence and then nutmegged their keeper. 2–0!

Gooooooooooooooooooooaaaaaaaaaaaaaaaaalllllllllllll lllllllllllllll!!!!!!!!!!!!!!!!!!!!

But Kylian had saved his best skills until last. On the edge of the penalty area, he had four defenders surrounding him. Surely, he couldn't escape with the ball! But with a stepover and a burst of speed, he did escape, and he scored too. 3–0!

'Man, you're so good it's not fair!' Irvin joked.

As Monaco lifted the cup, Kylian cheered and bounced up and down with his teammates, but he always kept one hand on the trophy. He didn't want to let it go, even though it would be the first of many.

CHAPTER 11

EUROPEAN CHAMPION

By July 2016, Kylian had become a star for club
and country. Because of his parents, he could have
chosen to play for Cameroon or Algeria, but instead,
he picked France. After all, that was where he was
born and where he had lived his whole life. It was
the French national anthem that a young Kylian had
sung loud and proud with his hand on his heart.
Plus, he wanted to be 'The New Henry'.

'If they want me, I want to play for *Les Bleus*,'
Kylian decided.

So, did they want him? Kylian played two
matches for the Under-17s but after that, his France
career stalled. The Under-18s coach, Jean-Claude

Giuntini, refused to select him. Just like his old Monaco youth coach, Giuntini thought Kylian was too inconsistent, too selfish, and not a team player.

Giuntini passed that on to the Under-19s coach, Ludovic Batelli, but luckily, he didn't listen. Yes, Kylian was still only seventeen years old, but he was already lighting up Ligue 1 with Monaco. Plus, Batelli really needed a new superstar because he had just lost his best player, Ousmane Dembélé, to the Under-21s.

'Come on, kid, let's see what you can do,' the coach told Kylian.

France were in the middle of qualification for the Under-19 European Championships. Only eight teams would make it to the big tournament in Germany. To get there, France needed to win their last three matches against Montenegro, Denmark and Serbia. Batelli's team had a strong core – Issa Diop in defence, Lucas Tousart and Ludovic Blas in midfield, Jean-Kévin Augustin in attack – but with Ousmane gone, they lacked flair. That's where Kylian came in...

'Welcome to the squad,' said Lucas, the captain. 'I've heard amazing things about you!'

Not only was Kylian the newest member of the squad, but he was also the youngest. Would he struggle to make friends? No, because he'd been playing with older age groups all his life.

'Are you sure you're only seventeen?' Jean-Kévin joked. 'You act more like you're *seventy-seven*, if you ask me!'

Kylian didn't play football like a seventy-seven-year-old, though. In the match against Montenegro, he was France's danger man. Whether he popped up on the left wing or the right, he was always a threat. He could and should have got a hat-trick of goals and a hat-trick of assists. But instead, it was Ludovic who scored the only goal of the game.

'Come on, where's the end product?' Kylian asked himself angrily. 'You've got to do better than that!'

He did, two days later against Denmark, scoring the first goal in a 4–0 thrashing. Now, France just needed one last win.

Against Serbia, Jean-Kévin dribbled forward and passed to Kylian out on the right wing. 'Finish this!' his brain was telling him. He took one touch to control the ball, then looked up and BANG!

Goooooooooooooooooooooaaaaaaaaaaaaaaaalllllllll lllllllllllllllllll!!!!!!!!!!!!!!!!!!!!

Kylian and Jean-Kévin high-fived. 'We're off to Germany!' they cheered together.

On the touchline, Batelli punched the air. His decision to pick Kylian was really paying off. Could France now go on and win the Under-19 Euros? Why not? The last time that *Les Bleus* had won it was 2010, when they had Antoine Griezmann and Alexandre Lacazette in attack. Now, they had Kylian and Jean-Kévin.

France were placed in Group B with England, Croatia and the Netherlands. Kylian never worried too much about his opponents. At his best, he knew that he was good enough to beat anyone. Unfortunately, he wasn't at his best in the first game against England. Batelli took him off after sixty minutes as France lost 2–1.

'Don't worry, we all have bad days,' his coach told him. 'In three days, we go again!'

Jean-Kévin scored France's first goal against Croatia, and Kylian scored their second. He controlled Issa's long ball beautifully, dribbled around the keeper and tapped it home. He made it look so easy.

*Goooooooooooooooooooooaaaaaaaaaaaaaaaaalllllllllll
lllllllllllllllll!!!!!!!!!!!!!!!!!!!!!*

'That's more like it!' Kylian shouted passionately as he sank to his knees on the grass.

There was no stopping France now, and especially their star strikeforce. They had a friendly rivalry going. Who could score more? Against the Netherlands, Kylian got two, but Jean-Kévin got three!

'I win this time,' the hat-trick hero said as he walked off with the matchball.

In the semi-finals against Portugal, it was Kylian's turn to shine. France were 1–0 down after just two minutes, but they fought back quickly. Dribbling way out on the left wing, Kylian looked like he was going nowhere. But suddenly, ZOOM! – he muscled his way past the Portugal right-back and played a great cross to Ludovic. 1–1!

'Come on!' Kylian cried out as the whole team hugged each other.

In the second half, Clément Michelin crossed from the right, and Kylian poked the ball in.

Goooooooooooooooooooooaaaaaaaaaaaaaaaaalllllllllll llllllllllllllll!!!!!!!!!!!!!!!!!!!!

2–1! He celebrated like his hero, with a jump and a spin.

'Nice one, Cristiano!' Ludovic teased.

Kylian's second goal was more like Ronaldo, though. He jumped up high to head the ball past the Portugal keeper. 3–1!

He was France's hero, leading them through to the European Championship final against Italy.

'Okay, you win this time,' Jean-Kévin admitted.

With one game to go, France's two top young attackers were tied on five goals each. Who would claim the Golden Boot?

Against Italy, Jean-Kévin scored his sixth goal in

the sixth minute of the match. 1–0 to France!

What about Kylian? He dribbled into the Italian penalty area, but his shot went wide. 'No!' he shouted, slapping his leg in frustration.

In the end, it was Jean-Kévin who got the Golden Boot and Best Player awards. Never mind that, though, because after a 4–0 win, France were the European Champions! And at the age of seventeen, Kylian had played a massive part in their success. He had another winners' medal to add to his collection.

'Well done!' Kylian's proud parents shouted when they met up with him afterwards.

'Great work!' said the AS Bondy president, Atmane Airouche, who congratulated him. He had come all the way to Germany to cheer his old player on. 'I hope you're having a big party tonight!'

Kylian shrugged. 'Some of the others are going out, but I'm tired. I might just go to bed.'

For Kylian, it was just another goal achieved. The next day, he would move straight on to his next target – winning more trophies at Monaco.

CHAPTER 12

HAT-TRICK HERO

In the space of six short months, Kylian had
played his first senior game, scored his first senior
goal, signed his first senior contract, and won the
Under-19 European Championships with France. All
of that, and he was still only seventeen!

So it was no wonder that Kylian was feeling pretty
confident as the 2016–17 Ligue 1 season kicked off.
He felt ready to fight for more game-time at Monaco.
He would show Jardim that he deserved to play more
than just the last twenty minutes of matches. He
wanted to play every minute of every match! To do
that, though, he needed to start the new season with
a BANG!

Kylian couldn't wait for the first game against

Guingamp. He was starting up front alongside Guido Carrillo, with Tiémoué and Thomas Lemar in midfield. Awesome! However, it soon turned into a nightmare.

First, Monaco went 2–0 down, and then as Kylian tried to turn things around for his team, he suffered a head injury and had to come off.

'What? No, I'm fine to play on!' he argued, but the team doctors stood firm. He couldn't continue in case there was a serious concussion.

For the next two months, Kylian had to wait and watch from the sidelines. Monaco were playing well without him, and they even beat PSG. When would Jardim put him back into the team? Kylian was still as impatient as ever.

Kylian finally returned to the starting line-up against Montpellier. Great, so what could he do to keep his place this time? As he dribbled into the penalty area, he had two defenders in front of him and no teammate to pass to. He faked to cross with his right foot but then switched it to his left. Just as he was about to shoot, one of the defenders fouled him. *Penalty!*

'Well done, mate!' Radamel Falcao said, helping him back to his feet.

Kylian scored Monaco's second goal himself with a clever flick header, and then set up the fourth goal for Valère Germain.

Surely Jardim couldn't drop him after that? But for the next two months, Kylian was in and out of the Monaco team. He would play one great game, and then one average game. That wasn't good enough. He knew that he needed to become more consistent with his goals and assists – and December 2016's League Cup match against Rennes was a good place to start.

Kylian sprinted onto Boschilia's through-ball and curled a shot past the keeper.

Goooooooooooooooooooooaaaaaaaaaaaaaaaaallllllllllll llllllllllllllllll!!!!!!!!!!!!!!!!!!

1–0! 'Come on!' he roared, pumping his fist at the crowd.

Just ten minutes later, Kylian tapped home Nabil Dirar's cross. 2–0!

'Nice one!' he cheered, jumping into Nabil's arms.

Kylian had seventy more minutes to complete
his first professional hat-trick. Surely he could do
it. The time ticked by quickly, but he didn't give up
hope. All he needed was one chance. Finally, in
the second half, João Moutinho played the perfect
pass and Kylian couldn't miss. 4–0 – he was a hat-
trick hero!

'Thanks!' Kylian called out, giving João a high-five
and a hug. What a way to celebrate his eighteenth
birthday, which was just days away!

Now, Kylian needed to take that red-hot scoring
form back into Ligue 1. There was no time to waste.
Against Metz, he lined up alongside João, Radamel,
Boschilia, Bernardo *and* Fabinho – what an awesome
attacking team! Yes, Kylian had a very good feeling
about this game...

João chipped a great pass over the top to Radamel,
who headed it down to Kylian. With his left foot, he
calmly placed his shot in the bottom corner. 1–0!

*Goooooooooooooooooooooaaaaaaaaaaaaaaaalllllllllll
lllllllllllllll!!!!!!!!!!!!!!!!!!!*

'Thanks, partner!' Kylian cheered happily, pointing

back at Radamel.

They were Monaco's new star strikeforce, just like Kylian and Jean-Kévin had been for the France Under-19s. Kylian's speed and skill, combined with Radamel's strength and experience – what could defenders do? Uh oh, Metz were in big trouble.

Radamel converted a cross from the right. 2–0!

Kylian raced onto Fabinho's long ball, cut onto his right foot and scored. 3–0!

'Come on!' he cried out, punching the air.

It was time to score another hat trick. Boschilia threaded a great pass through to Kylian. As the goalkeeper rushed out at his feet, he managed to poke it past him. 4–0 – hat-trick hero!

Kylian stood there with his left arm in the air and a huge grin on his face. What a feeling! The Monaco fans waved their red-and-white flags and chanted his name:

Mbappé! Mbappé! Mbappé!

There was even time for Radamel to grab a second goal. 5–0!

'If we keep this up, the title's ours for sure!' Kylian

cried out joyfully.

They were playing so well together. With thirteen games to go, Monaco were top of the Ligue 1 table, three points ahead of their rivals, PSG. The fans were full of hope, after seventeen years of disappointment. Kylian and his teammates couldn't let them down.

'Let's take it one game at a time,' Jardim told his players, 'and take our chances!'

Kylian did exactly what his manager asked. Against Nantes, he scored his first goal after four minutes. Then just before half-time, he steered Bernardo's incredible cross past the keeper.

Goooooooooooooooooooooaaaaaaaaaaaaaaaaallllllllllll llllllllllllllll!!!!!!!!!!!!!!!!!!!!

Kylian roared up at the crowd, pumping both fists. It was another special occasion for him. He had just scored his tenth Ligue 1 goal and he was the youngest player to have achieved that for thirty years. Forget the 'New Henry' nickname – Kylian was on track to become the best player ever!

'Are you surprised by how well Mbappé's playing?' the journalists asked Jardim. Suddenly,

everyone wanted to know everything about France's
latest wonderkid.

'No, not at all,' the Monaco manager replied. 'I've
worked with him every day since he was seventeen.
We know that he's a player of great quality with a
spectacular future ahead of him.'

Yes, what a season Kylian was having! His record
on the pitch was remarkable – a goal or an assist
every sixty minutes. But would he be able to keep
that up? Of course he could! He was feeling as
confident as ever.

CHAPTER 13

MAGIC VS MANCHESTER CITY

Scoring goals for fun in France was one thing, but what about in Europe? The Champions League was the greatest club competition in the world. That was where a star could become a *super*star. Messi, Cristiano, Neymar Jr... could Kylian be next?

In the group stage, however, he only played twenty-five minutes of Monaco's six matches: thirteen minutes against Bayer Leverkusen and twelve minutes against CSKA Moscow; it just wasn't enough time to shine.

'I'm quick, but I'm not that quick!' Kylian joked with Jirés.

But that was all before he became a hat-trick hero.

By the time the Round of 16 started in February 2017, he was one half of Monaco's star strikeforce – Radamel and Kylian. Would Jardim finally give him his first Champions League start, away at Pep Guardiola's Manchester City?

Yes! There was his name and shirt number on the teamsheet – 'MBAPPÉ 29'. Kylian wanted to run a victory lap around the training pitch but instead, he played it cool. Starting in the Champions League at the age of eighteen? No big deal!

'Thanks boss, I won't let you down,' Kylian said with a serious look on his young face.

Over 53,000 fans packed into Manchester City's Etihad Stadium for the biggest game of the season so far. As the teams walked out of the tunnel and onto the pitch, Kylian's whole body was buzzing. Both sets of supporters were making so much noise! It was even better than he'd imagined in his childhood dreams.

'Attack down the right wing whenever you can,' Radamel told Kylian as they waited to take the kick-off together. 'Fernandinho's a midfielder, not a left-back!'

'Will do!'

It was City who scored first, but Monaco kept fighting. They weren't the best team in defence but they were awesome in attack. Fabinho crossed to the back post and there was Radamel with a brilliant diving header. 1–1!

It was an end-to-end game, full of exciting football. The Manchester City defence couldn't handle Kylian's pace and movement. Radamel flicked the ball on and he sprinted past Yaya Touré and Nicolás Otamendi...

'Keep calm,' Kylian told himself.

He didn't want to waste it by shooting wildly, but unfortunately, that's exactly what he did.

'Hahahaha!' the City fans laughed, as the ball flew high and wide of the goal.

Kylian puffed out his cheeks. What a chance! He had to do better next time. He soon got a second chance. As Fabinho played the pass, Kylian raced into the penalty area, between the City centre-backs. The ball bounced up nicely for him to strike but Kylian didn't rush his finish this time. He slowed down and picked his spot – top corner. 2–1!

*Goooooooooooooooooooooaaaaaaaaaaaaaaaallllllllllll
lllllllllllllllll!!!!!!!!!!!!!!!!!!!!!*

Kylian threw his arms out wide and then slid across
the grass on his knees. 'Yesss!' he screamed. He had
scored his first Champions League goal, and it was one
of his best. Had he broken another record? No, not this
time. He was only the second youngest Frenchman to
score in the Champions League – Karim Benzema had
been three months younger. Never mind!

'What a shot, *Casse-bonbon!*' Benjamin Mendy
cheered. That was his new nickname for Kylian. It
was the French for 'pain in the neck'.

From then, Monaco's night should have got even
better. Radamel missed a penalty and Kylian missed
another good chance. But instead, City pulled off an
amazing comeback to win the first leg 5–3.

'I know you're disappointed,' Jardim told his
players in the dressing room, 'but those away goals
could be really important. Now, we have to go and
win the second leg at home!'

'Yeah!' they all cheered together. Their team spirit
was so strong.

Kylian had never heard such noise at the Stade Louis II. In one stand, the fans formed a wall of red and white.

'Monaco! Monaco! Monaco!' they chanted all night long.

Out on the pitch, the players did them proud. Kylian got his first chance in the sixth minute, but City's keeper made a good save.

'So close!' he groaned with his hands on his head. Still, it was a good sign...

Two minutes later, Bernardo crossed from the left and Kylian stuck out his right boot. Nutmeg! He poked the ball through the keeper's legs and into the net. 5–4!

Goooooooooooooooooooooaaaaaaaaaaaaaaaaalllllllllll llllllllllllllll!!!!!!!!!!!!!!!!!!!

Kylian hardly gave himself time to celebrate his second Champions League goal. 'Let's go!' he called out, beckoning his teammates to follow him back to the halfway line. They had more work to do.

That early goal gave Monaco lots of confidence. Soon, Benjamin crossed to Fabinho – 5–5! Kylian ran over to high-five the goalscorer.

'We're almost there!' he screamed.

However, when Leroy Sané scored for City, Monaco needed to get another goal, or they were out. They could do it; Kylian never stopped believing. With fifteen minutes to go, Fabinho won a free kick on the right wing. Thomas curled the ball into the box and Tiémoué headed it in. 6–6!   The whole Monaco team chased after their hero.

They would qualify on the 'away goals' rule. An away goal victory was a close as a Champions League tie could be, but Kylian didn't care.'Quarter-finals, here we come!' he yelled to the fans above.

At the final whistle, the players ran towards each other for a big team hug. Against the odds, they had beaten Manchester City!

It was a famous win for the club, and a famous night for Kylian too. He had just scored two goals in two games against one of the best teams in the world.

He was no longer just the talk of France; Kylian was now the talk of the whole football world.

CHAPTER 14

CHAMPIONS OF FRANCE

Kylian's first Champions League adventure didn't end there. He was becoming more and more consistent as the competition went on. In the quarter-finals against Borussia Dortmund in April 2017, he was Monaco's main man again.

Away in Germany, Thomas crossed and Kylian bundled the ball in. 1–0!

Then in the second half, he stole the ball off the Dortmund defence, steadied himself and slammed a shot into the top corner. 3–1!

Goooooooooooooooooooooaaaaaaaaaaaaaaaalllllllllll llllllllllllllll!!!!!!!!!!!!!!!!!!!!

It was time for Kylian's new celebration pose. He

slid on his knees, folded his arms across his chest, and tried to look as cool as possible. He had his younger brother to thank for the pose. That's what Ethan did whenever he beat Kylian at FIFA.

'You can't keep copying Ronaldo when you score,' Ethan told him. 'You're a superstar now. You need a move of your own!'

Kylian had to use his awesome new celebration pose again in the second leg against Dortmund. It was his fifth goal in four games – he was officially on fire! He scored one more in the semi-final against Juventus but that's where his amazing first Champions League journey came to an end – Monaco lost 4–1 on aggregate.

'I'll be back,' Kylian promised himself, 'and one day, I'm going to lift that trophy!'

He had to move on quickly, though, because Monaco had other prizes to fight for. PSG beat them in the French Cup semi-final and the League Cup final, but their Ligue 1 title dream was still alive.

Game after game, Monaco kept on winning because Kylian kept on scoring. He got the opening goal to beat Bordeaux, and then two more to conquer Caen. His composure was incredible.

'I wish all young players were as mature as you,' Radamel joked in training. 'You're got more sense than Benjamin and Tiémoué put together!'

But every time Monaco won, PSG won too. PSG were still only three points behind in second place. Every weekend, the pressure was on to perform well. One slip-up and the title race could be wide open again.

Monaco's trip to Lyon would be particularly tough. Lyon were fourth in Ligue 1 and they had a talented team featuring Memphis Depay, Mathieu Valbuena, and Kylian's old Under-19 captain, Lucas.

'Come on, six more wins and the title's ours!' Jardim reminded his players before kick-off.

Kylian was determined. They couldn't end their sensational season without a single trophy!

Against Lyon, Radamel scored first but they knew that one goal wouldn't be enough. Monaco needed a second to make things safe. Just before half-time, Bernardo found Kylian in space on the left wing.

Uh oh, Lyon were in big trouble. Kylian licked his

lips and raced forward at speed. He was so dangerous on the dribble. Lyon's centre-back Mouctar Diakhaby backed away and backed away, too scared to attempt a tackle.

Stepover to the left, a little hop, and then GO!

To finish, Kylian lifted the ball over the diving keeper and into the back of the net.

Goooooooooooooooooooooaaaaaaaaaaaaaaaallllllllllll llllllllllllllll!!!!!!!!!!!!!!!!!!!!!

2–0! Kylian skidded over to the corner flag, with his arms firmly folded. The fans were going wild up above, but not him. He stayed as cool as ever.

'What a hero!' Bernardo cried out when he caught up with his teammate.

Kylian nodded his head as he got back to his feet. Yes, he was a hero – Monaco's hero. And with his help, they were going to win that league title, no matter what.

'Five more wins!' Jardin urged his players on.

The next weekend, Monaco took on Toulouse on the Saturday. Again, Kylian's name was there on the teamsheet and again, it was there on the scoresheet too. There was just no stopping him, or his team. From 1–0 down, they fought back to win 3–1.

'We're nearly there!' Kylian shouted to the supporters at the final whistle.

That Monaco victory put the pressure back on PSG. Could they beat Nice on the Sunday? No, they lost 3–1!

'Two more wins!' Jardim told his players before their match against Lille. The finish line was in sight!

Just before half-time, Kylian found himself one-on-one with the left-back on the edge of the penalty area. Uh oh, Lille were in big trouble. Kylian twisted and turned, one way and then the other, with his fancy feet flashing. First right, then left, then right again. ZOOM! With a burst of speed, Kylian dribbled through and crossed to Bernardo. 2–0!

'Thanks, Kylian!'

In the second half, Thomas chipped a clever pass over the top to Kylian. He could have taken a touch to control it but no, he had a better idea. He could see Radamel waiting in the middle, so he crossed it first time on the volley. 3–0!

'Thanks, Kylian!'

One more win – that was all Monaco needed now. There was a tense atmosphere at the Stade Louis II ahead of their match against Saint-Étienne. Could they claim the title in front of their home crowd? It would be the perfect way to win it.

Monaco! Monaco! Monaco!

Kylian was desperate to be his team's hero yet again. He hit a powerful early strike but the Saint-Étienne goalkeeper made a good save.

'What a chance!' Kylian sighed heavily. Next time, he had to score.

Radamel played the perfect pass and Kylian was off, sprinting straight past the Saint-Étienne defence. Now he just had the keeper to beat. He looked up and picked his spot – bottom corner. He pulled back his right foot and…

…DUMMY!

As the goalkeeper dived, Kylian dribbled around him and passed the ball into the empty net. 1–0!

Goooooooooooooooooooaaaaaaaaaaaaaaaalllllllllll llllllllllllllll!!!!!!!!!!!!!!!!!!!

'Phew, I thought you were going to miss that!' Radamel said as they celebrated.

Kylian just laughed. 'Me? Never!'

Would one goal be enough? No, Monaco needed a second to make things safe but it didn't arrive until the last minute. Thomas crossed to Valère. 2–0!

By then, Kylian had been substituted, so he stood there clapping and cheering on the sidelines. Why wasn't the referee blowing the final whistle yet? He was ready to run back on for the big title celebrations.

The party had already started in the stadium. The fans waved their red-and-white flags and sang at the top of their voices:

Campiones, Campiones, Olé! Olé! Olé!

Finally, the match was over, and so was Monaco's seventeen-year wait. They were the Champions of France again!

Campiones, Campiones, Olé! Olé! Olé!

It was a moment that Kylian would never forget for as long as he lived. He was soon at the centre of the big team hug on the pitch. Monaco's superstars moved around the pitch together –

Radamel, Fabinho, Benjamin, Bernardo, Boschilia, Tiémoué, Thomas, Valère, and, of course, Kylian – all applauding the fans.

What an important part he had played in his first full season – 15 goals and 11 assists! And that was only in Ligue 1, where he was the clear winner of the Young Player of the Year award.

In total, Kylian had finished with 26 goals and 14 assists. All that, and he was still only eighteen years old. His stats were way better than Messi or Cristiano at that age. At this rate, Kylian would achieve his dream of becoming the best footballer ever.

Once they had collected their winners' medals and lifted the Ligue 1 trophy, the Monaco players returned to the dressing room to get ready for a big night out.

'Are you coming, mate?' Tiémoué asked.

Kylian shook his head. 'Sorry, I'm tired. I'm going to go home, but have fun!'

For him, the Ligue 1 title was just another goal achieved. The next day, he would move straight on to his next two targets – the Champions League and the World Cup.

CHAPTER 15

FRANCE'S NEW FLAIR PLAYER

'Mbappé for France!'

The Monaco fans had been calling for him ever since the start of the 2016–17 season. 'Yes, he's still young, but look how amazing he is *already*. He could win the World Cup for us in a few years!'

Didier Deschamps, the national team coach, wasn't so sure. What was the rush? At that stage, Kylian was still only seventeen. So, he didn't make the senior France squad for the qualifiers against Belarus in September 2016, or against Bulgaria and the Netherlands in October, or against Sweden in November either.

But by March 2017, Kylian had forced Deschamps to change his mind. How could he say no to

Monaco's young hat-trick hero, especially after his magic against Manchester City? France were crying out for a flair player like that.

'Who knows, maybe we wouldn't have lost the Euro 2016 final if we'd had Mbappé in the team!' his fans argued.

Kylian had watched that final on TV in Germany with the national Under-19s squad. It was France vs Portugal, his nation vs his hero, Cristiano. France were the clear favourites to win. They were playing at home at the Stade de France and their attacking trio – Olivier Giroud, Antoine Griezmann and Dimitri Payet – had looked awesome all tournament.

'Allez la France! Allez la France!' Kylian and his teammates cheered.

In the final, however, France's forwards just could not find a way past the Portugal defence. When Dimitri got injured, Deschamps brought on Kingsley Coman, but he couldn't change the game either. Neither could André-Pierre Gignac or Anthony Martial. In the end, it was Portugal's Eder who scored the winning goal.

'How on earth did we lose that?' France's junior stars asked each other in disbelief. Back home in Paris, their senior stars were asking themselves the exact same question.

'I could have changed that game' – Kylian didn't say it out loud but that's what he was thinking. He had the speed, the skill *and* the confidence. Two weeks later, he helped France to win the Under-19 Euros. If only...

But now, nine months after that Euro 2016 final, Kylian was about to skip straight to the French senior team. Deschamps named his squad for the World Cup qualifier against Luxembourg:

Hugo Lloris, Laurent Koscielny, Paul Pogba, Antoine Griezmann, Olivier Giroud, Dimitri Payet...

There were lots of older, experienced players on the list but there was also a new young star:

...Kylian Mbappé.

'Congratulations!' his proud parents cried down the phone.

'Well done, you deserve it!' his Monaco manager told him.

429

'You and me, *Casse-bonbon*,' his club teammate Benjamin cheered happily. It was his first call-up too. 'Let's do this!'

What an honour! Being called up to the national team was a dream come true for Kylian, but it wouldn't mean much unless he actually played. If he came on, would he become France's youngest-ever international? He loved breaking records. But no, it turned out Maryan Wisnieski had been thirty-three days younger when he made his debut in 1955!

Still, Kylian was desperate to play against Luxembourg. Hopefully, if France were winning comfortably, he would get his chance.

Djibril Sidibé cut the ball back to Olivier. 1–0!

On the sidelines, Kylian punched the air. They were off to a good start but five minutes later, Luxembourg won a penalty. 1–1!

'Maybe they'll need me to come on and change the game,' Kylian thought, trying to think positively.

But no, Antoine scored from the spot. 2–1!

Then Benjamin crossed to Olivier. 3–1!

Was that game over? Deschamps decided to take

off Dimitri and replace him with... Kylian! He was already warmed up and raring to go.

'Use your speed to attack down the left,' his manager told him.

Sure thing! Wearing the white 'Number 12' shirt, Kylian raced out onto the field. He didn't think about the fact that he was making his senior France debut, or about his talented new teammates. All he thought about was getting on the ball as quickly as possible. How much magic could he create in the last fifteen minutes?

Plenty! Ousmane Dembélé curled a great pass to Kylian as he ran down the wing. Uh oh, Luxembourg were in big trouble. He stayed calm and hit a powerful shot with his left foot, but the goalkeeper managed to tip it over the bar.

So close! Kylian winced. It was nearly the perfect start to his senior international career.

He didn't get another chance to shoot, but he did get the chance to show off his full range of fancy skills and stepovers.

'Hurray!' the France fans cheered. They loved their new flair player.

ZOOM! Kylian sprinted straight past Luxembourg's right-back and crossed the ball into the box. Olivier stretched out his right foot, but he couldn't quite reach it.

So close! Kylian winced again. He had nearly helped Olivier to get his hat-trick.

'Great ball!' the striker shouted, giving him a thumbs-up.

Kylian soon ran out of time but three days later, Deschamps picked him to start in the friendly match against Spain at the Stade de France in Paris.

'Thanks boss, you won't regret it!'

In his hometown, Kylian would get to play sixty, seventy, maybe even ninety minutes of football! He couldn't wait. In the tunnel, he looked as relaxed as ever, but once the match kicked off, he was fully focused on winning and scoring.

A cross came in from the left, and Kylian cleverly flicked it goalwards… but David De Gea made a super save!

So close! For a moment, Kylian stood there with his head in his hands, but then he chased back to get the ball again. He still had plenty of time left.

Kylian certainly didn't look like the new kid on the block. He was linking up really well with Antoine, playing one-twos all over the pitch. Was this the future of France's attack? The fans hoped so.

At half-time, Gerard Piqué even asked to swap shirts with him. What? The Barcelona centre-back had won pretty much everything there was to win in football – the World Cup, the Euros, the Champions League, the Spanish League. But now, Piqué wanted Kylian's shirt!

'Sure,' he replied, sounding as cool as ever.

After sixty-five minutes, Deschamps replaced Kylian with Olivier. At that point, the score was 0–0, but soon, France were 2–0 down.

'That's what happens when you take Mbappé off!' his supporters argued.

Oh well, Kylian's first international goal and assist would have to wait a little longer. That was okay; he would have plenty more chances to impress. At the age of eighteen, he was only just getting started.

CHAPTER 16

WHICH CLUB TO CHOOSE? PART II

After winning the Ligue 1 title for the 2016–17 season, what was next for Monaco? Would they grow stronger, or was it a one-off success? Would they be able to buy even better players, or would they lose their superstars? Unfortunately, it was a story with a sad ending.

Bernardo Silva was the first to go, moving to Manchester City in May 2017.

'I'm going to miss playing with you!' Kylian admitted as they said their goodbyes.

Next, Nabil Dirar went to Fenerbahçe, and Valère Germain went to Marseille, while in July, Tiémoué Bakayoko left to join Chelsea.

'Don't go!' Kylian begged his friend.

Then, to make matters even worse, Benjamin Mendy moved to Manchester City as well.

'No, not you too! Why is everyone abandoning me?' Kylian complained.

At this rate, it would just be him, Radamel Falcao, Thomas Lemar and Fabinho left! Monaco had no chance against the power of PSG, especially when their rivals signed Neymar Jr from Barcelona for £200 million.

'They'll win the league easily now!' Kylian thought to himself.

Was it time for Kylian to move on too? He loved his club but he wanted to win the top trophies. That didn't look very likely to happen at Monaco.

Kylian thought long and hard about what was best for his career. He was one of the top players in the world now, and the big clubs were queuing up to buy him once again. But which one would he choose?

Arsenal? Arsène Wenger had been trying to sign him for years but The Gunners weren't even in the Champions League anymore. Kylian had his eyes firmly fixed on that prize.

Liverpool? Kylian had an exciting conversation with their manager, Jürgen Klopp, but unfortunately, the club couldn't afford to buy him.

Manchester City? That was a possibility. Money wasn't a problem for them, and Kylian had really impressed Pep Guardiola with his Champions League magic.

'Come join our exciting project,' the City manager tried to persuade Kylian. 'Think about it – you, Sergio Agüero, Leroy Sané and Gabriel Jesus in attack, with Kevin De Bruyne and David Silva in midfield. We would win every trophy there is!'

Working with Guardiola would be an amazing experience, but playing in the Premier League? Kylian wasn't so sure about that – what other options did he have?

Barcelona? With Neymar Jr gone, was there a gap next to Lionel Messi and Luis Suárez? No, they eventually decided to sign his France teammate Ousmane Dembélé instead.

Real Madrid? How cool would it be if Kylian

and Cristiano could play together in the same star strikeforce. They would be unstoppable! Real's manager, Zidane, loved that idea and so did the club president, Florentino Pérez. He met with the Monaco chairman, Dmitry Rybolovlev, to agree a deal.

'We want £170 million for Mbappé.'

'We'll offer £130 million, plus an extra £25 million in bonuses.'

Pérez left France, feeling very confident. The deal wasn't quite done yet, but it seemed like only a matter of time before Real got their new Galáctico signing.

Kylian was excited too. He had dreamed of playing for the club ever since his first trip to Madrid for his fourteenth birthday – plus Real had just won the Spanish League *and* the Champions League.

'Don't get your hopes up yet,' his dad told him. 'There's still a lot to work out before you get to wear that famous white shirt!'

Wilfried was also now Kylian's agent and he travelled to Spain to meet with Pérez and the club directors. There was one important issue that he wanted to discuss: Kylian's role in the Real team. After all, he wasn't going to move to Madrid to just sit on the Bernabéu bench.

'So, where will my son fit into the starting line-up?' Wilfried asked.

It was a good question. Real already had their star strikeforce, 'BBC' - Karim Benzema, Gareth Bale and Cristiano. They also had two young talents waiting in the wings: Isco and Marco Asensio. Did they really have space for another wonderkid?

'Don't worry, we'll make room for Kylian,' Pérez promised.

However, by the middle of August, nothing had changed. Real still had all of their attacking stars.

'Sorry, son,' Wilfried said. 'I don't think that's a good move for you right now.'

There was one last option left – Kylian's hometown club, PSG. They were desperate for him to become the third member of their amazing new all-star attack. Forget Barcelona's 'MSN' or Real Madrid's 'BBC'; PSG were aiming for 'MCN': Kylian Mbappé, Edinson Cavani and Neymar Jr.

'With the three of you, we believe that we can win the Champions League,' PSG's manager, Unai Emery, declared confidently.

That was exactly what Kylian wanted to hear! Not only were PSG offering him regular first-team football, but they were building a top-quality team to take on Barcelona and Real Madrid. He would even get to play with one of his heroes, Neymar Jr! Kylian used to play as PSG on FIFA so that he could use the Brazilian to beat his brother Ethan.

'I'm in!' Kylian told his dad.

There was one big problem, though. Would Monaco really sell Kylian to their biggest Ligue 1 rivals? They didn't want to say yes, but PSG's offer was too good to say no to – the full asking price of £170 million. It wouldn't be paid straight away because PSG had already spent so much money on Neymar Jr, but they would take Kylian on loan for one year and then pay the full amount the next season.

Monaco could see that Kylian's mind was made up. He wanted to return home to Paris and there was no point trying to stop him. On 31 August 2017, the deal was done. Suddenly, his face was seen all over his city.

'Welcome Kylian,' said one poster.

'Paris loves Mbappé,' said another.

Another just showed his number – 29, the same shirt that he had worn at Monaco.

Kylian had already been famous but now that he was a PSG player, he was super-famous. Every time he tried to leave his house, fans surrounded him in seconds, asking for photos and autographs. It was crazy; he couldn't go anywhere anymore!

Oh well, Kylian would just have to get used to all the extra attention. For now, though, he was fully focused on football.

'I really wanted to be part of the club's project,' he had told the media. 'It's one of the most ambitious in Europe.'

It was time for PSG's stars to prove themselves. Kylian, Edinson and Neymar Jr – they were about to take on their greatest challenge together.

CHAPTER 17

OFF THE MARK FOR FRANCE

Before making his debut for his new club, PSG, however, Kylian had two more games to play for his country. A shock defeat to Sweden meant that France really needed two wins in their World Cup qualifiers against The Netherlands and Luxembourg.

'Let's do this!' Kylian told his old Monaco teammate, Thomas Lemar.

Kylian had only just signed for PSG but luckily, he didn't have far to travel for the first game. The Stade de France was only an hour's bus ride across Paris from the PSG ground at Parc des Princes. He was really looking forward to representing his country again. He was now the second most expensive player in the world, but his international record still stood at four games and zero goals. He had failed to score in twenty minutes against Sweden, or in ninety-five minutes against England.

'I've really got to do something about that,' Kylian told his teammates, with that serious look on his face.

The Netherlands team weren't as strong as they used to be but Didier Deschamps wasn't taking any risks. The France manager stuck with his usual formation – Kingsley Coman and Thomas Lemar on the wings, with Antoine Griezmann and Olivier Giroud up front. That left Kylian waiting impatiently on the bench again.

'Allez les Bleus!' he mumbled, shaking his restless legs. How long would he have to wait?

Antoine played a great one-two with Olivier and then nutmegged the keeper. 1–0!

Kylian slumped a little further down in his seat. If France's strikers kept playing like that, he wouldn't be needed at all! However, sixty minutes went by before Thomas made it 2–0 with a superstrike.

'Bring me on, bring me on!'

Kylian looked over at Deschamps. Was the manager ready to make a change? Yes, he was – and a few minutes later, Kylian finally came on to replace Olivier.

'Hurray, it's Mbappé!' the fans cheered.

Right – Kylian had twenty minutes to score his first goal for France. That seemed like plenty of time but it would soon fly by if he didn't take his chances...

He dribbled through the tired Dutch defence but the keeper saved his shot.

'Hey, look up!' Antoine shouted angrily, standing in lots of space.

'Sorry!'

The next time Kylian ran forward, Kylian did pass the ball to Djibril Sidibé, but he asked for it straight back.

'Now!' he cried out, sprinting into the penalty area.

Djibril's pass was perfect and so was Kylian's finish. This time, the keeper had no chance.

Goooooooooooooooooooooaaaaaaaaaaaaaaaaalllllllllll lllllllllllllll!!!!!!!!!!!!!!!!!!!!!

Kylian raced behind the goal with his arms and mouth wide open. At last, he was off the mark for France! It was another target achieved before his nineteenth birthday.

Kylian wasn't his country's youngest scorer ever but he was their youngest scorer for fifty-four years. That was a long, long time, and a good reason to crack out his trademark celebration pose. He stopped, folded his arms across his chest, and stood there looking as cool as possible.

'You're allowed to be excited, you know!' Thomas laughed.

The France players all came over to congratulate him – Djibril, Paul Pogba, Alexandre Lacazette. Kylian really felt part of the team now.

'Excellent victory yesterday,' he wrote on Instagram, next to a picture of his celebration.

At that stage, he was wearing France's Number 20 shirt, but hopefully that wouldn't be the case for long. Antoine wore Number 7 and Olivier wore

Number 9. Kylian had his eyes on Number 10. That shirt had belonged to Zidane, France's last World Cup hero.

A deadly display in the next match would surely do the trick. Kylian couldn't wait to start in attack with Antoine and Olivier against a nation ranked 136th in the world. Now that he was off the mark, the goals would surely start to flow. Uh oh, Luxembourg were in big trouble...

But no, it turned out to be a really frustrating night for France. They had so many chances, but they couldn't score a single one! Their composure had completely disappeared.

Kylian pulled the ball back to Antoine but he blasted it high over the bar. MISSED!

He played a quick one-two with Antoine but a defender got in the way of his shot. BLOCKED!

Kylian danced through the Luxembourg defence but then fired straight at the goalkeeper. SAVED!

He threw his arms up in frustration. What was going wrong? Were they trying too hard, or not hard enough? Kylian couldn't tell. He showed off his full range of tricks, flicks and stepovers, but none of it was working. The score was still 0–0. After sixty minutes, Deschamps took Kylian off and put Kingsley on the right wing instead.

'You were unlucky not to score today,' his manager told him, 'but you've got to learn to take your chances.'

It was a harsh but very important lesson for Kylian. Deschamps had so many talented attackers to choose from: Antoine and Olivier, but also Ousmane, Kingsley, Alexandre, Dimitri Payet, Nabil Fekir, Florian Thauvin and Anthony Martial. The pressure was really on to perform.

Kylian had a £170 million price-tag at club level, but that didn't mean anything at international level. In order to achieve his target of playing at the 2018 World Cup, he still had a lot to prove. Deschamps knew that he could be a gamechanger off the bench, but was that the role he wanted? No, Kylian wanted that Number 10 shirt; he wanted to be France's flair player right from the start.

CHAPTER 18

MCN: THE EARLY DAYS

The PSG fans couldn't wait to see Kylian, and 'MCN', in action, and in September 2017 they got their first opportunity. Uh oh, their first opponents Metz were soon in big trouble.

After thirty minutes, Neymar Jr slipped the ball through for his strike partners to chase. Kylian was desperate to score on his debut, but he let Edinson take the shot instead.

1– 0!

'Thanks!' the Uruguayan said, giving his teammate a big hug.

'No problem!'

'MCN' were going to need to work together

to succeed. They were three superstars but they couldn't be selfish. There was no 'I' in 'team', and especially not in 'great team'.

So, who would score next – Kylian or Neymar Jr? In the second half, Kylian chipped the ball forward to the Brazilian. A defender cleared it but it bounced straight back to Kylian. *BANG!*

Goooooooooooooooooooaaaaaaaaaaaaaaaaalllllllllll llllllllllllll!!!!!!!!!!!!!!!!!!!

2–1! 'Yes!' Kylian screamed out, throwing his arms out wide. One game, one goal – Kylian was already off the mark at PSG.

Who would score next? Neymar Jr, of course! He dribbled through and found the bottom corner. 3–1!

Edinson and Kylian jogged over to congratulate the Brazilian. One goal each for all three of them – what a start for 'MCN'! The 2017–18 season was only just beginning, but the future looked very bright for PSG...

...Just as long as they remembered to work together. The following week they were 1–0 up against Lyon when Kylian won a penalty.

'Hurray!' the supporters cheered at first, but that soon turned to:

'BOOOOOOOOOOOOOOOOOOOOOO!'

Edinson had been the team's penalty taker for ages and he was the fans' favourite. But Neymar Jr was trying to steal the spot-kick instead.

'Who does he think he is?' the PSG supporters spat angrily. 'He's only just arrived and he already thinks he owns the place!'

Eventually, Neymar Jr walked away but the Brazilian clearly wasn't happy. To make matters worse, Edinson's penalty then struck the crossbar.

'Come on, we're meant to be a *team!*' Kylian told his strike partners, trying to act as the peacemaker.

'MCN' needed each other. When Neymar Jr missed the next match against Montpellier, 'M' and 'C' couldn't score without him. Kylian had one shot blocked, one shot saved, and one shot cleared off the goal line.

'What's wrong with me today?' he groaned, wiping the sweat off his forehead.

When 'MCN' were reunited a week later against

Bordeaux, they made up for that goalless draw against Montpellier.

Neymar Jr scored a free kick. 1–0!

Edinson poked home the Brazilian's pass. 2–0!

Kylian fluffed his shot but right-back Thomas Meunier scored instead. 3–0!

Edinson let Neymar Jr take the penalty. 4–1!

Julian Draxler volleyed in Kylian's cross. 5–1 at half-time!

The only thing missing was a Kylian goal. He had to get at least one! He vowed he wasn't leaving the pitch until he had added his name to the scoresheet.

Julian returned the favour to Kylian in the second half. Kylian ran on to his pass and picked his spot – far bottom corner. 6–1!

'Finally!' he said to himself with a smile. Kylian dedicated his goal to his injured friend, Benjamin Mendy. He held up two fingers on each hand to make '22', Benjamin's shirt number at Manchester City.

In the dressing room afterwards, manager Unai Emery praised the PSG players. 'See, look what you can achieve when you help each other!'

By the Christmas break, they were nine points clear of Kylian's old club Monaco at the top of the Ligue 1 table. They had won 16 of their 19 games, scoring 58 goals along the way. That included 19 for Edinson, 11 for Neymar Jr and 8 for Kylian.

He wasn't always the star of the show for PSG, but Kylian was the youngest by far and he was just happy to be helping his team out. Along with his eight goals, he also had seven assists. Those were very good numbers and besides, he was looking for club trophies, not individual awards. So far, he was cruising to his second French league title in a row.

He was also learning lots. He had only just turned nineteen and yet he was playing alongside Edinson and Neymar Jr, plus Ángel Di María, Dani Alves, Thiago Silva, Marco Verratti... the list went on and on! With such experienced and talented teammates, Kylian was improving all the time.

'Hey, you're a superstar too, you know!' Neymar Jr kept reminding him.

The Brazilian was six years older than Kylian, but

they got on really well. They were always laughing, joking and posing for Instagram photos together – on airplanes, on the training ground, on the pitch celebrating goals, even at awards ceremonies dressed in smart suits.

'Smile for the followers!'

Kylian was careful not to lose his football focus, though. He was the second most expensive player in the world and the new 'Golden Boy', the best young player in Europe. That was a lot to live up to. Plus, with Ángel playing well, he had to keep fighting for his starting spot. He came off the bench against Dijon with twenty-five minutes to go. Plenty of time to win back his place!

PSG were already winning 5–0, so Kylian could go out onto the Parc des Princes pitch and enjoy himself. With 'MCN' playing together again, the crowd expected more. They got more! Neymar Jr scored the sixth and Kylian scored the seventh.

'Goal time!' he roared, jumping into the Brazilian's arms.

After the match, Kylian posted an Instagram photo

with one arm around Edinson, 'The Matador', and one arm around Neymar Jr, 'Crack x 4'.

Now that they were a happy family, were 'MCN' unstoppable? Not quite. It was easy to forget that Kylian was still so young. It felt like he had been playing football forever! Most of the time, he seemed very mature but occasionally, he did act like the teenager that he was. He was growing up in public and that wasn't always easy.

In the League Cup semi-final against Rennes in January 2018, PSG were winning 3–0 when Kylian took out his frustration on Ismaïla Sarr. It was a silly late tackle and, in a flash, he was surrounded by angry opponents.

'What did you do that for?' they asked, pushing him back.

'Ref, that was reckless. Send him off!' they shouted.

Red card! Kylian walked off slowly, shaking his head and removing his gloves.

'A player did that to me last week and what did he get? Nothing, not even a yellow!' he muttered moodily.

Once he had calmed down, however, Kylian felt guilty and embarrassed. He had let his team down and left them to defend with ten men. What a stupid error! Rennes scored twice, but at least PSG held on for the victory. *Phew!*

'I'm really sorry, that won't happen again,' Kylian promised his manager and teammates. He had definitely learnt his lesson.

'Don't worry, we still won,' Edinson reassured him.

'We all make mistakes,' Neymar Jr comforted him. 'Just try not to make any against Real Madrid in the Champions League, okay?'

CHAPTER 19

KYLIAN VS CRISTIANO

That's right – in the Champions League Round of 16, it was Kylian's 'MCN' vs Cristiano's 'BBC'. At last, he would come face-to-face with his childhood hero on the football pitch. What an exciting encounter! What a fascinating fixture! PSG were cruising to the Ligue 1 title but were they strong enough to challenge Real Madrid, the European Champions?

So far, so good! In the group stage, in the autumn of 2017, PSG had already thrashed Celtic 5–0 and 7–1, and Anderlecht 4–0 and 5–0. That was twenty-one goals scored in only four games!

Kylian's favourite game, however, was the 3–0 win over German giants Bayern Munich. That night, at the Parc des Princes, 'MCN' had been simply unstoppable. In the very first minute of the match, Neymar Jr dribbled all the way across the penalty area and set up Dani Alves to strike it. 1–0!

Most of the time, Kylian had two Bayern defenders marking his every move. No problem! He used his strength and skill to hold the ball up until Edinson arrived. 2–0!

Again and again, Kylian created great chances for his strike partners. Edinson and Neymar Jr could have both had hat-tricks, but in the end, they got one goal each.

As Kylian went to cross the ball, Bayern's left-back David Alaba jumped up to make the block. Just kidding! Kylian rolled the ball across to his other foot instead.

'Hurray!' cheered the PSG fans of his sublime skill.

Kylian dribbled between Alaba and Niklas Süle, and this time, he did cross to Neymar Jr. 3–0!

What a night it had been for all three members of 'MCN'! Although Kylian hadn't scored himself, he had set up two goals against one of the best teams in the world. Now, it was time to take on Real Madrid.

The first leg was played away at the Bernabéu. The PSG players were feeling confident as their plane landed in Spain. They were top of Ligue 1, whereas Real Madrid were only third in La Liga. At their best, PSG knew that they could beat anyone, even the European Champions.

'This is it, guys, the match you've been waiting for!' Emery told his team in the dressing room. 'I need you to be fearless out there tonight.'

Kylian looked around at Neymar Jr, Edinson, Marco, Dani Alves, Thiago Silva – yes, they were all fired up and raring to go.

'Let's win this!' the team cheered together.

Kylian liked to think that he was one of the coolest guys around, but even he was shocked by the atmosphere in the stadium. As he walked out onto the pitch, it was like being surrounded by four walls of deafening noise. So that was what 80,000 fans sounded like. Wow!

Looking up, Kylian could see an enormous blue

banner, reading 'VAMOS REAL!' Yes, they were in for their toughest battle yet.

Cristiano took the first shot, but it was PSG who scored the first goal. Out on the right wing, Kylian turned and skipped brilliantly past Marcelo. As he sprinted forward, he had Edinson at the front post and Neymar Jr at the back post. Thanks to Edinson's clever dummy, Kylian's cross ran all the way through to the Brazilian. His shot was blocked but eventually, the ball fell to Adrien Rabiot. 1–0!

'Yes!' Kylian yelled out, pumping his fists. He was playing his part for PSG.

The Bernabéu was stunned into silence, and Cristiano was furious. It wasn't a good idea to anger 'The Beast'. There was no way he was going to let his team lose like that. He scored a penalty just before half-time and then a tap-in with ten minutes to go. The first leg finished Real Madrid 3 PSG 1.

Kylian was hurting as he hugged Cristiano. 'Well played,' was all he could say to his hero.

In fact, 3–1 didn't feel like a fair result at all. PSG had wasted some excellent chances. On the flight home, Kylian couldn't help thinking back to the ones he had missed: the shot that flew straight at the keeper, the cross that he couldn't quite reach.

'Hey, it's not over yet,' Neymar Jr reassured him. 'We can beat them at home!'

The two teams reconvened in Paris the following month, March 2018. As the teams walked out of the tunnel, the Parc des Princes was covered in blue, white and red. They were the colours of PSG, and the colours of France. This time, Kylian looked up at an enormous red banner, reading, 'ENSEMBLE, ON VA LE FAIRE!'

'Together, we will do it.' That's right – teamwork was going to be a key part of PSG's gameplan. They had eleven players out there on the pitch; not just 'MCN'.

Real could have gone 4– or 5–1 up, but with half-time approaching, it was still 3–1. Neymar Jr slipped a great pass through to Kylian. Could he be the PSG hero? The angle was tight but he decided to shoot anyway… saved by the keeper!

'Why didn't you cross it?' Edinson screamed. He

was waiting in the middle for an easy finish.

Kylian put his head in his hands. He had definitely made the wrong decision. 'Sorry!'

It was exactly as Deschamps had told him after France's draw with Luxembourg – Kylian had to learn to take his chances. If he didn't, his team wouldn't win. Early in the second half, Cristiano scored a header: 4–1 to Real!

Kylian's heart sank. That was pretty much game over. Or was it? Edinson did pull one goal back, but that was nowhere near enough. They were out of the Champions League.

PSG 2 Real Madrid 5,

Kylian 0 Cristiano 3.

'Hey, this time we failed,' Thiago Silva comforted Kylian at the final whistle, 'but next time, we'll succeed, okay?'

Kylian nodded but in his head, he was still asking himself, 'Why didn't I square it to Edinson?'

It would take him a few days to get over the disappointment, but thankfully Kylian had other targets to aim for. PSG could still win another French treble.

CHAPTER 20

TROPHY TIME

PSG had won their first trophy of the 2017–18 season way back in July 2017 – the Champions Trophy. Kylian had played that day, but for the losing team, Monaco.

'That one doesn't count!' he decided, and Neymar Jr agreed. He hadn't played in the match at all. In fact, Edinson had been the only member of the 'MCN' trio at PSG at that point.

So, the team really needed to win some new trophies to make Kylian and Neymar Jr happy. PSG were out of the Champions League, but they were top of Ligue 1, through to the semi-finals of the French Cup, and through to the final of the League Cup.

Kylian planned to make the League Cup his PSG Trophy Number One. To lift it, however, he would have to beat his old club, Monaco. In the days before the final, in March 2018, there was lots of friendly banter between Kylian and his old teammates, Radamel, Fabinho and Thomas.

'MCN are coming for you!'

'Ha ha, we're not scared of your three-man team!'

'Yeah, enjoy your runners-up medal, mate!'

When the two teams had previously met in Ligue 1, Kylian played one of his worst games of the season. PSG won but he missed so many chances. This time, he was going to come back to haunt Monaco. With Neymar Jr out injured, the pressure was really on. He had to perform well.

In the eighth minute of the final, Kylian got the ball with his back to goal. He spun quickly and then ZOOM! he was off, dancing his way past Youri Tielemans…

then Jemerson…

then Fabinho…

until finally Kamil Glik fouled him.

'Hey!' Kylian cried out as he got back to his feet. 'That's a penalty. Check the VAR!'

The referee waited for the video assistant's verdict... *Penalty!* Edinson stepped up and scored. 1–0!

'Yes!' Kylian cheered, throwing both arms up in the air.

He was only just getting started. Soon, Kylian was on the ball again just outside his own box, and he raced forward on the counter-attack. His pace was so explosive that no-one could catch him. Just before the halfway line, Kylian looked up and spotted Ángel in space on the left. His pass was perfect. 2–0!

In the second half, Kylian dribbled towards goal again and this time, he poked a pass through to Edinson. 3–0!

Kylian was desperate to score a goal of his own, but a hat-trick of assists would definitely do. At the final whistle, he punched the air and then hugged his old teammates.

'Man, you tore us apart today!' Fabinho admitted.

Kylian smiled, 'Sorry, your messages just spurred me on!'

Instead of winner's medals, the PSG players got their own small versions of the League Cup.

'Well I know what I'm drinking out of tonight!' Dani Alves joked.

As he celebrated up on the stage, Kylian had his hands full. Not only was he holding a mini League Cup, but he also was also holding the Man of the Match award. As a big basketball fan, Kylian declared himself the 'MVP' on social media – the Most Valuable Player. What a night!

'Hurray!' he cried out, when captain Thiago Silva lifted the big gold trophy.

The next day, Kylian was already asking, 'Right, what's next?' His hunger was never satisfied.

Kylian's PSG Trophy Number Two would be the Ligue 1 title. They were just far too good for the rest of France. They had only lost two league games all season! The PSG squad was so full of stars that they didn't even miss Neymar Jr that much.

Kylian scored one goal with his left foot against

Metz, and then two goals with his right foot against Angers.

'We're nearly there!' he shouted as he celebrated with Edinson and left-back Layvin Kurzawa.

By mid-April, PSG were fourteen points clear at the top of the table. One more win would be enough to claim the title and who were their next opponents? Monaco!

Kylian was desperate to destroy his old club again but unfortunately, Emery picked Edinson, Ángel and Javier Pastore in attack instead. What? No way!

'Sorry, but we've got the French Cup semi-final coming up on Wednesday,' his manager explained to him. 'I need you fighting fit for that.'

Fine! Kylian sat grumpily with the other subs as his teammates scored goal after goal without him. By half-time, they were winning 4–1! He was so bored and frustrated that he started banging his head against the bench seat in front.

'This is torture!' he muttered.

Still, he joined in with the team celebrations at

the final whistle. 'CHAMPION LIGUE 1!' he posted on Instagram with a picture of all the PSG players.

The next day, he was already asking, 'Right, what's next?'

The answer – the French Cup, the final part of PSG's treble! After his rest against Monaco, Kylian was determined to be the star of the show in the semi-final. Uh oh, Caen were in big trouble.

Ángel passed it through to Edinson, who crossed to Kylian. 1–0!

Goooooooooooooooooooooooaaaaaaaaaaaaaaaaaallllllllllll lllllllllllllll!!!!!!!!!!!!!!!!!!!!!!

What a great team goal! Kylian leapt into Edinson's arms and punched the air. 'Come on!' he shouted.

Caen equalised just before half-time but PSG's amazing attackers weren't worried. They always believed that they could score another goal.

Ángel backheeled it to Edinson, who crossed to… Kylian again. 2–1!

They celebrated in the same way, except this time, Ángel jumped up on Kylian's back.

'We need a new name for the three of us,' the Argentine suggested. 'DMC?'

Edinson shook his head, and said, 'CMD.'

It was the MVP's turn to disagree. 'No way,' said Kylian, 'it's got to be MCD!'

Thanks to Kylian's twenty-first goal of the season, PSG were through to the French Cup final. Their opponents would be Les Herbiers.

'Who?' a lot of the PSG players and fans asked.

Even Kylian didn't know much about them, and he was the biggest football fan in France! However, he did know everything that he needed to know – PSG were going to beat them!

'Don't underestimate Les Herbiers today,' Emery warned his players before kick-off at the Stade de France. 'They will be so fired up for this!'

But so was Kylian. He really wanted his PSG Trophy Number Three. He was a hat-trick hero, after all.

In the first ten minutes, PSG hit the post twice – first Giovani Lo Celso, and then Kylian.

'How did that not go in?' he groaned, throwing his arms up in frustration.

Ángel headed over the bar and then Giovani clipped the post again! What was going on?

'Be patient,' Edinson told his teammates. 'We'll score soon.'

Giovani was third-time lucky. As he dribbled forward, Kylian made a clever run to create space for him. From the edge of the area, Giovani curled a shot into the bottom corner. 1–0!

'Finally!' Kylian said to himself.

His frustrations, however, continued in the second-half. Kylian thought he had made it 2–0, but no, the goal was disallowed for handball.

'Never, ref!' he protested but it was no use.

Luckily, Edinson soon scored a penalty to secure the win.

'Well done, guys!' Neymar Jr cheered. The Brazilian was still not fit enough to play in the final, but he was back in Paris and proudly wearing the PSG shirt.

'Let me hold it!' Neymar Jr begged as they paraded the French Cup trophy in front of the fans.

Kylian laughed and let his friend hold one of the

handles. Only one, though – he refused to let go of the whole trophy!

That was the end of Kylian's successful first season at PSG – twenty-one goals, fifteen assists and three trophies. A few days later, however, he posed with the four trophies that the club had won, holding up four fingers for the camera.

'You liar, you lost that Champions Trophy final!' Thiago Silva reminded Kylian with a big grin on his face. 'Or were you playing badly on purpose?'

CHAPTER 21

READY FOR RUSSIA

Although the 2017–18 club season was now over, Kylian still had a busy summer ahead of him. Instead of chilling out on a sunny beach somewhere, he would be playing for France at the 2018 World Cup. Hopefully...

Deschamps had so many amazing players to choose from, and only twenty-three of them would go to Russia. Would 'Mbappé' be one of the names that didn't make the list? Kylian would be so disappointed. He had dreamt of playing at a World Cup ever since watching Henry and Zidane back in 2006. It was the tournament of a lifetime and he really didn't want to miss out.

'See you in Russia!' said his Brazilian PSG teammates Neymar Jr, Thiago Silva and Marquinhos.

'See you in Russia!' said his Argentinian teammates Ángel and Giovani.

'See you in Russia!' said his Uruguayan teammate Edinson.

Kylian kept his fingers firmly crossed. He couldn't be the odd one out. France would need a young flair player in their squad! But had he done enough to show Deschamps that he was ready for Russia?

Maybe not in the World Cup qualifiers, but Kylian was still finding his feet at international level. There had been lots of exciting signs for the future. He hit the crossbar in a friendly against Wales, and then set up goals for Alexandre against Germany and Thomas against Colombia.

'Now you just need to start scoring goals for France like you do for PSG,' his younger brother Ethan said. He was now part of the club's youth team. 'I know you can do it!'

It was in the next friendly against the World Cup hosts Russia that Kylian had finally showed exactly what he was capable of. With Antoine and Olivier both on the bench, he was France's star striker and he was even wearing the Number 10 shirt. This was his big chance to impress his national team manager.

'Come on, let's show the old guys how it's done!' Kylian told his teammates Paul and Ousmane.

It was Paul who played the perfect pass to him just before half-time. Kylian sprinted between two defenders, cut inside and fired into the bottom corner. 1–0 to France!

Goooooooooooooooooooooaaaaaaaaaaaaaaaaalllllllllllll lllllllllllllllll!!!!!!!!!!!!!!!!!!!

'Easy!' he said with a big smile as he high-fived Paul.

In the second half, Kylian scored again and it was one of his favourite goals ever. On the left side of the penalty area, he skilled the Russian defender in two stylish steps:

1) stepover,

2) nutmeg!

It was actually a double nutmeg because his shot then flew through the keeper's legs.

Goooooooooooooooooooooaaaaaaaaaaaaaaaaalllllllllllll lllllllllllllllll!!!!!!!!!!!!!!!!!!!

The France fans in St Petersburg went wild for

Kylian's classic celebration.

'That's more like it, mate!' Paul teased, slapping his head playfully.

Deschamps was delighted with Kylian's performance. When he was substituted a few minutes later, he got a hug and a big pat on the back from his manager.

'When you play like that, you're unstoppable!'

That's why Kylian was feeling quietly confident as he waited for the France World Cup squad to be announced. With his speed and skill, his manager knew that he could be a real gamechanger.

At last, the list was out. The attackers would be: Antoine, Olivier, Ousmane, Nabil, Florian... and Kylian!

'My first World Cup,' he posted straight away on social media. 'A DREAM!'

When he first joined the national team, Kylian had felt like the new kid at school. Now, however, he couldn't wait to spend the summer with lots of his best friends in football. Benjamin, Thomas, Ousmane, Paul, Antoine – what a fun group of players France had!

Their World Cup preparations began at Kylian's old youth academy, Clairefontaine. They worked on their tactics and fitness, but most of all they worked on building up the team spirit.

'France feeling,' Benjamin wrote under an Instagram picture of him carrying Kylian around the training pitch on his back. In another photo, Kylian and Paul were wrestling each other on the grass.

Although they all had plenty of laughs together, the France players were deadly serious about winning the 2018 World Cup. Kylian hadn't played in the Euro 2016 final against Portugal but he still felt the pain of that disastrous defeat. It was their job to make the nation proud of their football team again.

Now that he was definitely in the squad, Kylian moved on to his next target – the first XI. After all, there was nothing he hated more than sitting on the boring bench!

Luckily for him, Kylian started all three of France's warm-up matches, and he scored in the last one against the USA. *Phew,* what a relief! So, would that be Deschamps' first-choice team, with Paul, N'Golo

Kanté and Blaise Matuidi in midfield, and Kylian, Antoine and Olivier in attack? He really hoped so.

When the squad numbers were announced, Kylian punched the air. He had got what he wanted – the Number 10 shirt! Everyone was happy: Paul had Number 6, Antoine had 7, Olivier had 9, Ousmane had 11 and Benjamin had 22.

'I've got a great feeling about this!' Kylian told his teammates as they set off for their World Cup adventure in Russia.

At their base camp in Moscow, the players had everything they needed – big luxurious beds, the best training facilities, and PlayStations for their competitive FIFA tournaments.

'Get comfortable because we're not going home until after we win the final!' Deschamps told his team confidently.

'Yeah!' they all cheered together.

France's first opponents in Group C would be Australia. They didn't have any famous superstars, but that didn't mean it would be an easy match; even Kylian knew that there was no such thing as an easy

World Cup match.

He waited impatiently for news of France's starting XI. At last, it arrived and it was… GOOD NEWS! He would be playing up front with Antoine and Ousmane.

'Come on!' Kylian shouted with his fists clenched.

What an honour it was to walk out onto the pitch and represent France at a World Cup. Kylian was desperate to make a big impact, but the Australia keeper saved his only shot of the first half.

'Keep making those runs!' Deschamps encouraged him.

Kylian did, but the pass never arrived. After seventy minutes, Olivier replaced Ousmane and rescued France. He used his strength to set up Paul's winning goal. What a relief! It had been a poor French performance but at least they had the victory they needed.

'We'll have to play way better than that against Peru,' captain Hugo Lloris warned them.

Deschamps' only change for that next game was moving Olivier into the starting line-up in place of

Ousmane. Phew! Kylian would have another chance to prove that he was ready for Russia.

In the middle of the first half against Peru, Paul won the ball in midfield and passed it through to Olivier. His shot bounced off a Peru defender, over the goalkeeper's head and straight to… Kylian! He tapped the ball into the empty net. 1–0!

Goooooooooooooooooooaaaaaaaaaaaaaaaalllllllllll llllllllllllllll!!!!!!!!!!!!!!!!!!!

What an amazing moment! At the age of nineteen, Kylian had his first ever World Cup goal! Not only that, but he was now France's youngest *ever* World Cup scorer. Hopefully he would score better goals but there was plenty of time ahead for that. For now, it was time to celebrate. Antoine joined him and copied his classic pose – arms folded, cool looks on their faces.

'*Allez Les Bleus! Allez Les Bleus!*' the fans chanted.

With Kylian off the mark, could France now go on and win the whole World Cup?

CHAPTER 22

AMAZING VS ARGENTINA

Deschamps decided to rest Kylian for the final group match against Denmark. It was a wise move because he wanted his young superstar to be as fresh as possible for France's Round of 16 tie with Argentina.

For the Argentina game, Kylian couldn't wait to face his PSG teammates Ángel and Giovani and, of course, Argentina's Number 10, Lionel Messi. Yes, Cristiano had been Kylian's number one childhood hero but Messi was definitely in his top five. The guy was a total legend!

Times were changing, though. Messi was now thirty-one and Cristiano was thirty-three. Kylian, on the other hand, was only nineteen. People saw him as the future of world football but he wanted to be

the present too. He was ready to become a World
Cup star, and what better way to show it than by
beating Messi's Argentina?

'Come on, if Croatia can thrash them, then so can
we!' Paul argued.

Deschamps, however, wasn't getting carried
away. 'Any team featuring Messi and Di Maria is
dangerous,' the France manager warned his players.
'Of course we can beat them but we need to stay
smart.'

The noise was deafening at the Kazan Arena as
the two teams walked out for kick-off. France had far
fewer fans than Argentina but they sang the national
anthem as loudly as they could. Out on the pitch,
Kylian did the same, just like he used to as a kid back
in Bondy. He was so proud to represent his country
at the World Cup.

Kylian started the game brilliantly. As soon as
he got the ball, he turned and ZOOM! – he burst
through the middle, dribbling all the way to the edge
of the penalty area. Eventually, Javier Mascherano
had to slide in and bring him down. Uh oh,

Argentina were in big trouble.

'Great work, mate!' Antoine clapped. His free kick bounced back off the crossbar. So close!

Never mind, France would get lots more chances because Kylian had done his homework. He knew that pace was Argentina's biggest weakness. At top speed, no-one would be able to catch him.

Five minutes later, Kylian got the ball deep in his own half, and ZOOM! he was off again…

past Éver Banega…

past Nicolás Tagliafico…

past Mascherano too.

What a run! Kylian only had the Argentina centre-back, Marcos Rojo, left to beat. No problem! He kicked the ball ahead of him and chased after it. In a sprint race, there was only going to be one winner. Rojo knew that and so he pulled Kylian to the floor. Penalty!

'Amazing! Are you alright?' Olivier asked as he helped his teammate up.

Kylian nodded glumly. It was so unfair; he was about to score another World Cup goal! At least

France had a penalty, and Antoine didn't miss. 1–0!

Kylian was having his best international match ever. A few minutes later, he sprinted through again and this time, he was fouled just outside the box. Unfortunately, Paul's free kick flew high and wide.

They could have been 3–0 up but instead, Ángel hit a stunning strike to make it 1–1 at half-time. Then, just after the restart, Argentina scored again. 2–1! Oh dear, suddenly France needed Kylian's magic more than ever.

Right-back Benjamin Pavard equalised for France with a glorious goal but they were playing knockout football now. If France didn't score another, the match would go to penalties...

No, Kylian wasn't going to let that happen. This was *his* World Cup. As the ball fell to him in the crowded box, he kept his cool.

First touch to control it,

Second touch to beat Rojo,

Third touch to shoot with his lethal left foot.

Gooooooooooooooooooooaaaaaaaaaaaaaaaaaalllllllllllll

!!

Kylian skidded across the grass on his knees, with his arms folded across his chest. No big deal! But it was a big deal; it was a *massive* deal. Soon Kylian was at the bottom of a full France squad hug, including all the substitutes.

'Nice one, *Casse-bonbon!*' Benjamin cheered.

Near the halfway line, Messi stared down at his feet, looking devastated.

'Watch out world – there's a new Number 10!' the commentator screamed on TV.

As Kylian jogged back for the restart, he bumped chests with Antoine. His confidence was sky-high and he wanted more. Just in case anyone had missed his first goal, he scored again four minutes later. Olivier fed the ball through and Kylian calmly buried it in the bottom corner. 4–2!

Goooooooooooooooooooaaaaaaaaaaaaaaaaallllllllllll !!!

The substitutes raced back on to celebrate with France's new World Cup hero. Thanks to Kylian's amazing man-of-the-match performance, they were through to the quarter-finals! Kylian bumped chests with Ousmane, and then thanked Olivier with a hug and a high-five.

'This game will go down in history!' Antoine predicted.

It certainly would because Kylian had become only the second teenager ever to score two goals in a World Cup match. The first? None other than 'The King of Football' himself, Pelé, back in 1958. Wow, what an honour!

With five minutes to go, Deschamps gave Kylian a well-deserved rest. It wasn't a popular decision, however. The supporters wanted Kylian to continue and so did he. He was on a hat-trick, after all! As he trudged off slowly, his name echoed around the stadium.

Mbappé! Mbappé! Mbappé!

Kylian clapped the fans and then accepted a hug from his proud manager.

'Incredible!' was all Deschamps could say.

After the final whistle, Kylian walked around the pitch with a big smile on his face. He didn't want this amazing moment to ever end. He shook hands with all the Argentina players, including their Number 10.

'Well played,' Kylian said, seeing the despair on Messi's face. Football could be a very cruel game sometimes.

'You too,' the Argentinian replied graciously. 'You were the best player on the pitch today.'

Messi's brilliant football career was far from over but that night, a new world superstar was born.

CHAPTER 23

WORLD CHAMPION

'How are you feeling, Thirty-Seven?' Florian asked as the France players prepared for their World Cup quarter-final against Uruguay.

That was Kylian's new nickname because during that amazing match against Argentina, he had reached a top speed of 37 kilometres per hour. That was as fast as Usain Bolt in the Olympic 100-metre sprint!

'Put it this way; you'll be calling me Forty soon!' Kylian replied confidently.

His teammates were relying on him to be their speedy superstar again in the quarter-finals. It was going to be France's toughest test yet. Uruguay had two deadly duos: Diego Godín and José Giménez at the back, and Luis Suárez and Kylian's PSG teammate Edinson up front.

Uruguay had already knocked out Cristiano's Portugal and now they wanted to do the same to France. Even without the injured Edinson, they were still going to be very dangerous opponents.

'But if we stick to our gameplan, we'll win this,' Deschamps assured his players before kick-off.

That gameplan was simple – stay organised, work hard and work together.

Just like against Argentina, the France fans were outnumbered in the stadium. It sounded like the whole of South America had travelled to Russia for the summer! But Kylian wasn't going to let a loud crowd faze him. He was 100 per cent focused on his target – leading France into the World Cup semi-finals.

Every time Paul or Antoine got the ball in the middle, they tried to set him free on goal. Although Uruguay's defenders were excellent, no-one could keep up with a sprinting Kylian! Olivier tried to set him up too. After fifteen minutes, he headed the ball across goal to Kylian.

'Go on, score!' the France fans urged him. The Argentina match had showed that Kylian was capable of anything.

He had enough time to bring the ball down and shoot, but he didn't realise until it was too late. His header looped up and over the bar.

'Noooo!' Kylian groaned with his head in his hands. What a good chance wasted!

Oh well, there was still plenty of time to make up for his mistake. Kylian ran and ran but this time, he wasn't France's matchwinner. That was okay, though, because winning a World Cup was a team effort. Raphaël Varane and Antoine Griezmann scored the goals to beat Uruguay. 2–0 – job done!

'See you in the semi-finals,' Kylian wrote on Instagram with a big thumbs-up.

But who would their opponents be? On the journey back to base camp, many of the players relaxed by playing cards or watching a movie, but Kylian watched the other big quarter-final between Belgium and Neymar Jr's Brazil on his phone. It was important homework because France would have to beat the winners. The match finished 2–1 to Belgium.

'Bring it on!' Kylian told Antoine on the airplane as he shared the news.

To become the best, France knew that they would have to beat the best. Belgium had an amazing attack too: Romelu Lukaku, Kevin de Bruyne and Kylian's rival Number 10, Eden Hazard. Wow, it was going to be a really great game.

Was Kylian feeling nervous ahead of the biggest game of his life? No, instead he fell fast asleep on the flight to St Petersburg! Benjamin took a sneaky photo and posted it on social media.

'*Casse-bonbon* needs his beauty sleep for the big match!' he joked.

In the World Cup semi-final, France stuck to their gameplan once again. As soon as Paul got the ball in midfield, ZOOM! Kylian was off, sprinting between the Belgium centre-backs. He won that race but sadly he couldn't quite beat their keeper Thibaut Courtois to the pass.

'Nearly!' Kylian thought to himself as he jogged

back into position. He knew that in such a tight semi-final, one goal might be enough to win it.

France had to score first. Antoine played the ball over the top to Kylian who crossed it first-time to Olivier. He stretched out his left leg but his shot trickled wide. They both stood there with their hands on their heads. How many more glorious chances would they get?

Kylian slipped a pass through to Benjamin Pavard but Courtois made a great save.

'Not again!' Kylian muttered to himself. But just when his frustration was growing, France scored, when Antoine curled in a corner-kick and Samuel Umtiti headed it past Courtois. 1–0!

Kylian grabbed the ball out of the net and booted it high into the air. 'Come on!' he screamed. France were forty minutes away from a place in the World Cup final.

Could they score a second goal to make things safe? Kylian flicked an incredible back-heel pass through to Olivier but his shot was blocked. In the end, it didn't matter because France held on until the final whistle.

Allez Les Bleus! Allez Les Bleus! Allez Les Bleus!

'Yesssss!' Kylian screamed, punching the air. All of the substitutes ran onto the pitch to join in the joyful celebrations. They were now only one step away from lifting the World Cup trophy.

'WHAT A DREAM!' Kylian wrote on Instagram next to photos from the match.

The stage was set for the biggest game of his career – France vs Croatia. At the age of nineteen, Kylian was about to play in his first World Cup final!

On the day of the final, he woke up with a phone full of good luck messages from friends, family, teammates and coaches. He didn't have time to reply to them all but they helped to fire Kylian up for his big day.

'Come on!' the France captain Hugo shouted, clapping his gloves together in the tunnel.

The atmosphere inside Moscow's Luzhniki Stadium was incredible. Supposedly, there were more Croatia fans than France fans, but you couldn't tell from the noise. Both national anthems were sung loudly and proudly. As the Croatia anthem ended, a roar went up around the stadium. It was time for the World Cup final to kick off!

The first half was full of drama but not for Kylian. The Croatia defence was keeping him quiet. Instead, it was Antoine who stole the show with a teasing free kick, and then a well-taken penalty. France 2 Croatia 1.

'We need to calm things down and take control of the game,' Deschamps told his players in the dressing room. 'Stay smart out there!'

That's exactly what France did in the second half. They were more solid in defence and they used Kylian's pace on the counter-attack.

Paul looked up and gave Kylian a great through-ball to chase onto. ZOOM! Kylian got there first, of course, and pulled it back to Antoine. He laid it off for Paul to strike. His first shot was poor but his second was perfect. 3–1!

Game over? No, there was still plenty of time left and Kylian was desperate to grab a goal of his own. When the ball came to him outside the box, he didn't hesitate. BANG! It was in the bottom corner before the keeper could even react.

Goooooooooooooooooooooaaaaaaaaaaaaaaaallllllllllll llllllllllllllll!!!!!!!!!!!!!!!!!!!!

There was just enough time for Kylian's trademark celebration pose before all his teammates jumped on him.

'You legend!'

'What a hit!'

'You did it, 37!'

Allez Les Bleus! Allez Les Bleus! Allez Les Bleus!

What a way for Kylian to end his terrific tournament! Four goals, twenty-one dribbles, one 37 kilometres-per-hour sprint, one Best Young Player award (although Croatia's Luka Modrić would win the Best Player award), and one World Cup winner's medal. All that and Kylian was now only the second teenager ever to score in a World Cup final. He was too old to beat Pelé's record, but the veteran 'King of Football' himself was still very impressed.

'Welcome to the club,' he messaged Kylian on social media, and then sent him a signed Santos shirt.

The next few days were a brilliant blur. But in between all the celebrations, Kylian found time to post not one but TWO photos of him kissing the World Cup trophy.

'HISTORY FOREVER!' he declared.

It took time for the achievement to really sink in – at nineteen years old, Kylian was already a World Champion.

'You might as well retire now!' his dad, Wilfried, joked.

Was there anything left for Kylian to win? Yes, plenty! Luckily, he was totally obsessed with that winning feeling.

After a short holiday in Ibiza, Kylian returned to Paris and moved straight on to his next target – winning the Champions League. Yes, the boy from Bondy had become a superstar, but he was only just getting started.

Continue for a sneak preview of
another brilliant football story by
Matt and Tom Oldfield. . .

SUPERSTARS: DE BRUYNE AND DELE ALLI

Available now!

CHAPTER 1

MANCHESTER CITY'S MAIN MAN

Stamford Bridge, 30 September 2017

There was great excitement all across the footballing world, but especially around the Stamford Bridge stadium in West London. It was a sell-out for the biggest game of the Premier League season so far – the champions, Chelsea, versus the most entertaining team in England, Manchester City.

So, who would win the battle of the best? Which manager would come out on top: Chelsea's Antonio Conte or City's Pep Guardiola? And which brilliant Belgian would shine the brightest: Chelsea's Eden Hazard or City's midfield maestro, Kevin De Bruyne?

For Kevin, the match meant more than just another three points for his team. Back in 2012, at the age of twenty, he had made the bold move from his Belgian club Genk to Chelsea, with high hopes of becoming 'the next Frank Lampard', or even 'the new Zinedine Zidane'.

Kevin's manager at Chelsea, José Mourinho, had promised him game-time but, instead, he spent two seasons either out on loan, or sitting on the bench. Kevin had always been a stubborn star. He was impatient and strong-willed too. When he saw that he had no chance at Chelsea, he decided to make a name for himself somewhere else. He went to Germany and quickly became 'The King of the Assists' at VfL Wolfsburg.

Now, Kevin was back in England, starring for a new club. He was the best player in the Premier League and Manchester City were the best team too. Kevin had no hard feelings towards his old club but nevertheless, he had a point to prove to some people. It was time to show, once and for all, that he wasn't a 'Chelsea flop'. Five years on, Kevin was a completely different playmaker – older, wiser, and a whole lot better.

'Let's win this, lads!' his captain David Silva clapped and cheered before kick-off.

That wouldn't be easy away at Stamford Bridge, but City were top of the table and playing with so much style and confidence. With Kevin starting every attack in central midfield, Pep's grand plan was working brilliantly. City had thrashed Liverpool 5–0, then Watford 6–0, then Crystal Palace 5–0. Could they thrash Chelsea too?

Kevin dropped deep to get the ball as often as possible. He had two fantastic feet, capable of creating magic. Sometimes, he curled beautiful long passes over the top for City's speedy winger Raheem Sterling to chase. Sometimes, he played clever one-twos with Raheem, David and right-back Kyle Walker. Sometimes he was on the right, sometimes he was on the left, and sometimes he was in the middle. Kevin was everywhere, doing everything to help his team to win.

His first chance to score came from a free kick. He had scored plenty in his career, even one against

Barcelona in the Champions League. This time, however, his Belgian international teammate Thibaut Courtois made a comfortable save.

'Aaaaaaaaaahhhhhhhhhh,' the City fans let out a groan of disappointment, like the air escaping from a balloon. Kevin was so talented that they expected him to get it right every time.

'Next time,' he thought to himself as he ran back into position. As the game went on, Kevin, and City, got better and better.

CHANCE! Kevin crossed to Gabriel Jesus but it was intercepted by a Chelsea defender.

CHANCE! Kevin delivered a dangerous corner kick but Gabriel headed wide.

CHANCE! Kevin chipped the ball towards Gabriel but he headed wide again.

The City fans were growing restless in their seats. Their team was creating lots and lots of chances – but without their star striker, Sergio Agüero, who was going to step up and score the winning goal?

Playing in his new deeper midfield role, Kevin hadn't scored yet that season. Pep wanted him to be the team's pass-master, using his amazing X-ray vision to set up goals for other players. But what if they couldn't score?

Kevin could strike a brilliant shot, full of power and swerve. Like his hero Zidane, he was the complete midfielder, and he was determined to prove himself as a big game player. A win against Chelsea would keep City top of the Premier League, above their local rivals, Manchester United. His team needed him more than ever...

'Attack!' Pep shouted from the sidelines. 'Attack!'

So, the next time that Kevin played a quick pass to Gabriel, he kept running forward for the one-two. Kevin got the ball back and burst through the Chelsea midfield. He was just outside the penalty area now, with plenty of space to...

'Shoot!' the City fans urged. 'Shoot!'

It was on his left foot but Kevin didn't really have a weaker foot, just two magic wands. He steadied himself, pulled his leg back and struck the ball sweetly. *Abracadabra!* It flew through the air and over Courtois's outstretched arms.

Goooooooooooooooooooaaaaaaaaaaaaaaaaalllllllllllll llllllllllllll!!!!!!!!!!!!!!!!!!!!

'DE BRUYNE!!' the TV commentator cried out. 'Oh, that's special!'

What an important goal! As the ball hit the back of the net, the City supporters went wild. Kevin ran towards them, shaking his finger and roaring like a lion. He was so pumped up with pride and joy. He wanted to win the Premier League title so much.

On the touchline, Pep punched the air with delight. Their Brazilian substitute Danilo couldn't contain his excitement. He ran straight onto the pitch to bump chests with their hero. Soon, Kevin was at the centre of a big team hug.

'Come on!' he called out to the supporters and, in reply, they sang their favourite song:

Ohhhhhhhh! Kevin De Bruyne!
Ohhhhhhhh! Kevin De Bruyne!

It was an amazing moment for Manchester City's main man, one that he would never forget. Kevin had scored his team's winning goal, and against Chelsea! It didn't get any better than that. Back at

Stamford Bridge, the Belgian had showed the world that he was now a superstar.

'Kev, you're the best!' his manager Pep Guardiola said with a huge smile on his face.

Mourinho might not have believed in him at Chelsea, but Guardiola certainly did at Manchester City. And most importantly, Kevin believed in himself. He had always known that he had the talent, the drive and the resilience to reach the very top, even during his early days in Drongen.

KYLIAN MBAPPÉ HONOURS

Monaco
🏆 Ligue 1: 2016–17

Paris Saint-Germain
🏆 Ligue 1: 2017–18, 2018-19, 2019-20
🏆 French Cup: 2017–18
🏆 League Cup: 2017–18

France U19
🏆 UEFA European Under-19 Championship: 2016

France
🏆 FIFA World Cup: 2018

Individual

🏆 UEFA European Under-19 Championship Team of the Tournament: 2016

🏆 UNFP Ligue 1 Young Player of the Year: 2016–17, 2017–18

🏆 UNFP Ligue 1 Team of the Year: 2016–17, 2017–18

🏆 UEFA Champions League Team of the Season: 2016–17

🏆 FIFA FIFPro World XI: 2018, 2019

🏆 Golden Boy: 2017

🏆 FIFA World Cup Best Young Player Award: 2018

MBAPPE

7 & 10 — THE FACTS

NAME: Kylian Mbappé Lottin

DATE OF BIRTH: 20 December 1998

AGE: 22

PLACE OF BIRTH: Bondy

NATIONALITY: French

BEST FRIEND: Benjamin Mendy

CURRENT CLUB: PSG

POSITION: RW

THE STATS

Height (cm):	178
Club appearances:	223
Club goals:	150
Club trophies:	12
International appearances:	41
International goals:	16
International trophies:	2
Ballon d'Ors:	0

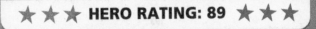

★ ★ ★ **HERO RATING: 89** ★ ★ ★

GREATEST MOMENTS

 **20 FEBRUARY 2016,
MONACO 3–1 TROYES**

Just months after his first-team debut and his
seventeenth birthday, Kylian achieved his next target –
his first senior goal! It wasn't his best strike but it still
meant the world to him because he had just become
Monaco's youngest-ever goalscorer! And whose record
had Kylian broken? Yes, that's right, his French hero,
Thierry Henry. A new superstar was born.

21 FEBRUARY 2017,
MANCHESTER CITY 5–3 MONACO

This was the night when Kylian went from being the talk of French football to the talk of world football. It was Manchester City who won this game, but Kylian's speed and skill caused them all kinds of problems. He even had the composure to score a fantastic first European goal.

31 MARCH 2018,
PSG 3–0 MONACO

Kylian made the big-money move to PSG in order to win more top trophies. In their first season together, 'MCN' didn't win the Champions League but they did win the French treble. Kylian was the man of the match in this League Cup final against his old club, Monaco. He won an early penalty with one of his deadly dribbles, and then set up goals for Ángel and Edinson. Neymar who?!

30 JUNE 2018,
FRANCE 4–3 ARGENTINA

Kylian's match-winning performance against Lionel Messi's Argentina will go down in World Cup history. His phenomenal pace won France an early penalty and in the second half, his two excellent finishes sent them through to the quarter-finals. Kylian became the first teenager since 'The King of Football', Pelé, to score a World Cup double.

15 JULY 2018,
FRANCE 4–2 CROATIA

Kylian wasn't at his awesome best against Croatia but he still got what he wanted – a World Cup final goal and a World Cup winner's medal. In the second half, Kylian got the ball just outside the box and buried his shot in the bottom corner. GOAL – what a way to finish off his first fantastic tournament for France!

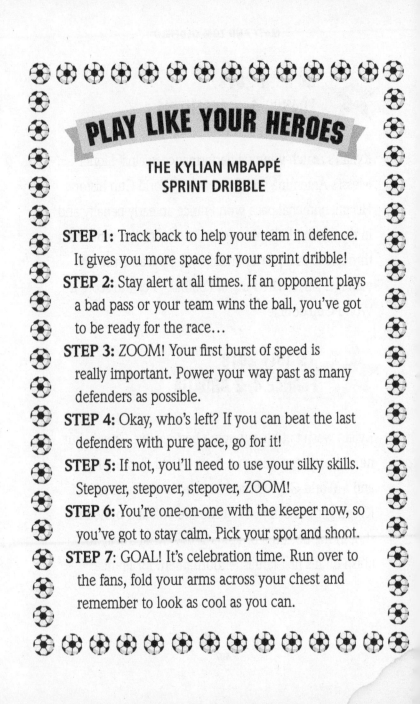

PLAY LIKE YOUR HEROES

THE KYLIAN MBAPPÉ
SPRINT DRIBBLE

STEP 1: Track back to help your team in defence. It gives you more space for your sprint dribble!

STEP 2: Stay alert at all times. If an opponent plays a bad pass or your team wins the ball, you've got to be ready for the race...

STEP 3: ZOOM! Your first burst of speed is really important. Power your way past as many defenders as possible.

STEP 4: Okay, who's left? If you can beat the last defenders with pure pace, go for it!

STEP 5: If not, you'll need to use your silky skills. Stepover, stepover, stepover, ZOOM!

STEP 6: You're one-on-one with the keeper now, so you've got to stay calm. Pick your spot and shoot.

STEP 7: GOAL! It's celebration time. Run over to the fans, fold your arms across your chest and remember to look as cool as you can.

TEST YOUR KNOWLEDGE

1. What sport did Kylian's mum play?

2. Who was Kylian's number-one childhood hero?

3. Which two top European clubs did Kylian visit before joining Monaco?

4. How old was Kylian when he made his Monaco first-team debut?

5. What was the name of Kylian's strike partner as France won the Under-19 Euros?

6. What was the name of Kylian's strike partner as Monaco won the Ligue 1 title?

7. Which country did Kylian make his senior France debut against?

8. Name two clubs (other than PSG!) who tried to sign Kylian in Summer 2018?

9. Kylian won four trophies in his first season at PSG – true or false?

10. How many goals did Kylian score at the 2018 World Cup?

11. Kylian won the FIFA World Cup Best Young Player award, but who won the FIFA Men's Player of the Year award?

Answers below. . . No cheating!

1. *Handball* 2. *Cristiano Ronaldo* 3. *Chelsea and Real Madrid* 4. *16 (16 years and 347 days to be exact!)* 5. *Jean-Kévin Augustin* 6. *Radamel Falcao* 7. *Luxembourg* 8. *Any of Arsenal, Liverpool, Manchester City and Real Madrid* 9. *False – he only won three but he posed with all four of PSG's trophies anyway!* 10. *Four* 11. *Luka Modrić*

CAN'T GET ENOUGH OF
ULTIMATE FOOTBALL HEROES?

**Check out heroesfootball.com
for quizzes, games, and competitions!**

**Plus join the Ultimate Football Heroes
Fan Club to score exclusive content
and be the first to hear about new
books and events.
heroesfootball.com/subscribe/**